I0815995

Royal Treatment

Royal Treatment

Jackie Robinson, Montreal, and the Breaking of Baseball's Color Barrier

SEAN J. MCLAUGHLIN

University of Nebraska Press • Lincoln

Manufactured in the United States of America

The University of Nebraska Press is part of a land-grant institution with campuses and programs on the past, present, and future homelands of the Pawnee, Ponca, Otoe-Missouria, Omaha, Dakota, Lakota, Kaw, Cheyenne, and Arapaho Peoples, as well as those of the relocated Ho-Chunk, Sac and Fox, and Iowa Peoples.

For customers in the EU with safety/GPSR concerns, contact:
gpsr@mare-nostrum.co.uk
Mare Nostrum Group BV
Mauritskade 21D
1091 GC Amsterdam
The Netherlands

Library of Congress Control Number: 2025042766

Set in Questa by A. Shahan.

To Slavko John Sapeta,
a fine catcher and a great friend.

Contents

Illustrations

Illustratons appear after page 98

Preface

Canada's most successful baseball players will candidly admit that they shifted their athletic focus to America's pastime only after it became apparent their NHL dreams were unlikely to ever come true. You will hear versions of this story from Matt Stairs, Larry Walker, and Justin Morneau—the journeyman slugger who hit 265 home runs for eleven franchises over nineteen seasons, the SpongeBob SquarePants–loving five-tool Hall of Famer, and the AL MVP in 2006 and NL batting champ in 2014—who all quite earnestly describe themselves as failed hockey players despite their many successes on the diamond. Such is that sport's hold over the Canadian imagination.

At the same time, there is no better way for foreign athletes to ingratiate themselves with Canadian sports fans than by picking up some hockey gear or throwing on a hockey sweater and smiling for the cameras. The further the players' actual sport of choice is from hockey, the better it all goes down from a public-relations perspective. Picture Expos legends Andre Dawson and Gary Carter in Montreal Canadiens sweaters at center ice in the Bell Centre waving to the adoring crowd or football players from the Calgary Stampeders, fresh off a Grey Cup victory, in Calgary Flames unis. The Toronto Raptors American superstar Vince Carter even donned a Maple Leafs sweater for the cover of a Canadian basketball magazine back in 2001. But it was the Blue Jays' universally beloved Puerto Rican slugger Carlos Delgado who took the biggest risk. He was as wobbly as a fawn and looked absolutely terrified on skates at a Leafs practice, but he got full marks for letting a camera crew from Sportsnet film him anyway. All the way from Vancouver Island to Newfoundland's Avalon Peninsula, the Canadian sporting public loves these visuals because it creates the impression that had he grown up here, our favorite athlete may well have hoisted a Stanley Cup or helped Team Canada to another Olympic gold medal.

It was much more than just a lark when Jackie Robinson grabbed a stick and assumed a goalie position in net for photographers at the Expo 67 Sports Pavilion in Montreal, though. Robinson was Georgia-born and California-raised, which meant that hockey was one of the few sports he never got to play growing up. It is a fair bet that he would have been a terrific skater given that we do know that he was talented enough to play professional football, tennis, or golf and that he excelled at track too.

Robinson had multiple business ventures and a busy schedule, but he still made a habit of coming back to Montreal from his home in Connecticut as often as he could after he retired from baseball at the conclusion of the 1956 season. Whether it was to sign the Golden Book at city hall, to watch a football game, or to step into the broadcast booth for the Expos, he was always finding reasons to come back to visit his old Minor League haunts and fondly reminisce over his time with the AAA Royals back in 1946. He never tired of telling Montrealers how good they had been to him and his wife, Rachel, while they briefly lived in the city during that one magical season, setting them up for all the success they later enjoyed in Brooklyn. This message became his mantra.

When he returned in September 1969, he did typical Jackie Robinson things. One of them was hugging a middle-aged housewife and Royals superfan who had taken twenty years to work up the courage to mail him her 1946 season tickets with a request that he autograph them for her.[1] But the main reason he came back was to visit the Expo 67 pavilions after the big crowds from its wildly successful opening two years earlier had thinned out. By this point, pretty much everyone who wanted to had already visited one of the biggest tourist draws of the decade, and his tour lined up with the dead period near the very end of the summer season. It was about as good of a time as any for a celebrity to walk around and get a taste of one of the most successful World's Fairs of all time before it closed for good.

Robinson was a very old fifty by this point, thicker and sporting a shock of white hair due to complications from diabetes. Anyone who saw him move gingerly or strain to read would be forgiven for not taking him for a retired athlete. If you forced someone who knew nothing about his background to guess, many would have thought he was closer to seventy than to the end of his playing days. One might even surmise that he probably knew there would not be too many more homecomings like this, making it all the more important to connect with old friends and smile for the camera.

Way back in 1946, most of Robinson's teammates on the Royals were Americans who gave him the cold shoulder, at least at first before he proved himself as the dynamic lynchpin of the best team in the Minor Leagues that year. By contrast, a handful of Habs players, Canadian Canadiens from the Prairie West to francophone Montreal, sought him out and included him as an equal in a gang of friends over the course of that summer. Maurice "Rocket" Richard, the best player in the NHL in 1946 and two years Robinson's junior, was completely in awe of the Royals' star player. He made a point of seeking Robinson out whenever he was back in town for various events and functions over subsequent decades.

Twenty-three years after his Montreal season, while he walked through the Expo 67 sports pavilion, it was an easy yes when a photographer asked Robinson if he could get a couple of quick pics of him out on the ice. Robinson loved Montreal, and Montrealers loved hockey, so he wanted to show his appreciation for a sport that mattered dearly to them. As he grabbed a Victoriaville Canadian stick and took his crouch in net, he might even have taken a split second to imagine himself as a young man out on the ice at the Montreal Forum in iconic Canadiens red, white, and blue alongside the Rocket, Toe Blake, Elmer Lach, and Bill Durnan. In that alternate Canadian timeline, competing in another sport mostly in a different country, he was always treated like a man and judged by the content of his character. Maybe that momentary fantasy explains why the photographer captured especially bright eyes and a wide smile on his face.

Royal Treatment

Introduction

As of this writing, it has been a decade since the release of the 2013 film *42*, an updated take on the Jackie Robinson origin story that delighted baseball fans and reminded its general audience that great social change in America typically comes first in the sporting realm before trickling down through the world of politics. There were star turns from the late great Chadwick Boseman in the lead role, alongside a perfectly cast Harrison Ford as Brooklyn Dodgers General Manager Branch Rickey, father of the Great Experiment to integrate Major League Baseball. We will never know how this version would have compared to the proposed Spike Lee biopic project that fell apart in the late 1990s, but filmgoers were mostly pleased with director Brian Helgeland's effort, and Warner Brothers turned a tidy profit off its investment.

Baseball's fan community shows off the best of its lawyerly tendencies when it turns its passions to big questions about who belongs in the Hall of Fame, who was the best X from Y era, and so on. There is no debate that Jackie Robinson integrated modern professional baseball in America after crude racists closed the door to Black players in the game's early years. (Defensive whiz Moses Fleetwood Walker caught for one season with the Toledo Blue Stockings of the American Association in 1884 and has the distinction of being the last Black player to compete at the non-Negro League Major League level until Robinson's Dodgers debut in 1947.) But when exactly did this profound milestone for baseball and the broader civil rights struggle actually take place?

The stock view is that baseball's color line collapsed when Robinson donned Dodger blue and white for Opening Day at Ebbets Field in Flatbush on April 15, 1947. Commissioner Bud Selig declared this date Jackie Robinson Day in 2004, and it has been marked league-wide ever since as both a remembrance celebration for a very special player and a gentle annual reminder that those in the game should aspire to being good and open-hearted.

There are, however, more compelling arguments that the real anniversary of this momentous change came much earlier, either when Robinson signed his first contract in "white" baseball with the AAA Montreal Royals of the International League on October 23, 1945, or when he first took to the field in a Montreal Royals uniform in Florida for a spring training game at City Island Ballpark in Daytona Beach on March 17, 1946, or when he made his regular-season debut as a Royal on the road at Roosevelt Stadium in Jersey City on April 18, 1946. Whichever you find most appropriate for a commemoration, one thing is clear: all roads go through Montreal. No wonder, then, that this defining moment in the Robinson story gets so little attention—for Americans, it unfolds not just in foreign Canada, but in its doubly foreign francophone cradle of Québec.

This brings us back to *42* and some plot-writing 101. Any good cinematic story typically involves a hero's triumph over adversity. As Chris Lamb so thoroughly shows in *Blackout: The Untold Story of Jackie Robinson's First Spring Training* (University of Nebraska Press, 2004), Robinson's first spring training in Jim Crow Florida in 1946 provided a full array of villains from which to choose. There was an ignorant mob that threatened violence, venal police officers who shared its beliefs, and city officials who went along with racial-discrimination ordinances because it seemed easier in the moment than getting on the right side of history. Robinson does indeed appear in a Royals uniform in *42*, but all of these scenes take place on hostile territory—the practice fields of central Florida—never north of the border on home turf during the Royals' march to a Junior World Series championship as the best AAA Minor League team of 1946.

At home in Québec, absolutely no tension at all was in the ballpark or among the white francophones in Villeray, the Robinsons' temporary home neighborhood; to the contrary, Montrealers immediately adored Jackie Robinson, he loved them back, and an unbreakable bond between the player and his new neighbors took root during his lone Minor League season.[1] Such was the hype surrounding his arrival that the stands for a cool Minor League home opener were filled with a who's who of the biggest names in Québec's political, cultural, and social life. Among them was twenty-four-year-old Maurice "Rocket" Richard, a fiery winger for the Canadiens, fresh off his second Stanley Cup victory. Here was an undisputed champion and francophone icon, the best player of his generation of the country's most beloved sport, cheering himself hoarse for Robinson along with a cross section of Montrealers who bridged every single one of Canada's linguistic, sectarian, and class divides.

It may be difficult for us today to imagine such a talented player as an underdog, but there were absolutely no guarantees of a big league future for Robinson when the 1946 Minor League season began. At a time when too many American voices still argued against change, Montrealers consciously chose to make a deep emotional investment in his success, and Robinson never forgot it. As Robinson himself admitted to a reporter from the CBC (Canadian Broadcasting Corporation) years later, "Had it not been for the fact that we broke in in Montreal, I doubt seriously if we would have made the grade so rapidly."[2]

Robinson's season in Montreal ended in a riot, but not the sort you might think. After leading his team to victory over the Louisville Colonels in the Junior World Series, hundreds of Royals fans blocked the exits to keep Robinson from leaving without a long curtain call for the home faithful. In unison, they roared a line from an old French soldier's song that came to the New World before the British conquest of New France in 1759. The first time he heard "*Il a gagné ses epaulettes!*" Robinson would not have known the crowd was telling him he had "won his stripes," but by the tenth chant he got the idea, which brought tears to his eyes. Flight home to catch or not, it is highly unlikely he would have gotten through this crowd and out of the park before midnight if not for skills he had honed on the gridiron with the UCLA Bruins. Sam Maltin, a Montrealer writing for the *Pittsburgh Courier*, memorialized the scene with a tragically beautiful passage: "To the large group of Louisville fans who came here with their team, it may be a lesson of goodwill among men. That it's the man and not his color, race or creed. They couldn't fail to tell others down South of the 'riots,' the chasing of a Negro—not because of hate but because of love."

Maltin is usually paraphrased as writing, "It was probably the only day in history that a black man ran from a white mob with love instead of lynching on its mind," a misquote that nevertheless captures the moment equally well.[3]

In that kindly mob was an understanding that everyone in the ballpark had been part of something very special, something that was so much bigger than baseball, and every individual member of it clung to the deep satisfaction this brought down to the last second. Montrealers still know this story today thanks in large part to the wonderful writing of Marcel Dugas and his social-media efforts to highlight the 1946 Royals. The proliferation of Jackie Robinson street art in different corners of the city testifies to the residual pride they take from their deep connection to him. Canada's baseball intellectuals who gather every summer for the induction ceremony at the Canadian Baseball Hall of Fame in the charming town of St. Marys, Ontario, are certainly quite familiar with the profound role a defunct Minor League baseball team from Québec played in the long American civil rights struggle. National sportswriters can usually be counted on to remind a wider English-speaking Canadian audience of the Royals footnote to the baseball integration story every spring around Jackie Robinson Day. And yet there will always be a chip on our shoulders until an American audience learns to appreciate this story along with us.

Many great Robinson biographies are in print already, and this book is not another one for the pile. Nor will it simply repeat in English the excellent work Dugas has already shared with francophone readers in *Jackie Robinson, un été à Montréal* (Éditions Hurtubise, 2019). Rather, it examines one pivotal juncture in his career and the legacy of the overwhelmingly positive relationship he had with the community that supported his rise to fame. In doing so, it brings the fan experience of Jackie Robinson directly into the foreground in a manner that centers Robinson within the context of the Black American expatriate community in Montreal in the era of the world wars. This is indeed a baseball story, but in the pages ahead will be many detours into early twentieth-century integration of various Canadian institutions, the city's vibrant jazz scene, and the civic aspirations of Montreal's business and community leaders. All of these sidebars paint a much clearer picture of why Montrealers embraced Robinson in 1946 to a far greater extent than residents of even America's most progressive cities could have at the time.

The worst approach to this story from this white Canadian writer would undoubtedly be the one that feeds snobbish binary myths of tolerant Canada as morally superior to hopelessly prejudiced America in pursuit of a narrative that celebrates an end to racism in Montreal or Canada as a whole. Jackie Robinson's sporting triumphs during his ephemeral presence electrified a city, but this was nowhere near enough to miraculously overturn nearly four centuries of ingrained prejudice and launch a new era of equal opportunity for Black Canadians. Henri Pardo's moving 2021 documentary *Dear Jackie* offers a cogent reminder that Black residents of Little Burgundy, a neighborhood that is to Montreal what Harlem is to New York, have always faced obstacles that are all too familiar to American readers. These include hard stereotypes about what jobs fit Black applicants, displacement in the name of urban renewal, and tense daily encounters with white neighbors who harbor unknown and hidden suspicions. This one urban neighborhood produced so much art and culture for the broader community to enjoy, and yet its Black residents have inherited lasting trauma from a legacy of discrimination that remains to this day.

Intolerance can be chipped away little by little, person by person, and an undeniable pocket of goodness did absolutely manifest itself through the deafening cheers for Robinson from thousands of Royals fans at Delorimier Stadium during his rookie season. Pardo's conscious appeal to the memory of Jackie Robinson is a reminder to his white viewers that they do have it in them to be more empathetic and inclusive when they want to, just like their forebearers were when they opened their hearts to a visiting Minor League baseball player who later became a star. As I tip my cap here to the Montreal fan community that rallied around Robinson, my admiration for them acknowledges that they represented a ripple of change rather than a tsunami in the grander picture of Canada's attempt to fulfill its aspirations of racial tolerance.

The first chapter to come, "Canada's Place in the Great Experiment," explains how the legacy of slavery differed in Canada relative to the United States. It charts the early twentieth-century growth of Montreal's Little Burgundy, the beating heart of Black Québec, and how its residents lived and worked. When Québec sat out the Prohibition experiment in the 1920s, Montreal became a sort of pre–Las Vegas entertainment escape for visiting Americans from nearby states who came en masse by train during the Roaring Twenties. This nightclub boom created a demand for entertainers that was filled by visiting Black American jazz musicians, who immediately delighted locals with their new sound and found unexpected freedoms to fully engage in all aspects of public life. The growth of a vibrant jazz scene, I argue, had a localized impact on how some white Montrealers viewed their Black neighbors. Old stereotypes that Black Montrealers were only suited for work as railway porters, port laborers, or domestic servants slightly gave way to a new idea that they were also in fact valued contributors to this city's cultural life. This helped soften attitudes about race a good two decades before Jackie Robinson arrived in town. I round out the chapter by surveying the blurry color line in Canadian baseball, which had integrated at least a generation before its American counterpart at the semiprofessional and amateur level.

The second chapter, "A Momentous Signing," covers developments leading up to Robinson's signing with the Royals in October 1945. It focuses on how Montreal fit into Branch Rickey's calculations and why he chose the Dodgers' foreign International League affiliate as Robinson's first stop in the organization. His Dixie clubs in Fort Worth and Mobile were obviously off the table, but he could have shipped Robinson out west to the AAA Saint Paul Saints of the American Association if not for its regular road stops in Jim Crow Louisville. More important, Royals President Hector Racine was an enthusiastic backer of the Great Experiment, and he played a major role in convincing Rickey that Montreal was the perfect host for Robinson. This chapter also surveys the war of words between sportswriters who championed Rickey's move and the regressive people who built straw men to justify the status quo of segregation during the run up to Robinson's debut.

The third chapter, "Coming through Adversity," dives into Robinson's start to the 1946 season with the Royals. It explores how his miserable spring training experience in Jim Crow Florida very nearly derailed the Great Experiment. It also covers the initial reaction of the Montreal press to his presence in Royals camp, which evolved from an almost blasé take in the fall on whether there would be any controversy when Robinson eventually took the field to downright indignation in the early spring when reporters learned of all the obstacles Florida officials put in front of him during the Royals training camp in the Daytona Beach area. The press initially expressed some concern that Robinson was competing for the job of hometown hero Stan Bréard, but this eventually gave way to disgusted reporting on how Jim Crow got in the way of baseball.

The fourth chapter, "Settling In," looks at how a very good Royals team on paper built up even more anticipation for its home fans thanks to Robinson's scorching start to the season during an extended twelve-game road trip. It explains how manager Clay Hopper overcame his prejudices and quickly transformed from a Robinson skeptic to a firm backer. It also discusses the struggles and demotions of two other Black players, Johnny Wright and Roy Partlow, who were signed by the Royals primarily in the hope that they would help Robinson feel less isolated in times of difficulty. Later, you will learn how Rachel Robinson managed her pregnancy as a newcomer in a mostly francophone neighborhood that showed her incredible grace. This chapter looks beyond baseball at the immediate impact Robinson had on other professional sports in Montreal. It explores the friendships he formed with Habs players who shared conditioning tips and included him in a goodwill hospital trip to meet wounded World War II veterans. It also looks into a very sincere but failed bid from the Montreal Alouettes of the Interprovincial Rugby Football Union (IRFU), the predecessor to the Canadian Football League, that, if successful, would have turned Robinson into the two-sport Bo Jackson of the post–World War II era. Counterfactual speculation aside, Robinson's success on the diamond did ultimately convince the club to integrate Canadian football, creating an opportunity for Herb Trawick to become a new city sporting icon after Robinson's departure.

The fifth chapter, "Glory," covers the late-season panic that set in when rumors started circulating that Branch Rickey would take Robinson away from Montrealers by calling him up to the big leagues to bolster the Dodgers' playoff push, at the Royals' expense. It provides a recap of Robinson's role in the Royals' championship run, highlighting the disgraceful conduct of Louisville Colonels fans and Royals fans' more vigorous response to it once the series moved north to Montreal. It concludes with the scene of mob joy that followed the Royals home victory in the final game of the Junior World Series.

The sixth chapter and final chapter, "Homecomings," explores Robinson's post-Royals player relationship with Montreal, which remained close right up until his death in 1972. His popularity there remained so high that as early as 1951 the Dodgers organization offered him his first managerial position with the Royals immediately after his retirement as a player. Robinson was flattered by the offer, but ultimately resisted while continuing to firmly advocate for MLB to desegregate its coaching ranks. In another fanciful what-if, Robinson did later agree to come back and manage a new Montreal team in the Continental League, an abortive attempt to create a third Major League in the late 1950s, which would have made him the first Black manager at the highest level in professional baseball had the project not collapsed before a single game was played. Regardless, Robinson returned to the city to a hero's welcome on numerous occasions, including a fall 1958 goodwill visit to sign the city's Golden Book, a city council honor for distinguished residents and visitors, and to catch up with Rocket Richard and others.

This chapter concludes with a look at how city officials and the Montreal Expos franchise posthumously amplified the public memory of Jackie Robinson through statuary at Olympic Stadium, along with events such as its 1982 All-Star Game tribute with his widow Rachel and Dodgers teammate Pee Wee Reese and a fiftieth anniversary celebration in 1996 of his lone Royals season. These efforts certainly contributed to the commissioner's decision to make Jackie Robinson Day an annual league-wide event. There is also an overview of how nongovernmental organizations have kept Robinson's memory alive, including the Jackie Robinson Heritage Minute (one in a series of long-running, widely viewed history commercials) from 1997. The tragic relocation of the Expos for Washington in 2004 robbed Montreal's fans of the joyful grind of a Major League baseball season, prompting the city's art community to refocus attention on Jackie Robinson's sojourn in the city through a series of delightful temporary and permanent installations.

1

Canada's Place in the Great Experiment

To gaze into another person's face is to do two things:
to recognize their humanity, and to assert your own.

—LAWRENCE HILL, *The Book of Negroes*

The histories of Canada and the United States have been intimately woven together from their colonial origins, though a much longer American shadow has cast itself across the northern border. Foreign visitors will often say that these two neighbors are the same but completely different, a statement that makes perfect sense to anyone who has spent even a short time in each country. This maxim applies to race relations just as well as any other national fault line. What follows here is a very brief summary of pre–Jackie Robinson Black Canadian history with an eye on how and why baseball integration came much earlier and met with less controversy in Canada than the United States.[1] For all of the cross-border similarities in values and attitudes, very particular factors in Canada, and Montreal more specifically, lined up particularly well for a groundbreaking experiment in integration of the most popular sport of the era.

Black faces were rare enough in Canada when Jackie Robinson first crossed the border in the fall of 1945 that the initial reaction of a good number of the whites who encountered them was a mixture of surprise and curiosity. White Canadian attitudes about race were not terribly different than in the United States or Britain at the time, though there certainly was less enthusiasm for enforcing the strictest forms of Jim Crow segregation found south of the border, in large part because numbers did not warrant it across most of the country. The blood lust that manifested itself in a plague of thousands of racially motivated lynchings was largely absent as well; Canadians handed out rough justice on occasion, but the targets were more often members of First Nations or white victims of sectarian violence.

The institution of slavery had followed a similar trajectory in Canada, one that did not break as cleanly and decisively after the American Revolution as many Canadians would like to imagine. Nearly 1,500 enslaved peoples of African origin were in colonial New France by the eighteenth century, most of whom came to Canada via native raiders who sold or gifted them to their French allies. They were incorporated into the British Empire, along with roughly seventy thousand French-speaking Europeans after the Conquest in 1759. Canada's Black population swelled a generation later when Loyalist refugees brought enslaved peoples across the border into rump British North America in the aftermath of their defeat in the American Revolution.

At the dawn of the nineteenth century, Canada was home to anywhere from two thousand to three thousand enslaved people, mostly in the Maritimes and in Upper Canada (present-day Ontario), who engaged more often in domestic or service work and skilled trades than as agricultural laborers. A majority of the colonies' most prominent white citizens of the era tarnished their historical legacy by small-scale involvement in the peculiar institution, which explains why colonial legislatures took until the 1820s to finally give in to considerable public pressure to end the institution of slavery. Upper Canada did albeit take significant action that still fell short of full abolition in 1793, outlawing the import of enslaved peoples and providing manumission for those in bondage once they reached age twenty-five.

The enslaved were joined by Black Revolutionary War veterans who had decided that Britain's offer of freedom was more convincing than that of the Continental Congress and thus could not return home to America without fear of reprisal. All told, they counted roughly four thousand. Most settled in picturesque but hardscrabble and windswept communities hugging the cold North Atlantic Coast in Canada's future Maritime provinces of Nova Scotia and New Brunswick. Postwar economic deprivation drove many to move on to London, England; freedman settlements in Sierra Leone; or British colonies in the Caribbean. Others stayed, and some of them migrated internally, seeking advantages in urban centers or on the new farmlands of Upper

Canada. A good number of their descendants similarly distinguished themselves on the battlefield a generation later in Runchey's Company of Coloured Men when American forces mounted an unsuccessful invasion of Canada during the War of 1812.

Still, it was not until 1834 that the Slavery Abolition Act brought a definitive legal end to the peculiar institution in all British colonies. This turning point set up a thirty-year period of stark legal differences between free Canada and a largely unfree United States, creating visions of British North America as a sanctuary in the imagination of enslaved Americans.

Runaways had begun trickling into Canada in small numbers as early as the 1790s, and some served on the British side during the War of 1812, fearing that American victory would lead to the reintroduction of slavery. Low-level migration picked up after the Underground Railroad network took root during the antebellum era. The work of American abolitionists who provided safe haven, food, and transportation to runaways grew exponentially in the aftermath of the 1850 Fugitive Slave Act, which gave enslavers a legal pathway to pursue enslaved runaways into Northern states that had long earlier banned slavery. The new law turned border states like Ohio and Pennsylvania into more tenuous refuges, forcing many of the formerly enslaved to press even further north as a survival strategy. All told, as many as forty thousand enslaved people fled into British Canada before the end of the American Civil War in 1865.

These newcomers quickly built agricultural communities-in-exile in rapidly growing Southern Ontario counties just a short distance from the American border. Snapshots of their lives were captured in the 1849 autobiography *The Life of Josiah Henson, Formerly a Slave, Now an Inhabitant of Canada, as Narrated by Himself*, which in turn motivated Harriet Beecher Stowe to publish *Uncle Tom's Cabin* three years later. Now considered problematic by many for fueling negative racial stereotypes, the work was at the time a great international bestseller that converted many thousands of readers into supporters of the abolitionist movement.

Henson's hometown of Dresden, Ontario, just seventy miles across Lake St. Clair from Detroit, was part of the Dawn Settlement founded at the terminus of the Underground Railroad in 1841. Within thirty years its population had swelled to seven hundred people, 72 percent of whom were Black.[2] Nearby Chatham, a modest inland county seat and trading center on the Thames River, was the hub of Black Canadian political life at the time. It most notably served as a staging ground for John Brown and his fellow revolutionaries, Black and white, before they launched their ill-fated raid on Harpers Ferry, Virginia, in October of 1859, one of the causes of the Civil War.

And then the wave receded just as quickly as it rolled in; roughly two-thirds of these new Canadian freedmen ultimately chose to return to the United States after Abraham Lincoln issued the Emancipation Proclamation in 1863. There were many different motivations for this mass homecoming, including a very understandable desire to serve in the Union Army and contribute to a military victory over Confederate enslavers back in their homeland. After the Civil War, others followed to reconnect with family members who had remained behind in the United States, to return to fairer climes, and, out of what in hindsight was a perhaps misguided hope, to find new opportunities that Reconstruction era politics would permanently open up for Black Americans.[3]

This outflow was slightly reversed in the early twentieth century when roughly 1,500 Black American homesteaders from the Jim Crow South migrated to the frozen expanses of Western Canada to take advantage of dirt-cheap land in Alberta and Saskatchewan that the government had been hoping to settle with winter hardy Ukrainians and Poles. Still, by the time World War I broke out, there were no more than twenty thousand Black Canadians in total, mostly concentrated in Montreal; a handful of communities in Nova Scotia, New Brunswick, and Southern Ontario; and even smaller settlements in the remote Prairie West. They accounted for less than 0.1 percent of a total population that had recently broken seven million, and their small villages and compact neighborhoods were in effect tiny, isolated dots on the map of a vast transcontinental dominion that stretched roughly four thousand miles end to end. As a result, they were often tucked away far from the main and easily overlooked by Canada's white majority.

Being better than America did not necessarily mean good, and Canada was never an easy place to make a home. The British had given

Black veterans of the Revolutionary War the most marginal land in the Maritimes and often never bothered to issue titles even after it had been in a family for generations. As the nineteenth century brought new technological innovations, white Canadians carried the same sort of prejudices as Americans, and those who did have interracial contacts pigeon-holed their Black neighbors into certain low-paying blue-collar jobs, particularly railway labor and domestic work. There was also de facto segregation in the schools of Upper Canada despite its early action to wind slavery down. But at the same time there was no formal Jim Crow, no lynchings, and no legal discrimination (yet) against Black Canadians.

Whatever their degree of tolerance, many white Canadians of the era took the passive role of choosing not to stand in the way of their Black neighbors who were attempting to earn a livelihood. This created some room for great success stories that likely would not have been possible in the United States in the nineteenth century. Dr. Anderson Ruffin Abbott, for example, was a Union Army volunteer who attended to Abraham Lincoln after he was fatally shot by John Wilkes Booth in the spring of 1865. He also happened to be the first licensed Black physician to come out of the University of Toronto. James Mink went on to build a transportation, mail, and hotel empire in Ontario that made him a millionaire before slavery was abolished in the United States.[4] A handful of outliers aside, the Black experience in Canada during this era was for the most part hardly different than that of any bordering American state.

The outbreak of World War I was a watershed moment for Black Americans and Canadians alike who saw military service as a patriotic opportunity to make a case for better treatment at home. Unsurprisingly, Black recruits for both the American and Canadian military were treated abysmally. Racism was so ingrained in the American Expeditionary Force that Black troops were either relegated to menial rear echelon work or, like those in the celebrated Ninety-Third Division, handed over to the French military because white American soldiers would not serve alongside them in combat. This indignity suited many enlisted men just fine after the transfer; they were given far more respect from the French officers who commanded them and were shown real gratitude from the local population while they were on leave in French villages and cities.

The Canadian military hardly did better, poorly threading a needle between an official policy of nondiscrimination and widespread de facto discrimination from recruiting officers on the ground. In the summer of 1914 Black Canadians were as enthusiastic about the war effort as their white neighbors and, like their American counterparts, also saw military service as a means of demonstrating their patriotism in a manner that would surely deliver new civil rights at home after the war. The Canadian military, however, was not particularly interested in using them, at least at first. Canada did not have an official anti-Black policy in World War I, but in practice recruiting officers had enough latitude to reject nearly every prospective Black Canadian enlistee on the grounds that they had no business fighting in a "white man's war."

Despite these barriers, over 1,400 Black Canadians did manage to serve in the military during the opening years of the war, often in combat roles. We can only assume that these individuals were able to sign up for duty thanks to some combination of meeting a rare enlightened recruiter, applying to join mixed-race units that already had recruits from Canada's First Nations, or giving particularly convincing intake interviews. After years of foot-dragging, Canada's military brass found a solution to its growing manpower needs and the reluctance of too many of its unit commanders to fully integrate: creating the all-Black No. Two Construction Battalion in Pictou, Nova Scotia, on July 5, 1916. Roughly six hundred men from Canada, the United States, and the British West Indies served with the No. Two from its deployment to wartime France in the spring of 1917 until the war's end a year and a half later.

Once this obstruction to large scale Black Canadian military service had been partially dislodged, something very profound unfolded on Canadian Expeditionary Force (CEF) camps in England, far from the hail of artillery shells along the front lines in contested northern France: Black and white Canadian soldiers starting regularly taking to the ball diamond as members of racially integrated baseball teams.

Baseball was hands down the most popular sport for all Canadian troops on rest or convalescent leave, and the military endorsed league play as a positive recreational outlet. In the eyes of the brass, the sport also seemed to encourage martial values of teamwork, self-sacrifice, and, at times, derring-do on the basepaths or in the field.[5] Soldiers took the game incredibly seriously, and the level of competition was quite high. Nevertheless, amateur and semiprofessional play back home in Canada had mimicked the so-called gentlemen's agreement and was as segregated as it was in the United States before the war, with only a handful of exceptions.

As the Great War stretched into years two, three, and four, however, some of the white Canadians troops who enlisted with the same racial prejudices as their American counterparts started to rethink them after preparing for the crucible of war alongside Black volunteers. We must keep in mind that this was, unlike in the United States, usually the first time most white troops had any sustained contact with their Black countrymen.

This sport integration began tentatively on military bases at home in Canada, then it accelerated rapidly after the great Canadian victory over Germany at the Battle of Vimy Ridge in Pas-de-Calais in mid-April 1917. Thirty Black soldiers had made their way into integrated units and contributed to what is widely viewed by conservative historians as a singular nation-making moment in Canadian history. Their valor did not go unnoticed back at home either.[6]

Ethelbert "Curley" Christian (1882–1954), for example, was an American immigrant and overaged volunteer serving with the Winnipeg Grenadiers. A savage artillery barrage during the Battle of Vimy Ridge left him buried alive in his trench, badly mangled by the time his comrades were able to dig him out forty-eight hours later. Two stretcher bearers were cut down by enemy bullets as they attempted to extract him from the battlefield, and gangrene had set in by the time he reached the hospital, forcing doctors to amputate both of his arms and legs in order to save his life.

And despite this horrific ordeal, Christian remained chipper and considered himself fortunate right to the end of his long life. He ultimately recovered from his injuries, got fitted for artificial limbs, married one of his caregivers, became a father, and then spent his remaining years as a nationally known advocate for Canada's World

War I veterans. On one famous occasion after the war, a woman who did not know who he was rudely observed that he had not removed his hat for the playing of the national anthem at a public event. He kept his cool and offered a classic reply: "Perhaps you would take it off for me. You see, I lost both arms fighting for the King."[7]

Christian's story was simply too miraculous and inspiring for Canadians of his generation to ignore. He returned to France in July 1936, alongside eight thousand fellow veterans, for King Edward VIII's dedication of the Canadian National Vimy Memorial. In the larger picture, the front-and-center role Christian played as advocate for Canada's World War I veterans was a constant low-level reminder that he was one of several thousand Black men who had willingly assumed the burden of war when their country needed them.

In the context of a protracted and bloody war that was upsetting many societal boundaries, historian Stephen Dame writes that "men of varied skin tones seemed to play ball together with less controversy in military settings than they did back on 'civvy street.'"[8] In the United States, by contrast, first and regular encounters had usually already happened predeployment on the home front, cementing harder racial ideas for white soldiers than in Canada, where these concepts were more abstract and easier to break. After having been conditioned for decades by minstrel shows, imperial British propaganda, racist newspaper reporting, then more immediately by D. W. Griffith's wildly popular 1915 pro-KKK film opus *Birth of a Nation*, white Canadian troops often found that the stereotypes they had bought into simply did not hold up after they finally had in-person contact with the Black "other." Such was the powerful effect of seeing another man willing to die fighting in the same uniform under the same flag.

As Dame shows, a handful of notable Black Canadian athletes of the era played integrated baseball in military leagues, including 1912 Olympic sprinter John Howard; Vimy Ridge veteran Gordon Johnson; Rankin Wheary, an experienced ballplayer who had competed in New Brunswick and New England; and Charlie Kelly, another two-way star from southern Ontario. Canadian teams fought hard for bragging rights for their respective units, and apparently they opened their rosters to the most talented players available regardless of race. Games were often attended in the thousands, with occasional pop-ins from curious royals, including the king and queen, adding to the pressure to compete at a high level.

Wheary was the star of an excellent Thirteenth Reserve Battalion team that came tantalizingly close to winning the 1917 Canadian Corps Championship, and he likely would have continued playing professionally back home had he not fallen at the Battle of Cambrai in the fall of 1918 at just twenty-two years old. A less-heralded all-Black team representing the No. Two Construction Battalion played regularly against all-white teams from other CEF units and against an integrated Forestry Battalion squad over the summer of 1918. Kelly's Foresters, also known as the Sawdust Kings, were talented enough to earn an invitation to join the newly created Anglo-American Baseball League in 1918 and compete against the best military-based teams in the London area. By contrast, American military play saw Black and white teams compete against each other, but there were no integrated teams within the American Expeditionary Forces (AEF).[9]

The most important aspect of this story insofar as it relates to Jackie Robinson's arrival in Montreal in 1946 is that baseball integration was most definitely not an ephemeral wartime phenomenon that gave way to the status quo once Canadian soldiers returned home. In the baseball hotbeds of the Maritimes, Québec, and Ontario, it was quite visibly there to stay even though racism did continue to rear its ugly head on the field far too often.

One of Canada's most legendary amateur teams of the early twentieth century was the Chatham Coloured All-Stars, founded as a mostly Black team in 1932 by the descendants of people in the Underground Railroad (and one resident of nearby Walpole Island First Nation Reserve) in a small county seat town in southern Ontario's rich agricultural belt. There was far too much talent on display at the park in the town's east end to limit this group to unorganized community play, so a local business owner and baseball enthusiast named Archie Stirling sponsored them and helped arrange head-to-head competition with all-white teams in the Ontario Baseball Amateur Association (OBA) starting in 1933.[10]

Out on the road, the All-Stars encountered their fair share of predictable obstacles, from rough opponents, crooked umpires, vicious language from opposing fans, and hoteliers who denied them accommodation, but none were great enough to stop them from going on a terrific run through the end of the decade. The home fans in Kent County were delighted by their electric play, and their rivals in other small- and medium-sized Ontario towns inevitably started to wonder about the great players they missed out on due to segregated rosters. Heidi L. M. Jacobs wonderfully chronicles the team's story in *1934: The Chatham Coloured All-Stars' Barrier-Breaking Year* (Biblioasis, 2023).

The All-Stars won an intermediate B provincial championship in 1934, took the Western Counties division title in 1935, and made an appearance in provincial finals once again in 1939. (This series was never actually played as a result of a dispute over which city should get hosting rights, and the All-Stars were denied a chance to win their second championship.) The team disbanded in 1939, dynasty intact, after several players signed up for military service during World War II. The team did not reassemble once peace returned in 1945, but a handful of veterans continued playing with other Chatham-based teams after the war.[11]

Canadian baseball fans have an instant and universal answer to the question of who was their country's greatest player of all time: Chatham's own Ferguson Jenkins, a nineteen-year Major League starting pitcher who won 284 games and accumulated 84.2 WAR (wins above replacement) over his impressive career from 1965 to 1983. The home fans all know him as a Hall of Famer who enjoyed his greatest success with the Chicago Cubs, but few are aware that he was the son of Ferguson Jenkins Sr., a talented defensive center fielder and accomplished hitter who often batted lead-off for the All-Stars once he joined the team in 1935. Fergie was born in 1941 after his father's playing days were over, but he kept one of his dad's OBA trophies close at hand in the bedroom of his childhood home.[12] Chatham's embrace of the All-Stars and the acquiescence of other Ontario towns to their participation in league play ultimately helped seed a love for baseball in one of Canada's finest athletes.

The city of Chatham has proudly honored the All-Stars legacy, starting in 1984 with a fifty-year anniversary celebration of their 1934 provincial championship. The Toronto Blue Jays paid tribute to these trailblazers in front of MLB fans as well, donning replica All-Stars uniforms once on the road in a Negro League tribute game at Shea Stadium against the Mets in 2001 and again at home in 2002 with Sagasta Harding and Don Tabron, the last two surviving members of the team, on hand to throw out the ceremonial first pitches. In more recent years, the Chatham area member of provincial parliament (the Canadian equivalent of a state house representative), Percy Hatfield, launched a valiant but failed campaign to pressure the Canadian Baseball Hall of Fame to enshrine the All-Stars while some of their children are still living.

The All-Stars were by no means the only players in Canada to ignore the color line after World War I. Down east in the Maritimes, baseball was the king of summertime, and prewar play had taken place in racially segregated leagues even though the region was home to Canada's oldest Black communities. This practice continued into peacetime, but Black teams first started regularly playing white ones as early as 1921 in Halifax, the biggest city in the region, and barnstorming Negro Leaguers soon added Maritimes cities to their circuit to the delight of local fans. In smaller towns away from Nova Scotia's capital, it became as common to see white players on the mostly Black Truro Sheiks as it was to see Black players on the mostly white Yarmouth Gateways.[13] This mixing was something that happened naturally and with little opposition, as fans collectively decided that they preferred watching better-quality play over upholding a nineteenth-century American segregation policy.

It was in Québec, however, that the most dramatic pre–Jackie Robinson progress toward integration at the semiprofessional and organized level took place. Baseball historian Christian Trudeau writes that "we find black players in white amateur teams as early as 1924, and since the news was covered so casually, there [is] a strong possibility that there were black players before then."[14] "Outlaw" league teams—the unaffiliated precursors to the successful Independent League teams that have sprouted up in recent decades to offer baseball to underserved communities—in fact brought in multiple Black players during the interwar years. Even within the system of organized baseball, the Montreal Royals notably flouted the National Association of Professional Baseball Leagues' ban on Black players in 1922, their first season playing in the newly founded Class-B Eastern Canada League.

Charlie Culver (1892–1970), also known as Charlie Calvert for his new francophone audience, was a mixed-race Buffalo native who played Negro League ball before relocating to Montreal and taking a Québécoise wife shortly after the end of the war. He was playing semipro baseball in the town of Saint-Hyacinthe just thirty miles east of downtown Montreal when tireless local baseball promoter Joe Page brought him over to the Royals, which he envisioned as the lynchpin franchise in the new four-team league. (The Eastern Canada League expanded into Vermont and then ultimately failed in 1924 after three seasons, but this is beside the point.)

Culver's story is little known, but it appears that he in fact integrated twentieth-century Minor League baseball, albeit at one of its lowest levels, twenty-four years before Jackie Robinson first suited up for the Montreal Royals in 1946. His professional career came to a regrettably premature end after just six total games despite solid results on the mound and at the dish and, thanks to Page's efforts, a profoundly significant April 30, 1922, appearance in a preseason home exhibition game against the visiting Boston Braves of the National League.

What appears to have ultimately done Culver in was a legal dispute over whether he had broken his contract with Saint-Hyacinthe when he signed with the Royals more so than a rude insistence on restoring the color line to professional baseball in Québec. Culver clearly had the talent for higher levels of competition and may well have been of Major League caliber in a different era, but he was forced to return to Saint-Hyacinthe and played semipro baseball in semiobscurity until 1930. He remained in Montreal until his death in 1970, spending decades as a highly respected coach at the youth and independent levels. Culver was inducted into the Canadian Baseball Hall of Fame in 2021.[15]

Trudeau's research shows that Negro League veterans such as Ted Page and Alphonso Lattimore came north to Montreal in the late 1920s to compete on city teams and that at least three Black players were on different clubs in the semiprofessional Provincial League in 1935. It was not just squads in cosmopolitan Montreal that integrated their rosters, either, but also small, less glamorous, and almost uniformly francophone outlying towns like Granby and Sorel. In 1936, South Carolina native and boundary crosser Chappie Johnson was so encouraged by the number of Black players in the Provincial League that he brought in Culver as player-manager for the newly formed Montreal Black Panthers, an all-Black squad made up of young American players from the Deep South.

The team itself did not do much winning against more experienced competition over its two short seasons, but three Panthers were selected for the Provincial League All-Star team that played an August 3, 1936, exhibition game against the Montreal Royals, which had rejoined the International League back in 1928. This could have been a landmark game on the long path to full integration in professional baseball, but two Royals from Dixie refused to take to the diamond against a team with Black players. The three Panthers were removed from the game, and only then did play begin. The Royals ultimately lost.[16] Had the Panthers players actually been allowed to take the field, this game would surely have gone down in history as one of the most significant sporting events of the early civil rights era.

At the same time, barnstorming American Negro Leaguers began adding more Canadian stops to their northern tours to take advantage of their growing popularity. There were no regional gaps to this demand at all; mono-color white prairie communities in Manitoba and Saskatchewan were just as eager to glimpse this American star power as residents of cosmopolitan urban centers in the East. Hospitable westerners in fact went a step further, opening their homes to these itinerant players, offering laundry, rooms in their homes, shared meals, packed lunches, and awestruck children to fawn over them.

As the postwar integration era ushered in an inevitable decline phase for the Negro Leagues by the 1950s, small clubs in the ManDak League, an independent, cross-border, five-club international circuit based in Manitoba and North Dakota, also offered healthy and regular pay for late-career Negro League veterans who faced dwindling opportunities stateside. At the other end of the age spectrum, the Western Canadian

League gave seventeen-year-old Californian Elijah "Pumpsie" Green his first professional action with the Medicine Hat Mohawks in 1951. Green is best known as a journeyman utility infielder who finally got called up to the show in 1959, when Tom Yawkey's Boston Red Sox club reluctantly became the last Major League team to integrate its roster, well over a decade after Jackie Robinson's debut for Brooklyn.[17]

To call the legendary Satchel Paige well-traveled would be a gross understatement; he played in many hundreds of Negro League, MLB, and Minor League parks, in addition to stints throughout the Caribbean and across North America as a barnstormer over his forty-year career. Paige started making multiple appearances in Canada every year from 1934 until he was finally on the cusp of retirement in 1964. These games usually pitted an accomplished group of traveling Negro Leaguers against any local side that was willing to pay to play them. Regardless of the frequent talent mismatch, these affairs often drew six thousand to eight thousand spectators, a number that would often have bettered Depression Era turnout for many Major League teams during the regular season.

Much of this jaw-dropping attendance was driven by Paige's star power, which was even bigger in Canada than at home. Historian Donald Spivey writes that "the ace from the USA was, during his era, the biggest single draw in Canadian baseball. . . . Canadians were coming out, in the main, to see him because he was a great pitcher and because he was black. He, like other black ballplayers, was a spectacle, a great ballplayer and an African-American, all in combination. He was a compelling attraction."[18]

Paige, power-hitting catcher Josh Gibson, and two-way Cuban phenom Martín Dihigo were three of the greatest what-ifs of the preintegration era, the greatest laments for fans who yearned for best-on-best competition, gentlemen's agreement be damned. Most Canadian fans were incredibly grateful for the brief glimpses they got of one of the greatest Negro Leagues stars and treated Paige like a conquering hero whenever he came to visit. Spivey quotes Paige's son, Robert Leroy Paige, speaking in his father's voice about his appreciation for Canada: "It's a place where I was treated like a man. You could stay at hotels, eat at restaurants, and I didn't have to enter backdoors. You know how I love the outdoors. I had many great fishing trips there, and loved hunting moose and caribou up north."[19]

By the World War II era, mainstream Canadian press coverage of Paige during his barnstorming tours through the country often included strident denunciations of baseball's color line and the persistent refusal of American authorities to allow integrated competition at the Major League level. Canadian fans had seen Paige pitch often, and they knew full well he had the talent to face Ted Williams or Stan Musial. These sentiments were much more aligned with those of the Black American press than that of conservative, mainstream, white outlets south of the border. There was general delight in Canadian baseball circles when a forty-two-year-old Paige finally got signed by the Cleveland Indians in 1948 as the oldest rookie in MLB history. It was no surprise to his Canadian backers when he threw 72.2 very effective innings mostly in relief that year and picked up a World Series ring for his trouble.

Baseball integration was indeed a broad national trend in post–World War I Canada, but unique factors were at play in Montreal specifically that augured particularly well for Branch Rickey's Great Experiment. Canada as a whole permitted much more Black participation in public life, especially when it came to entertainment and sports. Montreal, however, went even further when it refused to go along with the Prohibition experiment and, as a result, became a Las Vegas–type getaway destination in the 1920s for thirsty American tourists. The greatest Black jazz musicians of the day flocked to the city's nightclubs and played for packed audiences, discovering liberties that simply did not exist back home. Late at night, clustered around small tables in smoky nightclubs, many of their new white fans were coming round to a view that Black artists were a cherished part of the city's cultural life. The legacy of this mutual respect can still be seen every summer when Montreal welcomes roughly two million enthusiasts to congregate outdoors for the world's largest jazz festival.

Early twentieth-century Montreal was the unrivaled leader of Canada's cities, one of the country's earliest European settlements and home to a port that commanded a massive volume of trade with the growing communities further west in Ontario. There simply is no good American equivalent for the city, but the best description might be to imagine what would happen if you mixed French-speaking versions of New York and New Orleans in equal parts.

French explorer Samuel de Champlain first arrived on what came to be known as the Island of Montreal at the narrow base of the Saint Lawrence River, Canada's answer to the Mighty Mississippi, in 1603 and set up a trading post on the east side eight years later. Catholic missionaries determined to convert the local Iroquois soon followed. By the early 1640s, the first group of permanent settlers arrived, then soldiers came to protect them from attack from British-allied Iroquois who were determined to resist encroachment on their lands. It was a tenuous existence through to the end of the century, and a garrison mentality continued through the British Conquest in 1759, temporary American occupation during the opening months of the Revolution, and a successful defense against a second American invasion during the War of 1812.

The city truly began to flourish once international borders in the eastern half of North America were finally settled for good in the early nineteenth century. Upriver, pretty, refined Québec City's colonial ramparts and Old World charm served as a time capsule for New France, but Montreal transformed into the beating heart of a rapidly growing transcontinental nation. The port and surrounding industries had already made the city Canada's undisputed commercial hub, then the introduction of railways, canals, and bridges generated new wealth and facilitated deeper settler penetration of the country's vast interior.

English-speaking Protestant British merchants and American investors flooded in, often squeezing out and marginalizing old stock French speaking Catholics in a manner that created permanent and understandable bitterness. America divided itself by race and Canada by language and sectarianism. These deep frictions nevertheless turned the greater Montreal area into a raucous multinational hub of business and culture that blended French, British, American, and First Nations influences well before the massive waves of continental European migration began in the late nineteenth century. The city by all rights should have been picked as Canada's new capital on Confederation in 1867, out of a field of rivals that were deemed too French—Québec City—or too English—Kingston and Toronto—but it lost out to a much blander and less bilingual alternative, Ottawa, that was more palatable to the country's English-speaking majority, thanks to its location just across the river in the province of Ontario.

Then and now, the constants of Montreal life have always been brutally cold winters that begin in November and last through April, summer picnics in the park at Mount Royal, sprawling public markets, imposing, ancient-seeming cathedrals, political leaders that would be too flamboyant to win elections anywhere else in Canada, and a maze of boroughs that all look and feel very different. By the end of the nineteenth century, one of them, Petite-Bourgogne, or Little Burgundy to anglophones, carved out its niche as an English-speaking, working-class enclave where at one point 90 percent of its residents were Black.

Little Burgundy is wedged in along the Lachine Canal between tony Westmount, Ville-Marie, a vibrant downtown, and one-time fellow working-class neighborhoods Saint-Henri and Griffintown. Its proximity to the port made it a magnet for industry and low-wage laborers willing to put up with pollution and dilapidated housing. City officials tried to rebrand the neighborhood as Quartier Georges-Vanier in the 1980s as part of a failed attempt to break its association with immigrant poverty, but locals pushed back, and Little Burgundy it remains to the present day.

The canal unlocked seaborne trade further west down the Saint Lawrence River, but it was the arrival of the railways in the mid-nineteenth century that created mass demand for a new source of low-wage labor. The long-haul Pullman sleeper trains that arrived in 1870 each required service teams of porters and kitchen staff to keep passengers in luxury, and corporate decision-makers liked the optics of Black male laborers in a menial service role, so they recruited hundreds of them directly from the United States.

Incoming American porters, cooks, and waiters took these jobs and got rooms in the few shabby tenements near Windsor Station where Black tenants could legally take up rental properties. Black-owned businesses followed soon after, and then wives and families ultimately joined their porters in new homes up north in snowy Montreal. Their partners were largely pigeonholed into working as domestics for families in Westmount and other wealthier neighborhoods beyond the escarpment, often cobbling together two of these positions at a time, or they took low-wage work in the garment industry.

Roughly half of these new Black railway laborers were American, but they were joined by a large number of Caribbean migrants and a smaller cohort of Canadians who migrated into the city from the Maritimes. The West Indians considered themselves the best educated, the Americans thought they had a better knack for business, and both groups looked down on their Black Canadian neighbors as country bumpkins. Dorothy Williams, the doyenne of Black Montreal history, notes that by 1928, 90 percent of employed Black men in the city worked on the railways. Their jobs came with a measure of esteem, pensions, and, for the porters, clean suits, but racism could always rear its head when dealing with the public. Patrons referred to all porters as "boy" or "George," a nod to George M. Pullman, the American inventor who brought sleeping cars to Canada in the 1870s, without any consideration of how annoying this would be to working men with actual names of their own. More broadly, in the event of a dispute between a Black porter and a white traveler, there was little doubt whose version of events would be believed by the railway. This forced an excessive degree of caution. There was also an ambition-crushing low ceiling for promotion, based on the assumption that most white workers would not tolerate having a new Black supervisor.

The hours were long, the work was hard, and very real divisions were within the American and West Indian communities in and around Little Burgundy, but cherished local institutions like the Coloured Women's Club of Montreal, the Universal Negro Improvement Association, the Negro Community Centre, and the nondenominational Union Congregational Church—which later briefly had Jackie and Rachel Robinson as parishioners—helped paper them over to some degree. By Williams's account, prewar Black Montreal was gritty and poor, but united by a stronger sense of community than anywhere else in the city.[20]

Whatever one's immigrant origins, a shared outsider status came from more subtle forms of Canadians discrimination. Unlike in most American cities of comparable size, there were never any visible barriers as to where Black residents could go and which spaces were off limits. It was, for example, a common enough sight during the interwar years to see Black and white customers browsing for clothes together in the downtown Eaton's department store. That said, Black locals tended to learn quickly which establishments would not serve them, in the absence of explicit Jim Crow reminders. According to Gwen Lord, "[At] a whole lot of places . . . there weren't signs, but everyone knew. I guess you would have gone in there and sat for a while but they wouldn't serve you. So there would be no point going. You really wouldn't want to be in a place that didn't want you to be there."[21]

Up until the 1920s, most white Montrealers saw Black Montrealers as transient laborers with one very specific role to play in society. Outside of the railways, they hardly merited a second thought—that is, until outside factors drew legions of culture-seeking white Montrealers into Black spaces for the first time. Montreal was one of the few North American jurisdictions to pass on the disastrous Prohibition exhibition, which had a turbocharging effect on the city's already vibrant club scene. Revelers flocked to the city—aided by a direct train link, ten hours each way, with New York City—creating a thirst not just for drink but also quality entertainment in bars and clubs. This kindled a musical revolution that turned Montreal into a jazz mecca on par with New Orleans and Chicago, as talented local players were joined by scores of American musicians looking for opportunities to gig. Kostya Kennedy writes, "In the 1920s visitors came north to Montreal from the United States, briefly escaping Prohibition and creating a suddenly fervent nightlife where the lonely found love, and the misfits their kin, and the lights stayed on until dawn."[22]

Little Burgundy had emerged in the late nineteenth century as a Black neighborhood populated largely by younger men with some disposable railway income. Many of these migrants were either single or had not yet been joined by their families, which led to the rise of local entertainment venues that catered to vices, such as unlicensed boozing, gambling, and carousing with ladies of the evening. These pre–World War I clubs were unquestionably seedy dens of iniquity that earned the scorn of Little Burgundy's fledgling community associations and churches, but they catered almost exclusively to local residents rather than the city as a whole and were given some latitude by the authorities so long as the right palms were greased.

World War I stoked a minor youth rebellion in the 1920s not quite on par with the counterculture movement of the 1960s, but it was a significant component of the Roaring Twenties nonetheless. As older, conservative, white Québeckers railed against new forms of jazz music and the lascivious dance associated with it, the more their children were drawn to it. And it just so happened that the best venues for live, cutting-edge jazz in Montreal all were on Saint Antoine Street in Little Burgundy. Every trip came with a hint of exciting danger, breaking the taboos that came with crossing into a Black space. A handful of clubs took advantage of this new market opportunity early in the decade, but the most legendary of them all, Rockhead's Paradise, opened its doors in 1928 in a three-story building on the corner of Saint Antoine and Mountain Street.

The rumor of the day was that Rufus Rockhead, the West Indian immigrant who founded the eponymous club, had financed his new venture off the proceeds of his side business bootlegging into the United States while he was working as a cross-border railway porter. Rockhead cultivated an exclusive vibe, only allowing certain patrons to enter and the cream of the crop of Black musicians to take his stage. The white jazz bands that played hotel ballrooms were safe and boring to those who came to Rockhead's in search of a more uninhibited sound. For those up on stage, playing at Rockhead's never paid anywhere near as well as the mainstream venues uptown, but it certainly brought more street credibility within musician circles.

Less adventurous white Montrealers who lacked the courage to head down to Saint Antoine still flocked into major venues like the Ritz-Carlton hotel, where they lapped up an imported Black American style of music. The general rule was that Black bands played Black clubs for mixed audiences and white bands played white clubs for white audiences, but all of these boundaries fell apart in the wee hours, when musicians were free to play with whomever they liked in front of dwindling crowds of diehard jazz fans. Even the staid Ritz-Carlton got its comeuppance from the popular Johnny Holmes Orchestra when it refused to leave its Black pianist, a very young Oscar Peterson, son to a migrant West Indian porter and a domestic worker, offstage. Audience demand for one of the greatest jazz pianists of all time was so great that ownership had to rethink just how far it was willing to push to uphold the color line.[23]

It is an open question just how much of an impact the jazz boom had on hearts and minds across a sprawling city that was creeping up on a population of one million near mid-century. It most certainly did not make racially progressive converts of all Montrealers, who might have been much more open-minded than their country cousins but still lived within the confines of a stifling, Catholic-dominated social climate during the interwar years.

Jazz did, like wartime military service, create a new space where over the years thousands of Black and white Montrealers could interact regularly in a positive manner, which absolutely did challenge preexisting racial assumptions. By extension, those who had broken these boundaries were highly unlikely to teach their children that the old dividing lines had been natural and were worth maintaining. There is no great gap in the logic that someone who spent the decades of their twenties seeking out clubs that featured Black jazz musicians was already preconditioned to cheer on Jackie Robinson on the baseball field two decades later.

Music undoubtedly helped bring down racial boundaries in the decades immediately preceding Jackie Robinson's arrival in Montreal and so did baseball. It would be misleading, however, to paint a picture of sport as a universal salve for the wounds of racial discrimination in Canada in the first off of the twentieth century. Whereas Royals fans collectively showed their good-heartedness during Jackie Robinson's time with the club in 1946, prewar ball diamonds and hockey rinks across the country far too often remained a venue for an intolerant old guard to manifest its strength to the public.

The summer of 1933 was one of the lowest points in a long, painful depression that hurt Canadians just as badly as their American neighbors. Toronto had just surpassed Montreal as Canada's most populous city, and its rapid growth was similarly fueled by mass immigration from all corners and faiths from Europe. Unemployment rates in Toronto were less terrible than the country as a whole (17 to 30 percent), but wage stagnation and the pervasive fear of a sudden layoff hung over those fortunate enough to hold onto paid work. Desperation all too often breeds radicalism, and many citizens of Toronto the Good, a phrase coined by late nineteenth century Mayor William Holmes Howland, reached for a familiar scapegoat for the country's economic troubles.

Large gangs of fascist thugs who took inspiration from the Nazi Party's violent, stage-managed rise to power after Germany's March 1933 federal election began recruiting for Swastika Clubs all over Toronto. Then they began to flex their muscle with public displays of intimidation. They inevitably turned their attention to the city's Jewish population and chose an otherwise innocuous three-game softball playoff series between two teams of high schoolers, one Jewish and one Catholic, for one of the ugliest displays of civil unrest Canada had ever seen. The geopolitics of the day and a shared anti-Semitism made strange bedfellows out of roughneck elements from the city's dominant Anglo-Protestant community and the Italian Catholic immigrants they had long despised as they squared off together against a common enemy: anyone who came out to cheer on a team of teenaged Jewish ballplayers.

Game one between Harbord Collegiate Institute and St. Peter's School drew a massive crowd of over eleven thousand spectators on August 14 at the city's iconic Christie Pits ballpark, now home of the Toronto Maple Leafs of the Intercounty Baseball League. Soon after the first pitch, Swastika Club goons masquerading as St. Peter's fans made themselves known by unfurling a Nazi banner and lobbing "Heil Hitler" chants at the field whenever a Harbord player came to bat. The Harbord players provoked their rancor by refusing to take the bait and then ultimately prevailing in extra innings.

Fascist elements returned to the park the following day with white paint to deface the Christie Pits clubhouse roof with a swastika and Heil Hitler graffiti in advance of the second game in the series on the 16th. Despite every indication that there would be more unruly fan behavior, Toronto police dispatched just two officers to manage a crowd of ten thousand. This time, Harbord supporters had no intention of turning the other cheek. Everyone in the stands and on the long grassy knolls overlooking the field knew there was a high probability of violence; a good number of them came into the park with hidden makeshift weapons to unsheathe when it kicked off.

Harbord fans were thus prepared to go on the attack after "Heil Hitler" chants began from the other side. A massive brawl unfolded all around the field, and a handful of backup officers arrived on the scene, but the violence spun out of the park, down surrounding streets and alleys, and into residential backyards. The game somehow continued to a tight 6–5 victory for St. Peter's, despite the sprawling melee in all directions off the field. This was not enough to sate the city's bloodlust, and dozens of reinforcement fighters from surrounding neighborhoods poured into the combat zone, completely overrunning the handful of police officers. In one of the smaller victories of the battle, Harbord fans seized control of a swastika banner and ripped it to pieces.

It took nearly six hours before the fighting finally subsided in the wee hours of the morning, as the wounded and exhausted combatants finally retreated to their homes. The most surprising development was that despite hundreds of individual pipe and fistfights everyone walked away bruised but alive. The bloodied staggered individually into local hospitals for treatment over the course of the following days.

The series resumed a week later in a new park with paid admission only to keep the crowd size down to dozens rather than thousands. St. Peter's prevailed, 4–3, on a walk-off home run, then the players shook hands with a grace that eluded the purported fans who came out for them during the first two games of the series.[24]

The Christie Pits riot is viewed in public memory as one of Toronto's greatest embarrassments, a regretful and singular display of intolerance that does not truly represent the city's progressive inclinations. Yet it showed to all at the time that Canada's reputation for tolerance was, at worst, overplayed, or, at best, certainly had its limits. Insofar as it related to Jackie Robinson's Minor League assignment, the incident was perhaps a small factor that would have tempered loftier expectations about how smoothly high-profile integration would go rather than cause to put it off or abandon the idea of Canada as a host venue.

Back in Royals territory, too many conservatives in Québec had allowed themselves to be temporarily seduced by the appeal of European fascist movement in 1930s—including Montreal's flamboyant and popular mayor Camillien Houde—but the province was at least spared the ugliness of a public incident on par with the Christie Pits riot. There were however painfully obvious limits to how far the system would bend toward fairness, even in a cosmopolitan city like Montreal that stood out among its peers.

Hundreds of American jurisdictions from North to South enacted racist Jim Crow laws immediately in the aftermath of the Civil War, but the Canadian Supreme Court waited all the way until 1939 to issue a shameful ruling that gave businesses the legal right to discriminate by race. It all began in a Montreal bar three years earlier when a Canadiens superfan tried to sit down for a beer with his mates.

Fred Christie came to Montreal as a seventeen-year-old Jamaican immigrant in 1919 and made his living as a chauffeur. He married a local widow of German ancestry, Julie Osler, and they settled with his new stepchildren near the Montreal Forum in the Verdun neighborhood. Becoming a Canadiens diehard was part of Christie's assimilation process, and he was a regular visitor to the team's home arena, which operated the landmark York Tavern as a watering hole for the city's sports fans.

On July 11, 1936, he and friends tried to buy beers there after a Saturday-night boxing match, just as they had on many occasions without incident after Habs games, but this time he was declined by a sheepish bartender on the grounds that the York's new ownership had decided that it would no longer serve Black patrons. Christie and his two friends, Emile King and Steven St. Jean, were asked to leave the premises immediately. Incensed, he instead phoned the police and waited for officers to arrive on the scene so he could plead his case. They heard him out but ultimately concluded that the incident was not a police matter and escorted him from his favorite team's official bar in disgrace.

As cruel and disappointing as this encounter was, there is something slightly reassuring that even back in the 1930s Christie felt that he could appeal to local law enforcement against a blatantly discriminatory business and expect a sympathetic hearing. Christie refused to let the matter die and sued the York for $200 with the support from the city's Black community, including Union United Church and the city's railway porters. He won a partial victory with a lower court ruling in his favor that came with a $25 settlement, but the York appealed and won.

It took three years for the case to wind its way all the way up to the Supreme Court of Canada, which ruled four to one that the York had the right to choose whom it could deny service, establishing the legality of race-based discrimination by all businesses across the country.[25] Taken to its most ridiculous extreme, this precedent was later used as the basis of a tax-violation conviction of a pretty thirty-one-year-old Nova Scotia entrepreneur named Viola Desmond, who in 1946 bought a ticket for the Black section of a New Glasgow cinema and then moved into an open seat in the white section that would have cost one penny more had she been allowed to buy it. It was not until 1975 that Québec's new Charter of Human Rights and Freedoms finally outlawed discriminatory practices of the sort imposed on Fred Christie in 1936. The Canadian Charter of Rights and Freedoms followed at the federal level in the spring of 1982 to establish national nondiscrimination standards. Rather than run from a long-ago national embarrassment, the Bank of Canada added Desmond's portrait to the front of the newly designed Canadian ten-dollar bill in 2018.

Taken in sum, all of these developments indicated that Jackie Robinson and the Dodgers organization could reasonably have expected a relatively clean integration process on Canadian soil with the Royals in the fall of 1945. There were, however, enough red flags in the immediate history of Canadian race relations to indicate that this might not unfold without incident. It is still entirely reasonable to surmise that when looking north of the border in the most abstract sense Branch Rickey saw a much easier path forward for the Great Experiment in Québec, albeit one that still would not exactly qualify as easy. In the context of the times, finding a better option than sending Robinson out west to play for the AAA Saint Paul Saints of the American Association, which included the Louisville Colonels franchise in Jim Crow Kentucky, would have to be considered a win.

It was with a reserved optimism that the Royals finally introduced the man who would make sporting and civil rights history to the Montreal press corps on October 10.

2

A Momentous Signing

For Jackie Robinson and the city of Montreal,
it was love at first sight.
—JACKIE ROBINSON, *I Never Had It Made*

Heart disease finally caught up to MLB's first and longest-serving commissioner, Kenesaw Mountain Landis, a habitually scowling and craggy-faced patrician who died in hospital at age seventy-eight just two days after Thanksgiving in 1944. Landis was a sharp-elbowed, Ohio-born and Indiana-raised Republican lawyer who began practicing in Chicago at the twilight of the Gilded Age before taking on a very high-profile position as the Illinois Northern District Court judge in early 1905. He also happened to be a quietly immovable obstacle for those who wanted to integrate America's pastime.

Landis may well have been the most serious man in the baseball world before he assumed the commissionership in 1920. According to legend, as a young man he turned down a professional contract on the grounds that he played for the love of the game rather than money.[1] As a middle-aged judge in 1915, he purposely delayed ruling on an antitrust suit by the Federal League against the American and National Leagues in order to push this upstart competitor to financial ruin. Landis's inaction brought order and stability that made winners of wealthy owners and would-be owners in the established Major Leagues while also showing complete disregard for the hopes of fans mostly in second-tier Midwestern cities who yearned for top-quality baseball. This was a rigid, change-averse thinker if there ever was one.

The role of baseball commissioner was a necessary creation in the aftermath of the 1919 Black Sox scandal and a widespread perception that America's pastime had been corrupted by criminal gambling elements. Landis was indeed a serious candidate for the job who set the tone for his rule by issuing lifetime bans on eight White Sox players who he thought were involved in a scheme to throw the World Series and delivering a stern warning to owners with side interests in horse racing that they had to immediately divest themselves of these assets. He virtually had the power of an emperor over the sport at his zenith in the 1920s, and there was absolutely no ambiguity on where he stood on vice: it would not be tolerated.

Landis's exact views on race were more difficult to divine. He did issue a very public and lawyerly sounding July 1942 statement denying that owners were barred from signing Black players. There is good reason, however, to believe that he would not have permitted Branch Rickey's Great Experiment with Jackie Robinson to unfold as it did in 1946 and 1947. The kindest argument Landis's defenders have ever drummed up is that his values reflected his times.

Landis was as tight-lipped on his personal views on baseball's color line as one would expect from someone who had made a career in law, but he had a track record behind closed doors of leniency toward racists and intolerance toward integrationists. The view that he would have opposed Jackie Robinson's bid to join the Dodgers was seeded forty years ago in Jules Tygiel's *Baseball's Great Experiment* and has gained widespread acceptance in the intervening years. The Baseball Writers' Association of America (BBWAA) marked the centenary of the start of his reign as commissioner by voting to remove his name from the American and National League MVP awards after years of complaints from star players, Black and white, who felt that he did not deserve this honor.[2]

Before a road game against the White Sox at Comiskey Park in the summer of 1938, light-hitting Yankees backup outfielder Jake Powell responded to an innocuous pregame question from a WGN radio reporter about his offseason training regime with a bizarre claim that he kept fit by "cracking n——s over the head with [his] blackjack" as a cop back home in Dayton, Ohio. (As appalling as his words were, he had never even been a police officer; he was merely an applicant. Powell was in fact a petty criminal who died by suicide in a Washington DC police station in 1948 after being arrested for check fraud.) Under threat of a financially damaging boycott from the justifiably angry Black community, Landis reluctantly slapped Powell on the wrist with a ten-game suspension. This was the first time a player was suspended for a public display of bigotry—Powell, a crude anti-Semite, had escaped a well-deserved punishment for a deliberate collision that cost Detroit Tigers star and reigning AL MVP Hank Greenberg nearly all of the 1936 season—but this one in particular was applied to a bench jockey in the midst of a 0 WAR season who already rode the pine in almost two-thirds of his team's games, anyway.

No Major League executive was brave enough to openly challenge Landis over the color barrier by attempting to sign a Black player, but by the late 1930s there was a long list of high-profile owners, general managers, and dugout bosses who confessed that they saw the barrier as either anachronistic, an impediment to their team's success, or both. Their real feelings typically trickled out when they had been cornered by a new generation of more assertive Black and left-leaning sportswriters who asked bluntly how they felt about segregation in baseball.[3]

In due course, owners Clark Griffith of the Washington Senators, Phil Wrigley of the Chicago Cubs, and Grace Comiskey of the Chicago White Sox, along with legendary Athletics manager Connie Mack and his Cincinnati counterpart Bill McKechnie, all expressed qualified integrationist sentiment. Ford Frick, National League president, at least said the right things in public relatively early on, whether he believed them in his heart or not.[4] Among high-profile active players, Yankees outfielder Joe DiMaggio and Cardinals ace Dizzy Dean, both veterans of the postseason barnstorming circuit, advanced the argument that Negro Leagues stars such as Satchell Paige and Josh Gibson were absolutely qualified to play alongside them on Major League teams.[5] Two excellent Reds pitchers, 1939 NL MVP Bucky Walters and early-1940s ace Johnny Vander Meer, added their support to the idea of integration.[6]

Pie Traynor's good but not quite pennant-worthy Pittsburgh Pirates teams of the late 1930s were the most collectively enthusiastic about integration, in no small part because players were painfully familiar with the excess of star talent on the roster of the Pittsburgh Crawfords, a Negro Leagues powerhouse that played just two miles away over at Gus Greenlee Field. Toward the end of an uncharacteristically disappointing 1939 season, Wendell Smith of the *Pittsburgh Courier*, one of the country's leading Black newspapers, surveyed the skipper and most of his players on the race question. He certainly began the feature hoping to hear the right things, but the Pirates' own words supported his conclusion that the typical argument from ownership that they could not integrate without provoking a revolt from their white players was completely without foundation.

The general consensus around the Pirates' dugout was that aging Craws outfielder Cool Papa Bell, young slugging catcher Josh Gibson, and ace starter Satchel Paige were all easily big league quality players. This peer assessment came not just from reading box scores and game recaps but also after having actually competed against them on the off-season exhibit circuit. Left unsaid was the fact that all three played at positions of weakness for the Pirates, who could not quite keep pace with marginally better NL teams such as the Cubs, Cardinals, and Giants. Smith quoted Traynor with an unambiguous statement: "If given permission, I would certainly use a Negro player who had the ability to play in the majors."[7]

Support for the color line was clearly faltering when, a few seasons after the Powell incident, the Brooklyn Dodgers' colorful manager Leo Durocher went on record in July 1942 with the *Daily Worker*, a communist newspaper with a surprisingly good sports section, that he wanted to sign Black players and would do so straight away if not for "a grapevine understanding or subterranean rule" that this was forbidden.[8] Durocher was a scrappy middle infielder on the wrong side of thirty who took over as player-manager for the 1939 season, pulling the team out of doldrums that had lasted nearly as long as the Great Depression. Durocher proved to be an incredibly talented dugout boss, earning a Hall of Fame nod from the Veterans Committee for his twenty-four-year run as a manager. His Dodgers cleared .500 in 1939 and 1940, then they got great in 1941, winning 100 regular-season games and advancing to an anticlimactic World Series in which they lost to their archrival Yankees in five games by just seven total runs.

Durocher wanted to win badly in the hypercompetitive three-team New York market and saw the signing of Negro League players as an advantage in the Jim Crow era, similar to what the emphasis of on-base average was to moneyball enthusiasts decades later. He had, however, long bucked authority and perpetually seemed in danger of losing his livelihood through barely concealed philandering and associations with known gamblers, so he had little room for maneuver when Commissioner Landis summoned him in for a scolding, threatening him to change his tune if he hoped to stay in the game. Durocher ultimately emerged from Landis's dressing-down with a sheepish new story that he had in fact been misquoted by legendary Black sportswriter Wendell Smith and that no color line existed in baseball.[9] There is no record of what Landis actually said to Durocher—just plenty of circumstantial evidence that his words would not have been kind.

Aspiring owner Bill Veeck got his own private taste of Landis's appetite for changing the racial status quo. Veeck was an ultracharismatic wheeler-dealer and idea man who got into the business of baseball thanks to connections he made while his father was president of the Chicago Cubs. In 1940 he bought into the nearby sad-sack Milwaukee Brewers franchise of the AA American Association, and the team's fortunes shifted dramatically for the better almost immediately. Veeck spent most of his early years as a baseball owner overseas as a Marine Corps artilleryman until he lost his right leg in a battlefield injury in World War II. Nevertheless, he helped turn the cellar-dwelling Brewers of 1941 into a close runner-up in 1942 and then regular season American Association champs in 1943.

Veeck was a longtime fan of the run-and-gun Negro Leagues style of play who was unquestionably on the right side of history when he risked arrest by choosing to sit in the "colored section" of the Brewers spring training facility in Ocala, Florida. He told local law enforcement that if they followed through on the threat he would counter by pulling his team out of town, leaving it to deal with the subsequent loss of tourism revenue. Veeck was, however, an aspirational riser who wanted more than a stake in a Minor League club, so he engineered a bid to purchase the Philadelphia Phillies at the end of the 1942 season. Struggling would be an understatement for the

Phillies; the club had just reeled off six one-hundred-loss seasons over the previous seven years and no prospect of a turnaround was in sight. If any team needed an infusion of patented Veeck magic, this was it.

Veeck was more vocally progressive, but he had essentially reached the same conclusion as Durocher: it was time to bring in good players that made his team better, the color line be damned. He later claimed in his memoirs that if the purchase had gone through, he would have stocked the 1943 Phillies with Negro Leagues stars to help turn the team into instant winners. By his own contested account, he told Landis of his intention of breaking the color barrier, then had his deal to buy the club mysteriously blocked at the last minute. The Phillies as a result remained godawful through the end of the decade until Richie Ashburn and Robin Roberts emerged as stars, while Veeck had to wait until after Landis's death to finally get an opportunity to buy the Cleveland Indians at the end of the 1946 season as a consolation prize. He immediately thumbed his nose at Jim Crow Florida by moving his team's spring training facility to Tucson, Arizona, launching the Cactus League as a preseason alternative.[10] Shortly after, he integrated the American League in July 1947 when he signed twenty-three-year-old Newark Eagles star Larry Doby, a Hall of Famer whose excellent career was overshadowed by that of Jackie Robinson's by virtue of coming a close second among early Black players and toiling in a much smaller market. Veeck's Indians were World Series champions in 1948.

There are few greater authorities on Landis and the color line than John Thorn, a writer and Ken Burns collaborator who has been MLB's official historian since 2011. Thorn added his influential voice to the successful lobbying campaign to have the Negro Leagues categorized as a Major League in the statistical records. Thorn argues that Landis "was no more or less a racist than the owners he served, or of millions of other white Americans living in that era" and that he could have brought about integration at the height of his impressive power over the sport in the 1920s but chose not to. It is also his assessment that the silence of all attendees at the December 3, 1943, Winter Meetings at the Hotel Roosevelt in New York—after Landis claimed that no written color line was in baseball and teams were free to sign players of their choosing—reflected an implicit understanding that the status quo was to continue.

At the Winter Meetings in 1943, the morning panel was little more than a show Landis put on for invited members of the Black press in the hope of deflating the integrationist protest movement that posed a real threat to league revenue, particularly in New York and Chicago. Still, new Dodgers GM Branch Rickey alone made an unsuccessful attempt to press him for more specific details—after all, if there was no gentleman's agreement, why did every single club behave as though there was, to the obvious detriment of their on-field product?—but Landis clearly would not take the bait. In the end, the commissioner had merely thrown crumbs to invited members of the Black press in what Thorn describes as a "wink-and-nudge display of that hypocrisy."[11]

Rickey had seen multiple would-be integrationists fail unsuccessfully against an unjust system, so he opted for a cool, methodical approach to outplay Landis and maneuver his Kentucky-bred, Confederate-sympathizing successor Albert "Happy" Chandler into accepting the inevitability of change. Rickey was a baseball lifer who caught for Ohio Wesleyan University and was good enough to get the most starts behind the dish for a surprisingly decent St. Louis Browns team in 1906, but he backslid the following year with the New York Highlanders and was washed up as a player by age twenty-five. He spent much of the next decade coaching at the collegiate level before he got his second Major League break in St. Louis as manager of the Browns.

After a combat deployment to the Western Front as an army major during World War I, Rickey returned to the Gateway City in a new role as Cardinals manager. He brought some progress on the field, but ownership concluded Rickey's intellect would be better used as the team's business manager. Rickey protested, but the move was a good one for all parties in the end. He gained a reputation for being cheap to the point of cruelty in negotiations with players and conducted himself with a churchy moralism that many of those who called him "Mahatma" found off-putting, but he was as impactful of an innovator as any figure in the game during his era. He overhauled his new role and could be considered the first general manager of the modern era of baseball, creating the farm system and 20-80 grading scale, among other innovations.

Rickey waited until Jackie Robinson made his Major League debut in 1947 before explaining to the press why he had set out to break baseball's color line. By his telling, it came down to a moving encounter that took place during his early years as a coach at Ohio Wesleyan on a road trip to South Bend, Indiana, to play Notre Dame. Rickey's team had one Black player, Charles Johnson, and the result was foreseeable when he tried to rent a room in the hotel where the rest of the team was staying. Rickey interceded and convinced the clerk to at least let Johnson sleep on a cot in Rickey's room, which led to a scene later in the evening where the manager saw his player crying as he rubbed his hands and said, "Black skin. Black skin. If only I could make them white." All he could do in the moment was reply, "Come on, Tommy, snap out of it, buck up! We'll lick this one day, but we can't if you feel sorry for yourself."[12]

The city of St. Louis had given Rickey his first opportunity to become a baseball legend, and he had helped bring the Cardinals World Series titles in 1926, 1931, 1934, and 1942, but it was still an extremely conservative place as the Major League's southernmost outpost until expansion and relocation brought teams into Dixie in the early-to-mid-1960s. (The Cardinals eventually returned to glory in the 1960s thanks largely to their Black ace, Bob Gibson.) This was not the time nor place for a successful challenge to the color barrier, but Rickey's calculus changed when he took over as the Dodgers GM in 1943. New York, Brooklyn specifically, was a radically different environment from the southern-infused culture of the lower Midwest, and Rickey was finally free to put his plan into action.

The pre-Rickey Dodgers team was more of a cultural institution than a successful baseball franchise. Brooklyn was the most cosmopolitan borough in an incredibly cosmopolitan city; its heavy immigrant population was almost one-third Jewish and coming out to enjoy the circus-like atmosphere at Ebbets Field was a cherished component of the Americanization process for peoples who came from all across the world. Fans of "Dem Bums" during the lovable loser years of the 1930s were heavily working class and staunch backers of their Democratic Mayor Fiorello La Guardia and New Dealer President Franklin Roosevelt. They were also accustomed to low-cost tickets and guzzling plenty of cheap beer in the stands with their loud, boisterous comrades. Ebbets Field was severely hemmed in by Bedford Avenue beyond right field to the point that it was the smallest park of the era, a quirk that promoted both a physical and emotional closeness between players and fans. The Yankees and Giants certainly had their own diehards, but Dodgers fans were a breed apart.

The Dodgers on-field product took a major step forward when Larry MacPhail came in as general manager in 1939 after having overseen a successful rebuild of the Cincinnati Reds. MacPhail promptly found a new winning manager in Durocher, then brought in young cornerstone pieces, including slick-fielding shortstop and future hall of famer Pee Wee Reese. MacPhail's last prewar team went all the way to the World Series against the Yankees but lost four games to one, and each narrow defeat came in heartbreaking fashion. Victory was once an afterthought, but this club was definitely getting closer when the Pearl Harbor attack threw everyone's plans into disarray. MacPhail had been an artillery captain in the American Expeditionary Force during World War I and decided to do his patriotic duty once again at the end of the 1942 season, resigning his position with the Dodgers to take an officer's commission with the army and work out of the War Department though 1945. It was time to find a new boss who could build on his solid foundation.

Rickey arrived in Brooklyn from the Cardinals in time for the 1943 season as a seasoned executive with shoes just as big as MacPhail's. He had long wanted to integrate baseball, and with this move he found a fan base that was keenly receptive to it, along with ownership that was willing to green-light his search for a Black player. Rickey sold integration to George McLaughlin, a banker at the Brooklyn Trust Company who served as trustee for the Ebbets family and represented its 50 percent share in the club, by pitching it on purely business grounds. He convinced McLaughlin, who warned against integration for political or social motives but ultimately brought the other directors on board, that there was money to be made tapping into the Black Brooklyn market.[13]

New York was also the focal point of the pressure campaign to do more, faster—one million people had signed a *Daily Worker* petition to integrate baseball—and state and local politicians provided added legal cover by passing some of the era's most progressive civil rights ordinances.[14] New York Governor Thomas E. Dewey signed the Ives-Quinn Act that banned racial discrimination in hiring into state law on March 12, 1945, raising the question of whether New York–based MLB clubs would be open to legal action if they did not integrate their rosters relatively soon. It should not be forgotten that the war had decimated Rickey's roster—Reese and fellow Hall of Fame second baseman Billy Herman joined the navy, along with the Dodgers' most dependable reliever, Hugh Casey, while 1941 NL OPS leader Pete Reiser, staff ace Kirby Higbe, and dependable swing man Ed Head all left for the army—which also could have justified sending his scouts for a curious peek at Negro League talent as a wartime exigency.

Jackie Robinson was himself in uniform as a lieutenant in the U.S. Army when Rickey's Dodgers tenure began, and he was not considered among the earliest options for the Great Experiment. Rickey's interest was first piqued by a twenty-eight-year-old Cuban shortstop, Silvio García, who had enjoyed great success at home with the Elefantes de Cienfuegos and in the Mexican League with the Diablos Rojos. Why Rickey passed on him is up for debate, but it seems that he was deterred by some combination of pistol-carrying Mexican League jefe Jorge Pasquel's threats to his scout Tom Greenwade about the consequences of poaching players, as well as Greenwade's hasty scouting report that Garcia was a slap hitter who lacked maturity. In any event, Garcia was conscripted back into the Cuban military for a second tour and was unavailable anyway.[15]

After this unproductive Caribbean foray, Rickey reached the conclusion that best Black players were already close at hand in the American Negro Leagues. In due course, however, big names, worthy candidates all, came up, and each one was rejected in turn.

The legendary Satchel Paige was still in great form, but pushing forty—it was assumed, since no one really knew his age for sure until Cleveland Indians owner Bill Veeck actually went down to Mobile in search of his birth certificate before signing him in 1948—and had perhaps unfairly earned a reputation for a mercurial streak that caused concerns. Outfielder Monte Irvin of the Newark Eagles was the most exciting young player in the Negro Leagues at the time of the Pearl Harbor attack, but he was drafted into the army in 1942 and spent the next three years away from the game while he was on active duty. Fellow Eagle Don Newcombe had an electric arm and ace potential that he later fulfilled, but he was still just eighteen years old at the start of the 1944 season. The Baltimore Elite Giants young catcher Roy Campanella also seemed to have all of the talent in the world along with half-Italian parentage that would endear him to plenty of Brooklyn fans, but there were some doubts about his seriousness, given his known fondness for the night life. Both Newcombe and Campanella later joined and starred for the Dodgers, but in the meantime Rickey's search continued.[16]

Robinson came on the Dodgers radar as a tantalizing and raw prospect who nevertheless carried a fair bit of risk of his own. He was born into a sharecropper family in southern Georgia in 1919 and raised in Pasadena after his mother relocated the family out West to California when Robinson's father abandoned them. Robinson's older siblings oozed athletic talent. His brother Mack had tied the great Jesse Owens's Olympic-record time of 21.1 seconds in the 200m during the ominous 1936 Berlin games under Hitler's disapproving glare, walking away with a silver medal when Owens ran the race of his life in the final and set a new world record of 20.7 seconds. On his return to Pasadena, he could only find work as a street sweeper, so he wore his Team USA jacket on the job to remind his rich, white neighbors how the community rewarded its should-be heroes.

Jackie excelled at virtually every sport on offer at John Muir Technical High School, lettering in baseball, basketball, football, and track and field. He somehow also found time to excel in tennis and golf, sports in which he could be considered more of a casual dabbler. His head-turning performances continued at Pasadena Junior College in the fall of 1938, then he moved on after graduation to University of California, Los Angeles (UCLA), where he played in the backfield of an integrated football team that also featured future Los Angeles Rams Woody Strode and Kenny Washington, the first Black player in the

NFL. All of the familiar tales of Robinson's star-athlete tour at UCLA often neglect to mention that his scholarship forced him to divide his energies between some sports that meant little to him and that he was a four-sport letterman who still had to work part-time sweeping dorms as assistant janitor.[17] Robinson's hypercompetitive nature as an athlete was thus coupled with stoicism stemming from life experiences.

World War II military service did not necessarily mean a full break from athletics for America's star athletes; in fact, many of the nation's best baseball players managed to continue competing at a fairly high level, just without the familiar scrutiny of home-market sportswriters.[18] For example, a mix of not-yet-demobilized players largely from the high Minors and Negro Leagues took the field when the hotly contested 1945 GI World Series began in occupied Nuremberg in front of fifty thousand fans on September 2 at Stadion der Hitlerjugend (Hitler Youth Stadium), bedecked with American flags and converted to baseball from its previous use as a site for mass fascist rallies.[19] Surreal locale aside, this experience felt fairly close to the real thing for the players, given the circumstances. For Robinson, however, the war put baseball on hold for nearly two-and-a-half years, and he had little reason to believe he could ever make a living from it.

With marriage to classmate Rachel Isum on his mind, Robinson made a practical decision to leave UCLA before graduating to take a stable federal government job about two hundred miles up the coast in Atascadero as an assistant athletic director with the National Youth Administration. One of the other advantages of his new position in the months before the Pearl Harbor attack was that it allowed him to continue playing highly competitive integrated semiprofessional and professional football.

Robinson's college background should have put him on a fast track in an officer-training program after he was drafted into the army in 1942 and sent to join a segregated cavalry unit in Fort Riley, Kansas. The army, however, chose to slow roll Black applicants to the Officer Candidate School like Robinson and his new friend, legendary heavyweight boxer Joe Louis, prompting Robinson to file complaints that ultimately resulted in an intervention from Washington. This delay pushed Robinson's commission as second lieutenant back to January

1943, after which he was assigned to the 761st Black Panthers Tank Battalion in the heart of Jim Crow Texas at Fort Hood.

Robinson found that his new role as a morale officer for Fort Hood's Black troops entailed little more than providing them with entertainment, gum, and condoms. He could have continued playing football for the base team, but the Texas heat was so intense and the competition was so far below that of his last organized competition in the Pacific Coast Professional Football League that he chose to sit out what was probably his best sport. He did, however, try to join Fort Hood's baseball team, only to be turned away on the grounds that the color line would be maintained there. The officer who rejected him told him he was free to join an all-Black team, though both men understood that one did not exist on base. Up until this point, Robinson's West Coast experience in sports had been that whites generally found winning more important than maintaining racial boundaries. Texas provided a rude awakening.[20]

There was, however, one baseball-related silver lining to Robinson's military service: it led to a chance encounter while he was on medical leave at Camp Breckinridge in Kentucky with fellow soldier Ted Alexander, a journeyman pitcher from South Carolina who had most recently played for the elite Kansas City Monarchs of the Negro American League. (Through sheer coincidence, both men had been given the middle name Roosevelt in honor of America's twenty-sixth president.) Alexander convinced Robinson to write the Monarchs' owner Thomas Baird about the possibility of joining the team after he left the military. Baird obliged Robinson with an invitation to spring training in 1945 and an offer of $400 per month if he cracked the roster. This sum was modest, just barely above the median national income at the time, and Robinson was deterred by the prospect of long road trips by bus, Jim Crow obstacles to finding decent food and accommodation, and the negative impact distance would have on his relationship with his fiancée. But this was, after all, just a short-term commitment that would allow him to play at the highest level open to Black players at the time.[21]

Robinson had quite a lot of rust on him since a frustrating 1940 season with the UCLA Bruins when he apparently hit .097, but he indeed made the 1945 Monarchs without Alexander, who missed the season while his military service continued.[22] Then Robinson made an incredibly loud thirty-four-game professional debut at shortstop that forced Branch Rickey's scouts to take note: despite missing nearly four prime development years, Robinson put up a 1.049 OPS (.375/.449/.600), leading the league in doubles, home runs, extra-base hits, and position-player WAR. These gaudy numbers prompted Rickey to send a scout to Kansas City for an in-person look, armed with the cover story that he was scouting players for the new Brooklyn Brown Dodgers, a United States Negro Baseball League team that played mostly at Ebbets Field and the Minor League parks of teams in the Dodgers' system.[23]

As a player, Robinson held his own for the Monarchs as a shortstop, but his arm strength was a weakness that hinted at a future move over to the keystone. At the dish, he was a patient right-handed hitter with a wide, pigeon-toed stance who crowded the plate with his bat held high and straight. He worked deep counts, made great contact, and was very difficult to strike out, racking up an eye-watering total of over two-and-a-half times as many walks as strikeouts over the course of his Major League career. He also had extra-base power that might have translated into 20-plus home runs per season rather than his typical 10 to 20 if his home park, Ebbets Field, was not so heavily skewed to favor lefty pull hitters.

But it was on the bases where he really made his mark, importing an aggressive Negro Leagues style of running that was completely unprecedented in the white game, which emphasized the long ball and station-to-station play.[24] Robinson led the NL in steals in his first and third seasons, but the bigger problem for opposing pitchers was that he was in constant motion once he took his lead and created a source of distraction. His raw steal totals were impressive—including a Live Ball Era record of 19 steals of home—but the numbers do not fully show the fear and panic he created through constant sprints as though he was going to steal, followed by a quick halt and retreat to the bag. Whether he was seen as a skilled disrupter or a pest, there was full agreement that no base runner of the era could routinely throw pitchers off their game as well as Robinson.

On-field talent certainly mattered, but Robinson also seemed to nail all of the character criteria on Rickey's list. He had played in the spotlight at UCLA and was as prepared as anyone in the Negro Leagues for the double scrutiny of breaking a seemingly unbreakable barrier while at the same time playing in the glare of New York. Rickey saw his engagement to Rachel Isum and religious affiliation to the Methodist Church, to which Rickey was a near fanatical devotee, as two hugely important factors that would help keep him grounded when times inevitably turned rough. But it was the quiet dignity that Robinson maintained through his court-martial proceedings from the army that showed that he was capable of maintaining his cool in the face of injustice.

On July 6, 1944, Robinson had to leave the base at Fort Hood to see a doctor to obtain medical clearance for an old football-related ankle injury so he could accompany his 761st Tank Battalion on a fall deployment to France for the final Allied push into Nazi Germany. After the appointment wrapped up, he got on the nearly empty midnight bus back to base and saw a friend, Virginia Jones, the light-skinned wife of a fellow officer, four rows from the very back and decided to sit down beside her. The civilian bus driver decided that he saw a Black man sitting next to a White woman, so he stopped the bus and ordered Robinson to move all the way to the back row. In the ensuing argument, Mrs. Jones argued that two Black riders were already sitting in the Black section of the bus, while Robinson stridently rejected the notion that the civilian driver had any authority over him under military regulations. MPs were waiting for him by the time the bus arrived at the terminal.

Robinson was not arrested, but he was hauled in for an unsympathetic hearing with a provost marshal that resulted in court-martial charges for directing salty language at the officers who questioned him rather than accepting defeat and moving to the back of the bus. It took a full month before the actual hearing, during which time Robinson wrote letters about what had happened to him to the NAACP, California's two U.S. senators, the secretary of war, and friendly sportswriters from his UCLA days. His story subsequently blew up in newspapers across the country, and the army faced the prospect of major reputational damage with Black and liberal America if it wanted to press the case, so Robinson was quietly acquitted and put on permanent limited duty to rehab from his supposed ankle injury for the remainder of his tour. When his time was up, he requested and was granted an honorable discharge.[25] Meanwhile, the Black Panthers got a rousing pep talk from Gen. George S. Patton right before they started heroically punching their way through hotly contested German-held villages in eastern France that November without Robinson.

For some, the bus incident would have been a liability, but to Rickey it demonstrated that Robinson would absolutely stand up for himself when pushed and that he was unwilling to submit to injustice. This was exactly the sort of controlled backbone the GM was looking for in a player. Nevertheless, the question of whether Robinson was indeed the right man still had to be determined by Rickey's trusted scout, Clyde Sukeforth, who would make initial contact, and then ultimately Rickey himself.

Sukeforth was a Maine native and decent-hitting platoon catcher with the Reds from 1926 to 1931 who quietly finished out his playing days as a Dodger with three seasons of sporadic play then one last heroic eighteen-game swan song at age forty-three. His career came to a premature end thanks to an offseason hunting accident that left a pellet lodged in his right eye and impacted his vision for the rest of his life, but his college background at Georgetown and even temper hinted that he was better suited to front-office work. "Sukey" became a roving manager in the Dodgers' system before taking over the Royals from 1940 to 1942, a run that included an International League championship in 1941. One of Rickey's earliest moves as the Dodgers new GM was removing Sukeforth as Royals manager on the grounds that had been unable to fulfill the impossible task of keeping his players away from Montreal's legendary nightlife.[26] Nevertheless, Rickey still trusted Sukeforth's instincts as a coach and special-assignment scout, so he kept him in the organization with the big club in Brooklyn.

Tom Greenwade had scouted Robinson for the Dodgers over twenty games with the Monarchs, but Sukeforth was sent out to reel him in for contract talks with Rickey.[27] Sukeforth finally traveled west to Chicago in August 1945 to make his first approach to Robinson while the Monarchs were in town for a road series, but the scout had still not been fully apprised of Rickey's revolutionary intentions. When

Rickey informed Sukeforth that he was willing to travel to Chicago to meet Robinson rather than summon the player to Brooklyn, Sukeforth did, however, begin to sense that something bigger was afoot with Robinson than the routine signing of a new shortstop for a new Negro Leagues expansion team.

Rickey had authorized Sukeforth to offer Robinson reasonably generous terms—a $3,500 bonus plus $600 per month during the season—because he knew that he had to announce the signing of new Black player soon or risk losing all of the credit for years of groundbreaking work if Mayor La Guardia made a campaign-trail announcement demanding the integration of New York's three Major League teams.[28] That move would have made a profound, long-planned act seem as though it had instead come as a result of political fiat, creating a sense of urgency in the Dodgers front office. Neither Sukeforth nor Robinson knew what was coming next, but there was just enough on the table here to convince the player to join the scout in Toledo for a train trip to Brooklyn for the single-most momentous encounter in baseball history. Sukeforth deftly handled the initial meeting with Robinson in Chicago, sparing Rickey a trip that risked bringing his plans into the open before he was ready to reveal them.[29]

Just months before his death in 1972, Robinson wrote Sukeforth to thank his old friend one last time. "While there has not been enough said of your significant contribution in the Rickey-Robinson experiment, I consider your role, next to Mr. Rickey's and my wife's—yes, bigger than any other persons with whom I came in contact," he wrote. "I have always considered you to be one of the true giants in this initial endeavor in baseball, for which I am truly appreciative."[30]

By his own telling, Robinson arrived in Brooklyn for his meeting with Rickey on August 28 in full belief that he was actually being recruited for the Brown Dodgers.[31] Back during spring training, Robinson was lured up to Boston by a well-meaning Wendell Smith at the *Pittsburgh Courier*'s expense, along with two other Negro League stars, Sam Jethroe and Marvin Williams, for what was billed as a tryout for Red Sox scouts at Fenway Park. Smith probably believed he was advancing the cause, but the club only relented to a preseason charade because it was under pressure from a city councilman, Isadore H. Y. Muchnick, to integrate its roster or risk losing its license for Sunday games. Robinson later wrote, "Not for one minute did we believe the tryout was sincere," a correct assumption, given that neither general manager Eddie Collins nor field manager Joe Cronin had any intention of offering up any of these three invitees so much as a Minor League contract.[32]

Robinson's arrival at the cigar-smoke-filled Dodgers team office at 215 Montague Street in Brooklyn was shrouded in secrecy by Rickey's design and escaped the notice of the press. Perhaps the cloak-and-dagger was overblown—almost two weeks later Smith, the sportswriter who put Robinson on Rickey's radar, did report on the meeting in a *Courier* article that hinted suggestively that there was more at play than met the eye, but none of his colleagues at white papers perceived what was happening.[33] By the end of the encounter, Robinson agreed to join the Dodgers' system and sign a contract with their AAA affiliate in Montreal by November 1, though he was free to continue playing with the Monarchs (and briefly the Kansas City Royals barnstormers), provided he kept terms of his new deal to an incredibly tight inner circle right up until the ink hit paper.

Sukeforth was a mostly silent third-party observer in the room; he described the atmosphere as "electric." Both Rickey and Robinson took a good moment at the outset of the meeting to size each other up, then Rickey led off with a personal and complicated question about Robinson's romantic status. Rickey wanted to hear Robinson tell him that he indeed had a good woman to lean on for support during the trials ahead, but he got a complicated reply that Robinson thought he did, even if all of his time away from her while on the road left him with doubts. Rickey then proceeded straight to the set-up, asking Robinson if he knew why he had been summoned to Brooklyn. It was at this moment that Rickey revealed that Robinson was being presented with an opportunity to join the Dodgers' system with a trial in Montreal that would hopefully lead to a quick callup to the big club.

After dropping this bombshell, Rickey turned the conversation to a famously heated direction. Rickey explained to Robinson that he indeed had all of the physical tools to succeed but still questioned whether he had the courage to stand up to the racists that would try to block him at every turn. Before Robinson could answer, Rickey issued his famous challenge: "I'm looking for a ballplayer with guts enough not to fight." He then followed with the crudest, most full-throated role play of the sort of foul treatment Robinson could expect to immediately encounter from hotel clerks, waiters, opposing players, and every imaginable sort of white opponent of integration after he crossed the color line. Others would surely have lost their cool under Rickey's pressure test, but Robinson quickly grasped its purpose: to underline the point that these people wanted to provoke him into sabotaging himself by tempting him to fight fire with fire. Resistance on their terms would lead to defeat. No deep and meaningful conversation with Rickey would have been complete without some gospel, in this case a much softer Christian invocation to turn the other cheek in the face of provocations from lowlifes and scoundrels.[34] This initiation was shockingly direct and highly effective; within two hours both men had developed a full and lifelong trust in one another.

With the knowledge of what was coming, it was nearly impossible for Robinson to play out the string for the Monarchs after rejoining the team, leading him to try to negotiate his early release so he could return home to California after suiting up for a final time on September 21. The club was justifiably furious—he was its best position player after all—and it issued a sadly irrelevant threat that he was contractually bound to the Monarchs. This all-or-nothing gambit failed, and Robinson left the team to join the Kansas City Royals for some low-stakes barnstorming tune-ups back home in California through September and early October.[35]

In the weeks ahead, there would be howls of understandable protest that Rickey had no right to sign a player who was already under contract to a Negro Leagues team without at least offering fair-market compensation. These came from not just the Monarchs and sympathetic Black sportswriters but also various high-profile mainstream columnists. Nevertheless, Rickey rudely brushed aside this argument on the grounds that there was nothing organized about the Negro Leagues, with their irregular schedule and patchwork of league games and barnstorming appearances with local clubs and that their players were all effectively free agents at the end of every season. However unfair this was to Negro Leagues executives who did the best they could with limited resources for players who had no other domestic professional alternative, Robinson generally agreed with the Rickey line and never looked back.

He would not have known it at the time, but his future was about to be placed in extremely competent hands once he got to Montreal and joined the Royals.

Anyone who has given in to the cheap stereotype of Québec as a hockey-mad baseball backwater is only half right. Professional baseball arrived in Montreal in the late 1890s and was a solid gate draw even during its early years, which were characterized by a revolving door of short-lived teams competing at lower levels. By 1928 the city finally had a stable franchise, the Royals, at the highest level in the longest running Minor League, the International League, and a gleaming new home park that drew envy from visitors. Immediately after World War II, over half of Canada's Minor League baseball teams were located in Québec (eleven of eighteen). At the highest level, the Royals did have a solid International League rivalry with the Toronto Maple Leafs, a fringy outpost at the very westernmost boundary of International League territory, but Montreal clearly had the upper hand by the later 1930s. Toronto just did not have executives on par with those in Montreal, nor was the club ever able to figure out a stable, fruitful Major League affiliation that would keep it stocked with talent.[36]

The Royals' finances were relatively solid through the Great Depression, thanks to a major cash injection from Jean-Charles Emile Trudeau, aka "Charlie," a gregarious Montreal lawyer and businessman who made his fortune running a gas-station empire, and his investor partner Roméo J. Gauvreau.[37] Trudeau was the baseball superfan—he actually died in 1935 at just forty-seven from pneumonia during a trip down to Royals spring training in Florida—while Gauvreau was more of a well-connected engineer and investor with varied business interests across the city. They made a very shrewd decision to bring in Hector Racine, a forty-six-year-old business polyglot, as president in 1933, ushering in a long golden era in Royals history.[38]

Racine first affiliated the Royals with the Pittsburgh Pirates, a better than average National League team during the early-to-mid 1930s, but he shook them off after the 1938 season out of frustration with the parent club's unwillingness to share quality players. Before the breakup, he had started cultivating a relationship with Dodgers GM Larry MacPhail through constant invitations up to Québec for fishing trips and offered bonhomie to a top-rate executive whose team just so happened to be lacking a AA affiliate (the top Minor level until the AAA designation was created in 1946) of its own. Racine's long-game sales pitch ultimately worked, and the Royals switched affiliation to Brooklyn before the 1939 season, adopting the Dodgers' blue color scheme for their new uniforms, and, more important, tapping into the deep resources of a better-run organization.[39]

The Royals then got very good, very quickly. Brainy roving coach–scout Clyde Sukeforth brought the team up to .500 in 1940 after a couple of seasons near the cellar, then in 1941 he led them to an International League championship over the powerhouse Newark Bears. Less-fruitful playoff appearances followed in 1942 and once again after Sukeforth had been removed as manager in 1943. After a forgettable 1944 season, the Royals won the pennant in 1945 but lost the championship to Newark. All of this winning brought record attendance even in wartime, with a regular-season total of nearly four hundred thousand, plus another sixty thousand during the playoffs. This meant that the Royals outdrew a list of well-established Major League teams that included the Phillies, Reds, and Braves.

The Royals were an undisputed Minor League baseball powerhouse from 1946 to 1951, reeling off three International League pennants and two Junior World Series wins as overall AAA champs. No fewer than twelve members of the World Series–winning 1955 Dodgers were Royals alumni (five of whom were Black and four of whom earned Cooperstown honors), along with their manager Walter Alston.[40] Early-season cold weather aside, this was arguably the most desirable posting for any Minor Leaguer with big league aspirations in the immediate postwar years.

It was fortuitous that the Royals were such a welcoming, well-run organization because there was nowhere else in the Dodgers' system where Rickey could have dispatched Robinson for the 1946 season. Roy Campanella and Don Newcombe, who also signed with the organization that winter, were sent out to Class-B Nashua in the New England League, a safe place to play in a closed loop where the competition was too far beneath them to really serve their development. (Rickey slow-baked both of them—Campy finally came up at age twenty-six in 1948 and Newcombe at twenty-three in 1949—to stagger the arrival of his new Black players, wasting at least one season of productive Major League service for both of them.) As a slightly more developed prospect who dominated AAA play, Robinson would likely have hit better than .400 and posted comical numbers had this been his assignment. Nashua just was not an appropriate challenge.

None of the Dodgers other B league affiliates were options: the Danville Dodgers in Illinois were too remote, while the Meridian Peps in Mississippi, the Newport News Dodgers in Virginia, and the Asheville Tourists in North Carolina all played at home and on the road in the most rigorously enforced Jim Crow sections of the country. There was no way that Robinson could have taken the field for any of them in 1946 and escaped unharmed. It was the same story for the Dodgers AA affiliates, the Fort Worth Cats and the Mobile Bears. The Saint Paul Saints of the AAA American Association theoretically offered good competition in what was one of the more open-minded home markets in the northern states, but sending Robinson there would have forced him to play at least ten games on incredibly hostile territory in Kentucky against the Louisville Colonels. His first appearances there with the Royals in the Junior World Series at the end of the 1946 season were as incredibly ugly as the pessimists expected, vindicating Rickey's decision to avoid the American Association entirely. In the end, Montreal certainly had its assets, but Rickey ultimately chose it after crossing off all the other names on a list of Minor League alternatives.

The wider baseball world finally got its introduction to Jackie Robinson on a Tuesday-afternoon signing ceremony in front of the Montreal press corps on October 23. The Royals' bespeckled and long-serving president Hector Racine had summoned journalists to the team's headquarters at Delorimier Stadium with very little advance notice, hyping the press conference as "the biggest baseball story to ever hit this town." The start of the Canadiens hockey season was just four days away, and Montrealers were very much geared up for a revenge campaign against their archrival Toronto Maple Leafs after a disappointing semifinal NHL playoff exit that spring, but a robust contingent of local sportswriters came out of curiosity. None had even the remotest idea of what was about to unfold before them; secrecy-obsessed Rickey would almost certainly have been pleased to learn that all of their pre–press conference speculation centered on the possibility that Babe Ruth was going to become the team's new manager or, even better, that the Royals were about to be called up to the big leagues as a reward for their recent on-field success and strong gate numbers.[41]

Branch Rickey chose not to come to the city and take center stage at the press conference, leaving this momentous announcement to a group of francophone Québécois executives led by Racine that included club vice president Lt. Col. Roméo Gauvreau, GM Guy Moreau, treasurer Arthur Normandin, and club secretary Marcel Dufresne.[42] They were joined by just one visiting American, Branch Rickey Jr., the director of the Dodgers' farm system, who had traveled up from Brooklyn for the ceremony. It was Racine, not Rickey, who stood in front of the flash bulbs to make the official announcement on the Dodgers' behalf that baseball's color barrier was about to come crashing down. "We've brought you here tonight to tell you that we are signing a Black player who was highly recommended by Brooklyn Dodgers scouts," he said. "We have given him a healthy bonus to sign a contract and he will have a chance to make the roster in spring training in Florida."[43]

When Robinson was finally brought out, the room fell flat with disappointment, not so much with him personally but rather as an honest reaction to the realization there would be no Ruth or no big league baseball in town just yet. When Racine argued that segregation in baseball should end in part because of the patriotic contribution Black Americans had made to the Allied victory in World War II, the assembled local reporters took this justification as so obvious that they could skip past it entirely in favor of more practical questions. In fact, the first question Robinson took from a reporter was whether he was looking to take over the shortstop position at the expense of Stan Bréard, a wildly popular slick-fielding, no-bat Montreal native.[44] Some others even walked out of the press conference early, having given an offseason baseball story enough of their time with puck drop on the Canadiens' season looming.[45]

The magnitude of this event did, however, start to sink in by the time the assembled sportswriters made their way back to their respective newsrooms. The following day, Robinson coverage took up roughly half of the copy space on the first page of in the sports section of Montreal's biggest circulation English-language paper, *The Gazette*. Dink Carroll, one of Canada's most prominent sportswriters of the era, noted the historical significance of the event, both-sidesing the arguments for and against integration without offering his own take on the Royals and Dodgers' surprise move.[46] By the 25th, he summarized the general fan reaction in the city as "What's so big about that? I thought we were going to have a major league club here." Carroll, with a fair heaping of exaggeration, argued that this cavalier take was the result of "the absolute absence here of an anti-Negro sentiment among sports fans, which was what Mr. Rickey doubtless had in mind when he chose Montreal as the locale for his history-making experiment of introducing a colored player into the ranks of organized baseball."[47]

French-language papers tended to be more immediately enthusiastic about the Robinson experiment. *La Presse*, Montreal's leader, opened its story on the signing with the statement "A Black man will play next summer for the Montreal Royals! This fact, which might appear banal, constitutes probably the biggest news in the history of organized baseball." The article beamed with pride that baseball's color barrier was finally going to come down in Montreal rather than in the United States or any other Canadian city, viewing this development as an affirmation that Montrealers were more democratically spirited and less racially prejudiced than anywhere else in North America.[48] This paper immediately recognized that everyday Montrealers were central characters in an amazing story that had only just begun.

Elsewhere, *Montreal-matin* (Montreal morning) noted that Racine stood up for the principle "that a player of any nationality, race, or religion has the right to try out for an organized team."[49] Louis Gosselin at *La Patrie* (The nation) approvingly saluted Royals management for taking a bold step forward for both baseball and society as a whole. He correctly predicted that given how Montrealers long embraced great athletes from all corners, "it wouldn't make a lick of difference if the newest arrival, Robinson, was a bit more tan than the others."[50]

When Robinson took the microphone, he was fairly reserved and promised to make the most of his opportunity. "Of course, I can't begin to tell you how happy I am that I am the first member of my race in organized ball," he told them. "I realize how much it means to me, to my race and to baseball. I can only say I'll do my very best to come through in every way."[51] He wisely left it to Branch Rickey Jr. to speculate on how his new teammates would react to integrating the roster, and the Dodgers' farm director spoke to them directly and with less grace. "It may cost the Brooklyn organization a number of ballplayers. Some of them, particularly if they come from certain sections of the South, will steer away from a club with colored players on its rosters. Some players now with us may even quit, but they will be back in baseball after they work a year or two in a cotton mill."[52]

The plan was now in motion, and the unease of various figures in the game was left to marinate over the winter months. Negro League team owners all wanted to see a crossover Black player succeed, but they felt trepidation over the prospect that Robinson's success would lead to a mass exodus of star talent that ultimately would destroy their business. Judge William G. Bramham, the Kentucky-born longtime president of the National Association of Professional Baseball Leagues (NAPBL), the Minor Leagues' governing body, sarcastically mocked Rickey as Moses and said he was "using the Negro for [his] own selfish interests,"[53] but he did not use his powers to block Robinson's contract. The possibility that Robinson's career might well begin and end in the Minor Leagues was likely a factor in his decision not to attempt more draconian measures.

If there was one outside executive who unequivocally came out on the right side of history in the aftermath of the Robinson signing, it was International League President Frank Shaughnessy, who threw his public support behind the deal to clearly signal to franchise owners with reservations that they would find no help from him.[54] "Shag" was raised in a small town just west of Chicago and had multisport success in baseball and football as a player before becoming a coach and then an executive. He came to Montreal in 1912 and spent a decade and a half as the head coach of the McGill University football team, an assignment that could be considered a Canadian equivalent to that of an elite Ivy League school. He had a short stint as the Royals GM from 1932 to 1934 before becoming league president in 1936 and had a close relationship with all of the team's executives at the signing ceremony in 1945.

Most important, Shaughnessy had fallen in love with the city and, if asked, would have told Rickey that he had made the best possible choice by bringing Robinson into the Royals' organization. Even still, he quietly advised the Royals against letting Robinson play during early-season road games in Baltimore, a potential trouble spot where the fans had a well-earned reputation for bigotry.[55] His fears ultimately leaked out through the press during the off-season.

A week after the signing ceremony in Montreal, Robinson expressed his feelings on what lay ahead in a letter to his friend Wendell Smith at the *Pittsburgh Courier*. He believed that his glove would play and that he would ultimately be able to handle Major League pitching in time based on his experience coming up against Cleveland ace Bob Feller, the most dominant MLB pitcher of the 1940s, on the barnstorming circuit. Feller was openly dismissive of Robinson's chances of promotion to the big leagues, arguing that he was overly muscled and better suited to the gridiron.[56] Thus began a strange grudge that Feller held to his death in 2010. Robinson told Smith, "The few times I faced Feller has [*sic*] made me confident that the pitching I have faced in the Negro American League was as tough as any I will have to face if I stick with Montreal. There is one thing I would like to have made clear, just what does Feller really mean when he says I have 'football shoulders?'"[57]

Even after Robinson tore up the International League in 1946, Feller still stuck to his guns. He was asked by a reporter from *The Sporting News* whether there were any Black players he had seen on the barnstorming circuit of Major League talent. He replied, "I have seen none who combine the qualities of a big-league ballplayer—not even Jackie Robinson."[58] Roughly sixteen years later, Feller and Robinson stood side by side in Cooperstown on July 23, 1962, a delightful seventy-five-degree day, as they were inducted into the Hall of Fame together.

Robinson did not linger in Montreal after the press conference and zipped off to Venezuela soon after for some winter-ball action before the spring-training test began in March. As the snow and ice encroached across the land in mid-autumn, Montrealers pushed thoughts of baseball to the back of their minds and turned their attention to a very talented Canadiens team that was on its way to hoisting yet another Stanley Cup. While Robinson had ample time to prepare for his debut between the signing and first donning a Royals uniform on a Florida practice field the following spring, so did those who were determined to make their own stand against every goal Robinson, Rickey, and Royals were hoping to advance in the name of fairness.

3

Coming through Adversity

He was a sit-inner before sit-ins,
a freedom rider before freedom rides.

—MARTIN LUTHER KING JR.

Swedish sociologist and economist Gunnar Myrdal first visited the United States in 1929 for a year as a Rockefeller Fellow, then he returned home to Stockholm and began reeling off a series of books that established him as one of Europe's most compelling public intellectuals of the interwar period. He was very much a thinker on par with his famous British colleague John Maynard Keynes. Myrdal's pioneering work on wealth distribution and government intervention to heat and cool economies eventually drew the attention of the Carnegie Corporation, which induced him to begin a major new research project on the roots of American racial tensions. Myrdal was expected to bring a cool, outsider's perspective and present real solutions for his American readers and, after seven years of work assisted by an impressive team of scholars led by Richard Sterner and Arnold Rose, he finally published his 1,400-plus page, two-volume opus, *An American Dilemma: The Negro Problem and Modern Democracy* in 1944. At its heart, this widely discussed study argued that America could not lead the fight for democracy and freedom abroad during World War II while broadly operating as an apartheid state at home.

Myrdal put a very polished academic veneer on a widely held perception in the more cosmopolitan parts of Europe and Canada that America was hopelessly and reflexively bigoted. These places certainly had their fair share of crude racism, but they were at the same time home to plenty of people who thought Jim Crow was too extreme for a civilized society.

An American Dilemma was not without its faults, drawing a mix of praise and criticism from a range of leading Black cultural figures from W. E. B. Du Bois to Ralph Ellison, but it did succeed in explaining how long-standing biblical justifications for race-based oppression gave way to supposedly scientific ones during the era of Social Darwinism in the late nineteenth century. The result, to Myrdal, was that nearly all of white America held an unthinking and seemingly natural belief in universal Black inferiority. Myrdal writes, "This is a manifestation of the most primitive form of religion. There is fear of the unknown in this feeling, which is 'superstition' in the literal sense of this old word. Fear is only increased by the difficulties in expressing it in rational language and explaining it in such a way that it makes sense. So the Negro becomes a 'contrast conception.' He is 'the opposite race'—an inner enemy, 'antithesis of character and properties of the white man.'"[1]

Myrdal, along with leading Black activists of the era, including NAACP head Walter White and the powerful boss of the Brotherhood of Sleeping Car Porters, A. Philip Randolph, and some of America's leading progressive magazines, such as *The Nation*, wanted to believe that the shared sacrifices of war were going to have a meaningful liberalizing influence on white American views on race. How then, they all argued together, could Americans lead a global resistance to the vilest form of state-organized racism in world history without casting a critical eye to persistent systemic inequality at home?

This is what logic seemed to dictate to the optimists, even those who remembered that the end of the Great War a generation earlier was followed by a wave of savage white violence directed at Black communities everywhere, from small towns in Arizona and Georgia to Longview, Texas, and major urban centers, including Indianapolis and Chicago, during the Red Summer of 1919. These were not so much tragic and isolated incidents as the opening shots in a massive white backlash against more assertive Black demands for civil rights from a new generation led in large part by World War I veterans. Lingering memories of the massive KKK resurgence in the 1920s and the Tulsa Race Massacre of 1921, the bloodiest of them all, should have tempered expectations of what changes would come immediately after another world war.

The *Pittsburgh Courier*, one of America's most widely read Black papers, launched a Double V Campaign, with *V* standing for victory over fascism abroad, in addition to victory over racism and discrimination at home, just two months after the United States entered World War II. It all began with an impassioned letter to the editor from James G. Thompson, who asked a series of questions as a Black American of military age. "Should I sacrifice my life to live half American? Will things be better for the next generation in the peace to follow? Would it be demanding too much to demand full citizenship rights in exchange for the sacrificing of my life? Is the kind of America I know worth defending? Will America be a true and pure democracy after the war? Will Colored Americans suffer still the indignities that have been heaped upon them in the past?"

Thompson then went on to suggest the *V* for victory sign that featured prominently in the wartime propaganda of Allied countries be co-opted by Black America as a "the double V V for a double victory. The first V for victory over our enemies from without, the second V for victory over our enemies from within."[2] *The Courier* fully embraced the idea, urging its readers to provide their full backing for the war effort either in uniform or on the home front, while constantly pressuring the government to live up to the egalitarian principles of the Declaration of Independence and the Constitution. The paper was unsurprisingly one of the biggest boosters of baseball integration because of the great symbolic victory that would come from reforming America's pastime.

The reality, however, was that deeply entrenched prejudices remained and the war ultimately did little to change hearts and minds in white America. There were some victories for the civil rights movement, mostly notably the 1942 Fair Employment Act, which ordered an end to race-based discrimination in war industries, but the American military itself remained firmly segregated. The Red Cross even continued separating plasma by race through D-Day so as not to risk offending a wounded white soldier by saving his life with a transfusion of Black blood. If anything, the horrific Detroit Race Riot in June 1943, which left 34 dead and 675 injured in the worst incident of its kind since the bloody Tulsa Race Massacre in 1921, was an immediate and blinding reminder of the latent violent potential of white resistance to granting fair Black access to jobs and housing even in supposedly more enlightened parts of the country.

As Steven White, a political scientist at Syracuse University, argues, demobilized white veterans did tend to be more supportive of anti-lynching legislation and voting protections for Black Americans, but they nonetheless backed segregation at levels that were in line with the general population. In fact, while they were deployed in liberated Europe, they actively exported their own racial prejudices by feeding civilians with embellished warnings about the behavior of their Black service mates. The small minority of Southern veterans who took lessons from the war and the Holocaust that inspired them to join their Black counterparts in a campaign for civil rights faced a considerably larger cohort of other white veterans on the home front who were determined to maintain the status quo.

Also, a compelling body of literature suggests white attitudes did not begin to shift meaningfully in favor of legal equality until sustained national media coverage beginning in the mid-to-late 1950s—including powerful images on television—of the Rosa Parks–inspired bus boycott in Montgomery, the 101st Airborne deployment that was required to integrate Central High in Little Rock, lunch-counter sit-ins, the violent reprisals directed at those involved in the Freedom Rider campaign against segregation on interstate buses, the riot at Ole Miss when Air Force veteran James Meredith attempted to enroll, and then ultimately the vicious response of Birmingham first responders to civil rights protests in 1963 forced the issue into dinner-table conversations across the country.[3]

Multiple surveys of the era captured the hard attitudes that persisted through the war. One commissioned by the army in August 1944 found that 75 percent of white Northern soldiers and 85 percent from the South favored segregated training facilities. One commented, "White supremacy must be maintained. I'll fight if necessary to prevent racial equality. I'll never salute a negro officer and I'll not take orders from a negroe [*sic*]. I'm sick of the army's method of treating . . . [Black soldiers] as if they were human. Segregation of the races must continue."[4] In a separate survey, the National Opinion Research Center found that during the war just barely over a quarter of Americans supported integrated schools, only 40 percent agreed with the statement "Negroes should have as good a chance as White people to get any kind of job," just one-third "would not mind if [a] Negro with [the] same income and education moved on the same block," and a little under half supported a fairly innocuous move to integrated seating on public transportation.[5]

In practice, these attitudes helped perpetuate widespread state and municipal laws that were explicitly designed to hold Black Americans back as second-class citizens. Jim Crow was a catchall for any law or ordinance that segregated Americans by race and suppressed Black rights. The term itself came from a popular antebellum minstrel show in which Thomas D. Rice donned blackface and performed an exaggerated caricature of a Black American. Jim Crow laws were by no means an exclusively Southern phenomenon, but they tended to be harsher and were enforced more rigorously in the former Confederate states. The first were applied immediately after the Civil War, and the last remained in place until the passage of the Civil Rights Act in 1965.

Kentucky, home to this author and the Louisville Colonels team that will later emerge as the foil to Jackie Robinson's heroic 1946 Royals, had Jim Crow laws that were typical for the region. They generally focused on banning interracial relationships, keeping Black children out of better-resourced white schools, and segregating Black and white in public spaces. Specific examples included the 1904 Day Law, a state law that banned Black students from attending white colleges (deliberately aimed at Berea College, the only integrated postsecondary institution in the state at the time), the 1914 Louisville Residential Segregation Ordinance that prohibited Black families from buying or renting properties in white neighborhoods, and a whites-only admission policy at Louisville's Fontaine Ferry Park, the only amusement park in Kentucky's biggest city.

Jackie Robinson's path to Montreal in early 1946 ran directly through Royals and Dodgers spring training facilities in small east-central

Florida towns that are now exurbs between Orlando and Daytona Beach. Here, he faced the most restrictive version of the Old South that promised to throw down every sort of challenge imaginable, from passive laws such as those previously listed and active measures from local law enforcement, elected officials, and their hard racist allies among the citizenry. Anyone who has read Chris Lamb's *Blackout: The Untold Story of Jackie Robinson's First Spring Training* (University of Nebraska Press, 2006) would agree that there is no hyperbole to the suggestion that this challenge easily could have derailed the entire Robinson-Rickey effort to integrate Major League baseball.

Robinson had to attend to two things before he could travel to spring training and the biggest test of his life—one baseball-related and one personal.

One of Robinson's biggest liabilities heading into his first full, six-month season of baseball in 1946 was that he had not yet had the opportunity to test his stamina over the 150-plus game grind he was about to face. He signed on with the Royals just a few months shy of his twenty-seventh birthday, but he was still incredibly green as a baseball player. He had only played a few games at UCLA, then missed out on organized play entirely during his army years, and his valuable Monarchs sojourn in 1945 still only amounted to 137 plate appearances. Concerns about how he would hold up over a full season were well justified; his body did betray him, and he missed 30 of the Royals 154 games in 1946. In the short term, Robinson badly needed to find some outlet for high-level competition over the winter months before reporting to spring training, preferably somewhere he could play without all the added media scrutiny and pressure that would come from an American audience. Venezuela was the answer.

Mexico, Cuba, and Venezuela had for decades taken an open-door approach to baseball that provided valuable opportunities for Americans, particularly Negro Leagues players, to compete and earn over the winter months when they would otherwise have been idle. These sojourners generally found passionate fans, delightful weather, and warm local hospitality. On the cusp of the inaugural season of the Liga Venezolana de Béisbol Profesional (LVBP), Robinson decided to head to Caracas with a team of Negro Leaguers to participate in a fourteen-game round-robin against the Caribbean All-Stars (in fact, mostly B-team Venezuelans with two Americans and two Dominicans) and a Venezuelan squad made up mostly of regulars from the stacked Cervecería de Caracas team.

He was joined on the talented Las Estrellas Negras roster by future Dodgers teammate Roy Campanella, 1950 NL Rookie of the Year Sam Jethroe, and an aging Buck Leonard, a perennial All-Star for the Homestead Grays who was just a few years too old to get his own chance to break into the Major Leagues. The tournament's promoters, Luis Jesús Blanco Chataing and Bernardo Vizcaya, orchestrated American participation as a recruiting tool and ultimately succeeded in convincing seven participating Negro Leaguers to stick around and join local teams for the upcoming LVBP season.[6]

Robinson's teammates would have been forgiven for any jealousy they felt over the opportunity that Branch Rickey had presented him, but they instead rallied around the newcomer and gave him a crash course in some of the finer points of the game they had picked up over the years. Gene Benson, a longtime defensive wizard in center field for the Philadelphia Stars in the 1930s and '40s, was particularly invested in mentoring Robinson with the little time they would share together in Caracas.

Benson was one of hundreds of Negro Leaguers who aged out before Robinson's 1947 Dodgers debut and sadly missed his chance to cross over into the integrated Major Leagues, but he did enjoy local-legend status back in Philadelphia. History has largely overlooked him in favor of his power-hitting Negro League contemporaries, but he complimented unparalleled range and arm strength as a defender with a high-contact and low-power opposite-field approach as a hitter that brought him a run of four .300 average seasons toward the end of his career. Rickey encouraged him to work with Robinson down in Venezuela, and Benson happily obliged as a hybrid roommate-coach.

Benson was a sublime drag bunter, a skill that Robinson later added to his own arsenal, and also shared valuable insight on pitch recognition for breaking balls, an area of weakness for Robinson heading into 1946.[7] But the most valuable advice Benson ever gave came when Robinson shared his doubts about whether he would ultimately be able to crack the Dodgers' roster. Benson provided Robinson with cool reassurance that he would ultimately harness his potential and prevail when his moment came. This was a cosmic moment when an eager pupil collided with a kindhearted teacher and both came out much the better from their interaction.

After Robinson wrapped up a very productive sojourn down in Venezuela, he flew back to Los Angeles just two weeks before shipping out for spring training for a very important event on February 10, 1946: his wedding to former UCLA classmate Rachel Isum.

In the half century since her husband's passing, baseball fans have come to know Rachel Robinson very well as a formidable and dignified woman who has given back to the game and her community in many different ways. Carl Erskine, a Dodgers pitcher whose career overlapped with Robinson's, passed down a legend that encapsulates Rachel's role in Jackie's life. He claims that Buzzie Bavasi, a Minor League executive in the Dodgers' system who worked his way up to GM of the big club, sat down in the stands to watch a Royals game with Rachel early in the 1946 season. After his first encounter with Mrs. Robinson, he reportedly told Branch Rickey, "If Jackie was smart enough to pick Rachel as his wife, he's the guy you want."[8]

Rachel Robinson was very much a pioneer in her own right as one of the few Black graduates from the nursing program at UCLA in 1945. She spent the entirety of her husband's playing career raising their children, but when they grew older, she resumed her studies and completed a master's degree in psychiatric nursing at New York University in 1961. She spent years conducting valuable research at the Albert Einstein College of Medicine in the Bronx on the feasibility of providing home care combined with in-patient treatment for psychiatric patients, then she took on high-profile roles as the director of nursing at the Connecticut Mental Health Center and as an assistant professor at Yale University. She held these positions while simultaneously providing care to her elderly mother and her husband, whose health was rapidly declining by the late 1960s from diabetes-related complications.

Despite all these weighty responsibilities, she still found time to actively fight discrimination in the housing market in the Robinson's adopted home of Stamford, Connecticut, and even set up a construction company to build affordable housing. Her philanthropic pursuits took up more of her time after she established the Jackie Robinson Foundation in 1973, distributing over $100 million worth of grants to upward of 1,800 individual recipients over the next four decades. She was of course on hand, at age one hundred, with oversized Dodger blue scissors to cut the ribbon that marked the opening of the Jackie Robinson Museum in Manhattan in July 2022.

Back in the beginning, Rachel and Jackie met on campus at UCLA and clicked immediately despite having very different college goals in mind. She was an ever-studious nursing major, while he was a man about campus whose athletic exploits brought a degree of fame many would have found intimidating. She has said that one of the qualities that attracted her most was the pride that came from a fashion choice: he regularly wore white shirts that accentuated his Blackness rather than hid from it. He was relieved to find that she was not the least bit starstruck and was surprisingly easy to talk to. Their relationship developed out of an easy compatibility that led to a quick engagement by 1941.

Jackie's military service forced them into a long-distance relationship that was at times difficult despite his best efforts to remind Rachel he was thinking of her with a regular Friday package of chocolates by mail. At one point, he badly misread her intentions and demanded that she not join the Army Nursing Corps—he was all too familiar with the sort of men she would end up surrounded by, thanks to his time on a base in Texas—but Rachel was not the sort to be told what to do. She responded by returning his engagement ring in the mail, which had a helpful eye-opening effect on her future husband.

Their long-distance relationship continued following Jackie's discharge, his sojourn with the Monarchs, and trips to Brooklyn, Montreal, and then Venezuela before they could finally be together permanently in early 1946. The wedding itself was a grander ceremony than Rachel had wanted, but her mother insisted that they go big after years of deprivation and separation during the war. She did, after all, have a gorgeous white wedding dress from Saks Fifth Avenue in New York City to show off. After the wedding, they could at long last be together, albeit living in temporary guest quarters down in Florida. Once spring training wrapped up, Montreal would become the first place—finally—that they could call home as a married couple.

Branch Rickey was a serious man, and he ran Dodgers spring training as a serious business. By his order, player wives were not permitted to accompany their husbands down to sunny Florida, so the team could focus on the upcoming season without any familial distractions. This was not a holiday. He did, however, make one special exception in 1946 for Rachel Robinson. She surrendered to optimism before they departed Los Angeles and imagined the experience turning into a long and well-deserved honeymoon. She had never before traveled to the South, whereas Georgia-born Jackie was better prepared, thanks to his time in the army and on the road with the KC Monarchs for games in Memphis and Birmingham. Rickey had a good sense of what was to come and knew full well that Jackie's prospects of making it through a month in Jim Crow Florida would be infinitely better with Rachel at his side. Jackie would later confess that he could easily have lost his temper at any number of provocations and ended up in some Florida jail if she had not been there to cool him off.

Commercial aviation was still in its infancy in early 1946, but the Robinsons did have a fairly straightforward route on American Airlines to the Dodgers' spring training facility: a long-haul overnight flight from Los Angeles to New Orleans, then a short ride across the panhandle on a puddle jumper to Pensacola for a quick refueling stop before the last leg down the Atlantic Coast to Daytona Beach. Yet the trip still went all wrong almost immediately after they landed at their first stop in the elegant art deco confines of Lakefront Airport on Lake Pontchartrain.

On arrival in New Orleans, the Robinsons proceeded to the line for their connecting flight to Pensacola only to be told there were no seats for them on the plane. Despite having secured their tickets in advance, they were bumped in favor of two white passengers. Reluctantly accepting the inevitable, they attempted to kill time before the next available flight twelve hours later by sitting down to a meal in the airport restaurant, which turned out to be as segregated as any other in Louisiana at the time and which denied them service. Rachel was mortified that hunger eventually reduced them to eating fried chicken out of a shoebox lovingly packed by family back in Los Angeles who had anticipated this sort of hardship. This experience was painfully familiar to Jackie and was a regular occurrence on every road trip for generations of other Negro Leaguers nearly everywhere they played in America.

Rachel was disoriented by her first experience with overt displays of Jim Crow at Lakefront. She later recalled, "I'd never seen signs on restrooms, on water faucets and that kind of thing, so I went into the white ladies' bathroom just so I could recover my own sense of myself and I walked into there and did what I had to do and nodded at the ladies and walked out."[9] The journey had to go on.

Pensacola was supposed to be a quick pit stop before their final leg to Daytona Beach, but after the plane touched down, the Robinsons were ushered off the plane along with a Mexican woman. Their flight attendant gave the three of them an initially plausible-sounding story that the plane had to drop weight before adding enough extra fuel to safely fly through a patch of rough Florida weather. Selecting three nonwhite passengers for removal was a clear indication of which customers the airline valued least, but this indignity was compounded when the Robinsons watched helplessly as new white passengers boarded in their place. For the second time the airline lied to their face and then made no effort to conceal the real reason why they had been bumped. Jackie had had his fill of flying for the time being.

Pensacola is four hundred miles from Daytona Beach, and no one with cash in hand would have chosen a Greyhound bus in the pre-air-conditioning era over a short flight without good reason. At least traveling by bus theoretically offered the Robinsons the possibility of reclining and catching up on some badly needed sleep. They had a brief respite until the bus made its first stop and the driver ordered them to vacate their front row seats as incoming white passengers waited to take their places. For Jackie, there were echoes of his court-martial in Texas when the driver called him "boy" to get him moving more quickly, but this time he had little alternative but to quietly acquiesce. The plane debacles had already made him late for spring training, where he would be the center of attention. A confrontation on the bus, however justifiable, would have only have put him even further behind schedule.

Rachel later remembered this part of their supposed honeymoon. "We went to the back of the bus, and when it got dark, I started to cry because I felt my great husband who had been a fighter and a dignified person had been reduced by discrimination and by segregation. He had sort of caved in to what the society wanted in the South."[10] When Jackie finally arrived in Daytona Beach thirty-six hours after departing Los Angeles, he immediately told *Pittsburgh Courier* journalist Wendell Smith and photographer Billy Rowe that he was ready to pack it in on the spot and return to the Negro Leagues. They heard him out, then appealed for patience.[11]

Today, we often think of Florida as geographically part of the South, but not necessarily Southern in terms of culture and values, owing to generations of mass migration from cold-weather Northern states (accelerated by the spread of residential air-conditioning post–World War II) and the Spanish-speaking Caribbean. Florida acquired statehood in 1845 and was home to just 140,000 people when the Civil War broke out in 1861. Roughly half of its people were enslaved in a plantation-driven economy, and the state legislature enthusiastically joined the Confederacy in 1861. But Florida contributed just fifteen thousand troops to the war effort, and there were few significant military engagements there.

Still, white Floridians marched in lockstep with their neighbors in Georgia and Alabama on issues of race well into the twentieth century. By World War II, Florida was home to one of America's most restrictive Jim Crow regimes, one comparable to that of the Deep South, and race-based lynchings still happened on occasion. Just over a quarter of Florida's population was Black, and heavily discriminatory practices reigned from the Georgia line to the Keys and from the Atlantic Coast to the Caribbean.

There simply was no oasis away from Jim Crow in the Sunshine State. Racism manifested itself daily in subtle ways, such as a massive funding gap between Black and white schools and the unwillingness of local authorities to tie homes in Black neighborhoods into sewers or provide adequate garbage collection. It also came in loud and hot.

In Tampa, the state's third-most populous city, the White Municipal Party maintained a stranglehold on the mayor's office from 1910 to 1951 thanks to an explicitly pro–Jim Crow platform. An armed white mob in Miami set up barricades and burned crosses to prevent Black residents from moving into slightly better housing as late as 1945.[12]

The war shone a spotlight on Florida's long-standing racial tensions. As Gary Mormino shows, navy enlistment flyers in Florida papers made clear that Black sailors would be confined to work as mess attendants. When the Marines finally opened to Black men in 1942, it did so by creating the segregated Marine Corps Negro Battalion rather than integrating existing units. One of the state's congressmen complained to the navy in writing on behalf of constituents who opposed integrated sleeping quarters at Pensacola Naval Air Station. Black veterans were even barred from marching in Jacksonville's postwar victory parade that November.

For the most part, transportation and facilities such as commissaries, lavatories, churches, medical clinics, and recreation centers remained segregated in contravention of military guidelines. White MPs almost always responded with an excessively heavy hand whenever there were street fights involving soldiers and civilians in Frenchtown, the Black section of Tallahassee and Florida's primary military hub, and the authorities routinely handed out more severe punishments to Black soldiers for disciplinary issues. Black servicemen had little success in their attempts to draw media attention to these issues. In fact, as James Schnur writes, "White owned publications did little to dispel widely believed rumors that African-Americans plotted to rape white women and to resort to violence after most white men had entered military service overseas."[13] Protests against Deep South treatment, which was particularly jarring for Black recruits from northern states, always came to nothing in the end, and the climate in Florida on the eve of Jackie Robinson's arrival was oppressive in more ways than one.[14]

Branch Rickey had been led to believe that Daytona Beach was the most progressive of potential spring training sites, with a Black middle class, college, and ball field in the middle of its Black neighborhood. It did not have all the baseball amenities the Dodgers needed for hundreds of players, however, which meant that part of the organization's training would have to move to an overflow field in nearby Sanford, hometown of the Dodgers' radio announcer Red Barber and now an Orlando suburb. Barber assured the team on the eve of spring training that Sanford would move past Jim Crow and give all of the visiting Dodgers players a warm Southern welcome, but he spent the rest of his life bitterly disappointed at the embarrassment that came when his neighbors proved him wrong after Robinson first arrived.[15]

If the town's name sounds familiar, it is likely because Sanford was all over American television screens in late February 2012 following news reports that George Zimmerman, an overzealous neighborhood watch captain, had shot and killed unarmed Black teenager Trayvon Martin, who was walking back to the home of a family member with candy and iced tea he had just bought at a nearby convenience store. Zimmerman was ultimately found not guilty of second-degree murder, sparking the creation of the Black Lives Matter movement.

Quebéc's sportswriters were not looking for Royals copy just yet as spring training began in early March, particularly with the Canadiens on the cusp of finishing first overall in the NHL standings by a comfortable margin and playoffs about to begin right after St. Patrick's Day. One of the rare midwinter dispatches about Robinson from Caracas noted that he had been hitting well in Venezuela against poor-quality pitching and had shown "the arm of a bank manager" while playing shortstop.[16] His wedding got a very brief mention, no more than a paragraph in just a couple papers. Up north, January and February clearly belonged to hockey.

Sportswriters' early reporting as practices began tended to focus on Robinson's ultimate position when the Royals came north rather than the more serious issue of how he would navigate Jim Crow regulations in Florida. The early view was that manager Clay Hopper would leave shortstop to switch-hitting Stan Bréard, a defensive whiz and hometown favorite, shifting Robinson to second, where his arm strength would be less of a liability.[17]

Bréard's status was a particularly sensitive issue after two Québec-born heroes of the 1945 International League champion Royals left or flirted with leaving for Mexico to earn better money than they would in the Dodgers' organization. Slugging corner man Roland Gladu, author of a healthy .925 OPS, signed up to play in the Mexican League in early February, and Jean-Pierre Roy, the staff ace, was seriously considering the idea of following him after both were offered double their Royals salary to jump ship. Both players were coming to terms with their status as aging AAAA players—clearly too good for the top level of the Minors, yet still not quite able to capture a roster spot on a solid big league club—and the lure of a bigger paycheck in Mexico outweighed their dimming hopes of making the Dodgers out of camp.[18]

The 1945 Royals were unusually flush with three homegrown stars in Gladu, Roy, and Bréard, all of whom played pivotal roles on a championship club, but it looked briefly for a few weeks in early March as though they might begin the 1946 season with just one of them, and he would be reduced to a backup role. The club had just enjoyed one of its most successful seasons while featuring the most Québécois content ever on its roster, a double delight for Montrealers, and no one wanted the good times to end. (Roy's epic 1945 season probably all but ended his big league dreams at age twenty-six. He threw 293 innings over forty-one games, leading the IL with 25 wins. His workload was a 101-inning spike from his previous career high in 1945, and he was ineffective in 1946, missed all of 1947, and struggled through demotions until finally hanging up his cleats in 1955.) Paul Parizeau of *Le Canada* warned over the winter that there would be "angry consequences" if Robinson ended up dislodging Bréard from shortstop because the Dodgers disregarded Royals fans' understandable desire to see homegrown stars on their roster.[19]

Once positional jockeying and Bréard's status with the team were clear and Jim Crow began to rear its ugly face, the Québec-based and francophone press corps began to close ranks around Robinson as an underdog whose success did not threaten one of their own. Over the course of the next month, some members started taking shots at Rickey and their American counterparts whenever they felt that Robinson was either being insufficiently defended or unfairly attacked down South in spring training. What began to emerge among the press corps and the fan base, slowly and into the early part of the regular season, was a sense that with Gladu gone, Roy on the outs for having flirted with the idea of following him, and Bréard more of a sentimental favorite rather than a legitimate talent, Robinson would fill the void as Montreal's new star player in 1946.

Florida's Jim Crow laws were well understood and widely viewed as absurd in Québec, but it remained to be seen before spring training started whether they would actually hold up to a direct challenge from the Dodgers. *Le Front Ouvrier* (*The Workers' Front*), a working-class paper, had briefly noted to its readers back on January 5 that "the mentality and the laws have not changed in Daytona Beach and Black people are not well regarded down there. . . . Jackie Robinson will have to abide by Daytona Beach's segregation laws [that] won't let him stay in the same hotel as the Royals' white players. The city also provides separate buses, theaters, restaurants and other services for Blacks."[20]

Not until Robinson finally reported to camp in the first week of March did Canada's French-language sports reporters really take notice of what this would mean for their incoming star. Charlie Daoust, the sports editor of *Le Droit* in Ottawa, 125 miles east of Montreal and very much part of its sports orbit, led off his March 1 column with a lament that "Jackie Robinson, shortstop, and John Wright, pitcher, the two first black players in professional baseball with whites, retired to private families of their color in Sanford, Florida, while the other candidates for the Montreal Royals stayed in a hotel by the lake. . . . President Branch Rickey of the Dodgers invites whites to treat their two colored teammates well . . . but why put them in quarantine in the black neighborhood? . . . O democracy!"[21]

Paul Parizeau of *Le Canada* did note approvingly that Robinson and Wright were able to take to the practice field without "causing a rowdy demonstration" even though their separate lodgings and changing room had pointed toward friction.[22] Branch Rickey's opening appeal to prospective Royals players, which began with a firm assertion that his overriding goal was for the Royals to win a championship but emphasized that "if an elephant could play centerfield better than a player, I would start the elephant," did not impress Québécois reporters.[23] Syd Thomas of the news agency Canadian Press relayed Rickey's appeal to the Royals to treat Robinson and Wright as gentlemen, arguing that "it was a good gesture, but emphasizing the color distinction as though Wright and Robinson were a different type of species from white ballplayers doesn't help matters any. The boys will get a fair chance all right, but the sooner everyone forgets their race and accepts them as just ordinary ballchasers without all the fanfare, the sooner the problem will be solved."[24]

What did not make it into the papers surely would have infuriated them. Branch Rickey had arranged for Wendell Smith to serve double duty as Robinson's local fixer while he was covering spring training for the *Pittsburgh Courier*, while photographer Billy Rowe would tag along to document Robinson and Wright's historic spring training. Robinson and Wright were billeted in a private home in the Black neighborhood, Georgetown, on the east side of Sanford, while their white teammates stayed at the Mayfair Hotel, a local landmark. It took until just their second day of practice before the spokesmen from a local white mob arrived at the porch of their billet house to deliver a warning to Smith and Rowe: "We want you to get the n———s out of town . . . by nightfall." The consequences of noncompliance were quite clear from their tone.

Immediately after this encounter, Smith made a panicked call to Branch Rickey, who told him to get the Robinsons and Wright packed and out of Sanford at once. Smith gave them no explanation for their rapid evacuation until they were well on the road for Daytona Beach—Robinson was actually left wondering if he had been cut from the team already—and then he chose not to publicize the incident via the *Courier* out of concern that it would only inflame matters. Rickey too opted for complete radio silence, and all the other Royals players were kept in the dark, along with the sportswriters on the Dodgers beat.[25]

La Presse picked up on racial tensions within the Royals camp fairly early on, in March, noting that as player cliques formed, Robinson and Wright were very much isolated from the rest of the team. It quoted Robinson saying, "I don't know if we're waiting for the others to come to us rather than going to them [but] I think it's better to do this." The paper reported that Robinson had been repeatedly forced to give up his seat on planes and buses en route from California to Florida—a story that Rickey had chosen not to publicize—but when asked the rhetorical question of whether it was because he was Black, he still responded implausibly that he "didn't know and didn't want to know." After their relocation from Sanford, they were again billeted with a new set of local Black families rather than given rooms with the rest of the team. Hopper had offered them his manager's office as a changing room on account of overcrowding. Robinson took great care not to say anything that might be read as a complaint, saying his teammates were nice and he chatted with those who wanted to talk and gave some distance to those who preferred to keep to themselves.[26]

One of Robinson's fellow Minor Leaguers that year was Brooklyn-born Chuck Connors, a power-hitting first baseman who was assigned to the Mobile Bears at the end of camp and years later got a small taste of Major League action with the Dodgers then the Cubs. Americans of television-watching age in the late 1950s and early 1960s remember him fondly as the star of the hit ABC western *The Rifleman*, which ran for five seasons. Fifty years later, Connors was an eager participant in public Robinson commemoration events in Montreal, telling reporters about one particularly vivid memory from a practice game during the spring of 1946. Robinson had reached base and was darting back and forth off first in an effort to distract the opposing pitcher when the Royals hitter, Robinson's teammate, called time and barked to the umpire, "Get that fucking n—— to stop dancing out there or I'll kill him." Connors declined to name who made the remark.[27]

However much Robinson wanted to play the diplomat, he could plainly see that many of his new teammates were annoyed by his presence in an overstuffed camp with far too many hungry returning veterans competing for far too few roster spots. Dodgers coach George Sisler, a living legend who held the single-season hits record with 257 and racked up a pair of .400 seasons with the Browns in the early 1920s, was devoting much of his time to helping Robinson learn first base during the early part of camp when his ultimate position was still up in the air. Rickey was guarding an investment into which he had devoted all his reputational capital, but many players were jealous over what they saw as special treatment for Robinson. Lou Rochelli, one of the unsung heroes of Robinson's early tenure as a Royal who was in the process of being displaced by him as Montreal's second baseman, was actually the friendliest of the bunch. He still took time away from his own routine to work with Robinson on his fielding, particularly double play pivots.[28]

Some players resented all of the attention the press gave Robinson, while others were understandably bothered when other teams canceled games with the Royals on dubious, transparently Jim Crow grounds. However unfair the circumstances, it was easy to view each lost at bat as one less chance to shine and earn a promotion to Brooklyn. In retrospect, many would have later conceded that the Rickey-Robinson experiment was a big prize that was worthy of small, collective sacrifices, but it would not have been reasonable in the moment to expect players engaged in a highly competitive endeavor to acknowledge their role as peripheral figures in a grander story.[29]

One oft-repeated early camp prediction among Québec-based reporters that did not hold up too well in hindsight was that unheralded Johnny Wright was actually the better of the two new Black players on the Royals. Credit him for a hot start, but Wright only got into two games for the Royals in 1946 before his demotion to the Class-C Trois-Rivières Royals of the Canadian-American League. There was also a charmingly misguided hope on the sports pages of some of middle Québec's papers that Robinson would *not* make the Montreal Royals and earn a lower assignment in Trois-Rivières, which had a great downriver rivalry with the Québec Alouettes, a Cubs affiliate. This was in no way a byproduct of hopes that Robinson would stumble, but rather wish-casting from fans in proud but smaller Québec cities who wanted more opportunities to see him play closer to home in the upcoming season.[30]

Robinson finally got to take the field for the Royals in a Sunday-afternoon March 17 exhibition game against the big club at City Island Ballpark in Daytona Beach, marking the first integrated baseball game in the South and the first integrated professional baseball game involving a Major League team since the 1880s.

It was not a particularly inspired performance from Robinson, who reached base just once on a fielder's choice, stole a base, and then scored, but it was profoundly notable simply for having taken place. Rickey had ensured that local officials would not interfere, and the robust presence of the press corps deterred anyone who considered blocking Robinson and Wright from taking the field. The park was bursting with four thousand spectators, a quarter of whom were Black, and Robinson got the cheers he deserved rather than the booing he expected.[31] City Island was renamed Jackie Robinson Ballpark in 1990 and is now home to the NCAA Division I Bethune-Cookman Wildcats and the Daytona Tortugas, the Cincinnati Reds' Single-A affiliate.

Shortly thereafter, a bit of intrigue arrived in camp in mid-late March when it was reported that Mexican baseball magnate Jorge Pasquel "had sent a spy to see the sixty Montreal players currently in training." After having already landed Gladu, Pasquel had every reason to believe he could tempt other blocked prospects to come down to Mexico for a hearty salary. Clyde Sukeforth and fellow scout George Sisler had been ordered to investigate, apparently discovering that Pasquel's representative had offered Jackie Robinson a juicy $6,000 salary (roughly $96,000 in 2024 dollars, double the current minimum for AAA players after a favorable collective bargaining revision in the spring of 2023) to quit the Royals and join a Mexican team. Robinson was reported to have been uninterested in the proffer, which he "refused categorically."[32]

Defiantly turning down more money and better weather obviously endeared Robinson to Royals fans, but this tempest in a teapot still prompted Zotique Lespérance at *La Patrie* to take a well-deserved shot at Rickey for calling foul on Pasquel for "poaching" MLB players when Rickey had just done the same by bringing in Robinson from the KC Monarchs without offering any compensation. Issues of fair pay were particularly sensitive for writers based in Québec, which would become Canada's most heavily unionized province. Rickey had not endeared himself to them when he offered Gladu, the chronically underappreciated Montreal-born hero of the 1945 International League champion Royals, a $50 per month pay *cut* for his promotion to Dodgers, an insult that had made it much easier for him to take up Pasquel's offer to play in the Mexican League.[33]

Royals spring training began with roughly three weeks of practices and intersquad games before exhibitions began in earnest. Rickey had successfully negotiated permission for Robinson and Wright to play in home games in Daytona Beach and assumed that the arrangement would hold until the Royals headed north, but it was an open question what would happen in outlying towns where Jim Crow rules were less flexible. Rickey ultimately made a calculated gamble to send the entire team, Robinson and Wright included, out on the road to see whether local officials would actually try to enforce Jim Crow restrictions on interracial athletic competition under the glare of the national press. If they did, the Royals would abide by the law. If they did not, he would chalk it up as a victory. The first test case was scheduled for March 20 in Jacksonville with a game against the Royals' International League rivals, the Jersey City Giants.

Jacksonville's Durkee Field, as it was known in 1946, had been in use for three decades, with varied tenants, including a pair of local Negro Leagues teams, a handful of Minor League clubs, and several Major League teams during spring training. Right before the scheduled Royals-Giants tilt, the city's park director, George Robinson, informed the Jersey City Giants that local laws barred interracial competition, prompting a very last-minute dialogue among various Major and Minor League executives in the Dodgers and Giants systems. The New York Giants' Charles Stoneham "Chub" Feeney asked the Royals how they wanted to proceed. When the Montreal players indicated they intended to play, local officials responded that the ban on Robinson and Wright would hold. Jersey City president Steve Freel made a futile protest, but George Robinson ordered the game canceled and had the field padlocked to emphasize that he would not back down. The game was off, and the Royals could do nothing.

Jackie Robinson was unprepared for the worst to actually come to pass and responded to the game's cancellation by blowing up in front of his wife, Wendel Smith, Billy Rowe, and Johnny Wright. If there was one saving grace, it came when Rickey decided to change tack and opt for a full team boycott of any road game in which Robinson and Wright were denied access to the field.[34]

This display of backbone was a partial success. The team would stand behind all of its players, but Rickey's declaration did not entirely force a behavioral change from overly zealous Jim Crow enforcers outside Daytona Beach. During an April 7 game back in hostile Sanford against the all-white Saint Paul Saints, the Dodgers other AAA affiliate,

Robinson took up his position and went to bat without incident. He had a nice start to the game, singling, swiping second, then scoring a run in the second inning, prompting an intervention from a local police officer who escorted him off the field under threat of arrest if he resisted.[35] The *Gazette* reported that "one hundred fans attended to see Robinson play," but apparently their views counted for nothing to law enforcement.[36]

The ensuing standoff over whether Robinson and Wright could take the field in spring training exhibition games cost the team dearly over the final week of camp. The Royals had five of their games canceled or boycotted—one in Jacksonville on the April 9, two in Savannah on the 12th and 14th, and one more in Richmond—and a road game in Deland had to be relocated to Daytona Beach at the last minute.[37] They instead opted to scrimmage with other Dodgers affiliates, an unusual move due to the talent mismatch between levels, but it did at least allow them to salvage something from their last few days in Florida.

Royals management was unambiguous in its support of Robinson and Wright throughout this whole trying affair that undermined the team's preparations for the upcoming season. In the beginning, Hector Racine declared, "It will be all or nothing with the Montreal club. Jackie Robinson and John Wright come with the club or there's no game."[38] This earned an approving word on the editorial page of *Le Soleil*. "We know that blacks are viewed badly in many regions of the Promised Land of democracy. It's excellent that Mr. Racine, who protests against racial prejudice in the United States, is a French Canadian. . . . [His actions] show that nazi doctrines of a 'master race' don't play in the province of Québec."[39] Similarly, Charles Daoust of *Le Droit* wrote, "We congratulate Royals management for having canceled their exhibition game in Jacksonville tomorrow against the Jersey City Little Giants. . . . Montrealers will not stomach this gesture of intolerance."[40]

By the later stages of spring training, the American press tended to focus on how Robinson was visibly struggling on the field at times—which he was, due to too much positional rotation around the diamond, a nagging injury to his throwing arm, and the extreme stress of having to work within the constraints of unjust Florida laws.[41] But

Québec's French-language papers tended to write instead on how he was improving on a daily basis to the point where it was becoming easier to see him as a major contributor once the season began.[42] Québec-based and Canadian papers also frequently ran photos of Robinson with their Royals spring training updates, whereas their major American counterparts did not for fear of offending racist elements within their readership. In general, Robinson coverage in mainstream Canadian papers was starting to tilt more toward that of the Black American press—a genuine enthusiasm for the Great Experiment—and away from that of their white American counterparts, which observed neutrally or expressed skepticism.

It certainly got easier for the media in Québec to see Robinson for the talent that he was once it became clearer in later March that he was not a threat to dislodge Bréard as the starting shortstop. His playing time would come at the expense of good-guy second sacker Lou Rochelli. Still, the press was rather surprised that with roughly two full weeks left in camp Racine made an early announcement that Robinson "was practically assured" a spot as the Royals second baseman.[43] It was finally announced in the papers on April 9 that light-hitting Rochelli had lost his roster spot on the Royals and would be dispatched to the Saint Paul Saints of the American Association, which was not quite as competitive as the International League.[44] Rochelli never was able to play his way back to the Majors after a brief wartime cup of coffee with the Dodgers, but he did earn himself an important footnote in history for embracing change even if it came at his own expense.

As spring training began to wind down and Robinson's Minor League assignment to Montreal was all but official, Rickey felt secure enough that the organization had held together to make another massive announcement: the signings of two more high impact Black prospects, Roy Campanella and Don Newcombe, both of whom would immediately be dispatched to the Class-B Nashua Dodgers of the New England League. Plenty of bigots had hoped to see Robinson falter so badly that it would put off talk of integration entirely, but adding these two players to the organization amounted to a declaration from the Dodgers that the Great Experiment would no longer hinge entirely on Robinson. Black players, plural, were on their way up to Brooklyn.

One thing Nashua had going for it in the eyes of Dodgers executives was a heavy French-Canadian character that they hoped would translate into greater tolerance for Black players in a gesture of outsider solidarity. There is always a danger in sweeping cultural assumptions like this, but Buzzie Bavasi's hunch was proven correct, just as it had been regarding Montreal's reception for Robinson. Nashua today is a commutable drive to central Boston, about forty-five miles north, but in the immediate post–World War II era it still had a heavily blue-collar mill-town dynamic and plenty of second-generation French speakers born to job-seeking Catholic migrants from Québec among its thirty-five thousand or so residents. (One of the greatest writers in mid-twentieth-century America was Jack Kerouac, author of *On the Road* and the French-speaking son of Québécois immigrants in nearby Lowell, Massachusetts.) Even American-born citizens like backup catcher Oscar "Gus" Gallipeau were usually otherized locally as French Canadians.[45]

Campanella and Newcombe were probably ready for the challenge of the International League as early as 1946 and could have played alongside Robinson on the Royals, but Nashua was another great stepping-stone toward integrated baseball in a relatively small, insulated northeastern loop. They arrived in New Hampshire expecting Jim Crow but were pleasantly surprised to find the freedom to eat and rent accommodations anywhere they liked. Their teammates were almost universally locals who had grown up in all-white towns, which made it easier for them to welcome their new teammates without the inherited racial baggage that normally came from Southerners who had grown up under strict segregation regimes.[46] Campy and Newk had a certain novelty about them that undercut any perception that their presence was a threat to their adopted community.

Gallipeau and Campanella became fast friends, and the Nashua Dodgers went on to a very satisfying league championship over the Lynn Red Sox, which had been an isolated source of ugly racist incidents during the regular season. Campy was promoted to the Royals the following year and had another excellent season (hitting .273/.371/.432 as the everyday catcher) before finally beginning his Hall of Fame run with the Dodgers in early 1948. He was a tremendous hitter with home run power and gaudy on-base averages who picked up NL MVP awards in 1951, 1953, and 1955. A terrible rollover accident after he drove through a patch of ice in late January 1958 prematurely ended his playing career and left him wheelchair-bound, but he still remained engaged with the Dodgers for the rest of his life. In 2006 the Dodgers created the Roy Campanella Award as an annual tribute to the player who best exemplifies his leadership and team spirit.

Newcombe hung back unnecessarily for another dominant turn in Nashua before finally getting promoted to Montreal in 1948. He went on to win the NL Rookie of the Year Award in 1949 and turned in an epic 27-win season in 1956 to earn a Cy Young and MVP Award, the first player in MLB history to win both simultaneously and a feat only ten others have accomplished since. (In retrospect, the Dodgers probably ran him too hard that year—over 268 regular-season innings—and he never quite returned to form.) Many argue that Newcombe would have a strong Hall of Fame case if not for his delayed big league call-up and two lost years to military service during the Korean War. With Robinson fading by 1955 when the great postwar Dodgers dynasty finally won a World Series over their hated Yankees rivals, Campanella and Newcombe were very much the backbone of one of the greatest teams in Dodgers history.

Back in Daytona Beach in April 1946, the Royals' roster could not yet be finalized until the Dodgers set theirs first, but Racine gave an enthusiastic endorsement to Robinson, whom he deemed "marvelous in the field and quick on the bases." So far as his hitting was concerned, Racine added, "He'll probably start racking up plenty of base hits sooner or later."[47] That later was to come in less than a week on the 18th during the Royals' opener at Roosevelt Stadium in Jersey City, when Robinson made clear his bat was more than good enough for the International League.

Before then, by mid-April, Robinson's position was secure, and his backers could start thinking ahead to the next step in his career and what it would actually mean for the sport of baseball when he put on a Montreal uniform in regular-season games. Whatever happened during those first few weeks out on the road before his home debut, Québécois baseball fans had firmly rallied around him. On the cusp of the Royals' opener on the road in Jersey City, *Le Droit* finally put the season to come in aspirational, revolutionary terms: "French Canada, which has always been the asylum of the oppressed . . . , [has] the chance in 1946 to break the links of ethnic intolerance. In baseball, Montreal will destroy color bias."[48] It would be easy to take such a statement as flowery and dismissible rhetoric, but something very special and little understood to outsiders was in fact happening in the world of Québec baseball.

Robinson's AAA success in 1946 and the enthusiastic home reception he received prompted Rickey to bring Campanella up to the Royals in 1947. He too wowed home fans as the only Black player in the International League and a gregarious personality who excelled at a challenging position. Newcombe followed him in 1948 and jointly emerged as the Royals' staff ace (17-6 record, 3.14 ERA over 189 innings) alongside Jack Banta, after an uneven start to his season. The Royals had become a dynasty thanks to these three successive Black stars and took the Junior World Series title as Minor League champs in both 1946 and 1948, coming up just a half game shy of the Jersey City Giants for the regular-season title in 1947. Even after Jackie Robinson left for the Dodgers, attendance continued to jump to the point that Montreal had to be taken seriously as a possible host for an MLB expansion team, a dream that finally came true for all Canadian fans in 1969.[49] In the bigger picture, these three Black stars on the Royals created the conditions for Major League baseball to come to Canada.

Robinson, Campanella, and Newcombe deservedly got the limelight, but by Jon Stott's count eighty-six Black players of lesser renown suited up for integrated teams in the lower-level Provincial League of Québec from 1881 to 1960. This number included a good many Negro League veterans, some of whom made it all the way to the Majors, such as Puerto Rican infielder-outfielder Vic Power, who played over 1,600 big league games, and utility outfielder Dave Pope, a productive bench player into his mid-thirties.

Another milestone of great importance unfolded in Québec when Sam Bankhead took over as dugout boss of the Farnham Pirates, a Class-C Pittsburgh affiliate, in 1951 to become the first Black manager in the Minor Leagues. All of these historic firsts are a testament to the inclusive baseball community that had been developing across Canada, specifically in Québec, long before Americans were ready to accept integration.[50]

Some might argue that Minor League detours through Montreal unnecessarily cost Robinson, Campanella, and Newcombe money and Major League counting stats, but the Larry Doby counterfactual case suggests that Rickey's conservative approach of preparing his Negro Leagues prospects for the Dodgers with a year in a friendly AAA city was ultimately worth the delay.

South Carolina native Larry Doby was one of the finest players of his generation and deservedly won a plaque in the Hall of Fame very late in life in 1998 thanks to a favorable review from the Veterans Committee. Doby made the Newark Eagles at seventeen and sandwiched parts of four Negro League seasons with the club around his navy service toward the end of World War II. He was signed by the Cleveland Indians midway through the 1947 season, becoming the first Black player in the American League just three months after Robinson's Dodgers debut, but he scuffled badly over his rookie season after coming up directly from Newark.

Doby was a fixture in center field for Cleveland for a decade, a perennial All-Star from 1948 to 1955 who won down-ballot MVP votes for four separate seasons. He was a quintessential Steady Eddie in the middle of a strong lineup, delivering 20 to 30 home runs, 100 RBI, and averages near .400 on-base average on a regular basis. He led the AL in on-base average in 1950 (.442), home runs in 1952 and 1954, slugging in 1952 (.541), and RBI in 1954 (126). He was a key cog in the 1948 World Series champion Indians and the 1954 team that won 111 regular-season games before being swept by the Giants in the World Series. The only outstanding question about a fine career from a true gentleman is whether he might have put up slightly better counting stats and earned a quicker Hall of Fame induction had his integration been handled better.

Cleveland Indians owner Bill Veeck was different from Branch Rickey in nearly every way. He was demonstrably progressive, visibly impatient with injustice, and at times confrontational, whereas Rickey was shrewd, patient, and calculating. Both had the same goal of bringing about integration, but were very different in their methods. Their main tactical difference was that Rickey meticulously laid the groundwork for Robinson's promotion to the big leagues by getting a solid buy-in from his Minor League executives, running him through a difficult spring training, then giving him a full integrated season in AAA before calling him up to the Dodgers. Robinson had enough time to acclimate and hit the ground running for the 1947 Dodgers.

Veeck, by contrast, saw Doby as a toolsy twenty-two-year-old who was also one of the finest Negro League hitters of 1946 (.365/.437/.592) with a glove that could play at premium positions in the middle infield or the outfield. Cleveland scouts were already raving about Doby before he got off to another blistering start with the Newark Eagles in 1947, so Veeck decided to pounce given that Rickey and Robinson had already opened the door to Black players. Cleveland was a good team in 1947 and won at a .519 clip, but the club was in no position to challenge Yankees dominance for the AL pennant. The middle infield was already set with two of the team's best hitters, Joe Gordon (135 OPS+) at second and player-manager Lou Boudreau (128 OPS+) at short, so Doby's fastest path to playing time was shifting to the outfield, where center and right were occupied by placeholders.

From a development and organizational perspective, there was no pressing need to rush Doby to the majors in 1947 given his youth and the need for a positional change, but Veeck did it anyway for political and emotional reasons. Being the first AL team to integrate still counted for something to an owner with solidly progressive bona fides.

In Veeck's defense, Cleveland's AAA affiliate, the Baltimore Orioles, had earned a well-deserved reputation during Robinson's 1946 season for having one of the most racially intolerant and abusive fan bases on the International League circuit. Moving Doby down a rung was not a solution, either; Cleveland's AA affiliate played in Jim Crow Oklahoma City. A good argument could thus have been made for sparing Doby what almost certainly would have been a miserable, inhospitable year in the Minors in favor of bringing him straight to Cleveland. The signing was finalized in secret on July 3—Veeck did, to his credit, compensate Eagles owner Effa Manley for taking on Doby's contract, albeit at approximately one-tenth of his free-market value—and then, after spending his Fourth of July on a Chicago-bound train from Newark, Doby was in a Cleveland uniform ready to debut in a road game against the White Sox two days later.

Veeck was on hand to meet Doby on his arrival in Chicago and gave him an effusively warm welcome followed by a condensed version of the speech Rickey had given Robinson in the fall of 1945 about making the hard choice to turn the other cheek when provoked.[51] The following day, Doby headed to the ballpark. Many of Doby's new teammates were taken aback by the surprise announcement he was joining the team and did not react well on their first meeting with him in the dugout. He called years later, "I walked down that line, stuck out my hand, and very few hands came back in return. Most of the ones that did were cold-fish handshakes, along with a look that said, 'You don't belong here . . .' Now, I couldn't believe how this was. I put on my uniform, and I went out on the field to warm up, but nobody wanted to warm up with me. I had never been so alone in my life."[52]

Joe Gordon broke the ice and offered to play catch with Doby, who was flooded with relief knowing he would not be completely isolated during his time in Cleveland. A close friendship developed between them, but Doby could never forget the sinking feeling that came when some of his other teammates went even further than declining a handshake and actually turned their back on him rather than acknowledge the arrival of a Black player.

The following day, Sunday, July 6, Cleveland had a doubleheader at Comiskey Park, and Boudreau wanted Doby to get a full game in, so he tried to slot him in at first, a position Doby had played some in Newark. In the rapid shuffle to join the team in Chicago, however, Doby did not bring a first baseman's glove. Cleveland's regular first baseman was a very pedestrian-hitting (at the time) twenty-six-year-old named Eddie Robinson, who also happened to be right-handed and had already played all of the early game, but for reasons that were entirely his own he refused to share his mitt with Doby. Cleveland ace Bob Feller tried to downplay the incident on the grounds that players are justifiably protective of their equipment, but the White Sox dugout was willing to provide Doby with a loaner so he could take the field.[53] The opposing team's good sportsmanship here was completely overshadowed by an unnecessary humiliation.

Doby and Jackie Robinson formed a tight bond despite playing in different leagues, and they spent many hours on the phone together over the course of the 1947 season. Still, Veeck's experiment was clearly not going nearly as well as Rickey's at the outset. Doby played irregularly—just 33 plate appearances over 29 games during the final three months of the season—and he scuffled horribly (.156/.182/.188 with just a double as his sole extra-base hit). That doubleheader game in July was his only start of the season, and it certainly seemed as though Boudreau did not initially see Doby as a viable Major League player. Doby nevertheless kept his dignity and fought his way through a very difficult initiation. He refused to name his tormentors even late in life, but his sudden arrival in Cleveland and the cold shoulder he received from too many of his teammates clearly had a negative impact on his early development.

With the winter to process the experience and a full spring training with the team, he roared back to his full potential in 1948 as one of the team's best hitters the year it won its most recent World Series trophy. He was a fixture in the two hole—the skipper Boudreau usually provided protection at three—and he had a stellar .301/.384/.490 season in 500 plate appearances that would have won him a Rookie of the Year Award had he not burned his eligibility riding the pine the previous season. Ted Williams called him on March 3, 1998, to relay the news of his Hall of Fame election, prompting Doby to respond, "I feel like a bale of cotton has been lifted from my shoulders."[54]

There was considerable excitement all around heading into the start of baseball's regular season in 1946. Stars such as Ted Williams, Stan Musial, Joe DiMaggio, Warren Spahn, and Bob Feller had demobilized from the military and were finally able to rejoin their teams for a full season, bringing the quality of play back up to pre–Pearl Harbor levels. Traditional powerhouses New York, Boston, and Detroit were predicted to trade blows over a tough AL season, while St. Louis and Brooklyn were expected to be neck and neck over in the Senior Circuit. But perhaps most important and best of all, the echoey half-empty parks of the war years were going to fill back up again with screaming, sun-drenched fans, as normalcy returned to America's pastime.

This sense of optimism filtered down to the Minor Leagues, where the most anticipated date on the early AAA calendar was without a doubt Jackie Robinson's Royals debut in an Opening Day road game against the Jersey City Giants on April 18. Roosevelt Stadium was a big, modern AAA park with a seating capacity of twenty-four thousand, but Giants ownership took full advantage of the opportunity to cash in on Robinson curiosity and allegedly sold nearly fifty-two thousand tickets.[55] The game atmosphere was decidedly Major League, and those who came out to cheer on Robinson—a good number of those in attendance—witnessed what the United Press described as "a sensational start today in his ambition to become in baseball what Joe Louis has been to boxing, Jesse Owens to track, Buddy Young to football and Isaac Murphy to racing."[56]

It was as though all of Robinson's pent-up anticipation for this moment came bursting forth at once during a high-pressure game in front of a packed house. He came up to "a slight round of applause" for his first plate appearance but ended his afternoon in a mob of young autograph- and handshake-seeking fans who "almost pulled the shirt off [his] back."[57] His first time up at bat he ripped a hard groundout to short, but that was the only time he recorded an out in an epic afternoon that showed off all his offensive tools. He picked up 4 hits, including a three-run home run down the left-field line and a drag-bunt single; stole 2 bases; collected 4 RBI; and scored 4 runs, one of which came when he used his disruptive presence on the bases to force the opposing pitcher to balk him in from third. His Royals trounced Jersey City, 14–1; a loud statement had been made to all of the doubters.

One of the most memorable moments on a historic day came when Robinson touched home plate at the end of his first home run trot. There to greet him was the on-deck hitter, George "Shotgun" Shuba, who threw out a meaty handshake under the glare of all of the flashbulbs in the stadium after the two runners Robinson drove in retreated to the dugout rather than wait for him at home as baseball tradition dictated. Photographs would go out the following day in all the papers willing to print images of interracial solidarity; most of the published photos caught a smiling Robinson at a three-quarters angle while Shuba's profile faced him or his head was fully turned away from the camera. Sixty years later, Shuba remembered, "I couldn't care less if Jackie was Technicolor. We'd spent thirty days at spring training, and we all knew that Jackie had been a great athlete at UCLA. As far as I was concerned, he was a great ballplayer—our best. I had no problem going to the plate to shake his hand instead of waiting for him to come by me in the on-deck circle."[58]

This gesture, recently memorialized in a bronze statue of the two players mid-handshake in Shuba's hometown of Youngstown, Ohio, was doubly significant, given that twenty-one-year-old Shuba was competing with Robinson for playing time at second base. After a slow start, he was shipped down to AA Mobile and started playing the outfield to give him a better, but still mostly blocked, path to a Dodgers club that was spoiled by an abundance of riches. Shuba and Robinson became Dodgers teammates once again for a spell in 1948, but Shuba was up and down every year until 1952, when he carved out a permanent role as a utility player. He had shown that he had nothing left to prove after years of beating the tar out of baseballs in parks all the way from the Gulf of Mexico to the Laurentian Mountains of Québec. "If you are ever put on the spot, just do the right thing and everything will work out fine," he liked to say.[59] And it did.

Robinson's Royals debut was a truly ecstatic moment across the Black American press, particularly for reporters who had invested years of effort into bringing about baseball integration. Wendell Smith told his *Pittsburgh Courier* readers that "the hopes of fourteen million Negroes [were] resting on his big broad shoulders . . . [as] Jolting Jackie Robinson, the 'California Comet' [emerged] as the newest and most spectacular satellite to blaze across the International League baseball heavens in a decade."[60]

This enthusiasm percolated north of the border, where Montrealers were left with an agonizing wait of almost two more weeks before they could finally see Robinson play in person on May 1. *The Gazette* teased them, reporting that "Robinson was so excited [in the locker room after the game that] he had to tie his necktie three or four times but he was as happy as a kid on Christmas morning."[61] Baz O'Meara of the *Daily Star* stoked their anticipation by describing his debut in Jersey City as "another Emancipation Day for the Negro race . . . a day Abraham Lincoln would like."[62]

South of the border, their colleague, Wendell Smith, knew better than they did that Robinson's Royals debut was just the beginning of a great story in which a great community of Montreal baseball fans would unwittingly play a central role. He wrote, "Never in history have two players had so many people pulling for them to make good. . . . But at the same time, never in history have two ballplayers been so dependent on these same fans who are pulling for them, for they could very easily make or break Montreal's Robinson or Wright."[63]

FIG. 1. Robinson signs with the Royals on October 24, 1945. At left are Royals executives Lt. Col. Romeo Gauvreau and Hector Racine. Branch Rickey Jr. is standing. Bibliothèque et Archives nationales du Québec (BANQ).

FIG. 2. Jackie and Rachel Robinson on February 26, 1946, shortly after their wedding. BANQ.

FIG. 3. Robinson, spring training 1946, in Florida. Manager Clay Hopper and Dodgers GM Branch Rickey look on. Library and Archives Canada (LAC).

FIG. 4. Robinson, July 9, 1946. Photo by Conrad Poirer. BANQ.

FIG. 5. Robinson flanked by teammates Roy Portlow (*left*) and Johnny Wright (*right*) on August 6, 1946. BANQ.

FIG. 6. Robinson takes in a game with football star Herb Trawick. LAC.

FIG. 7. The Robinsons in the stands. LAC.

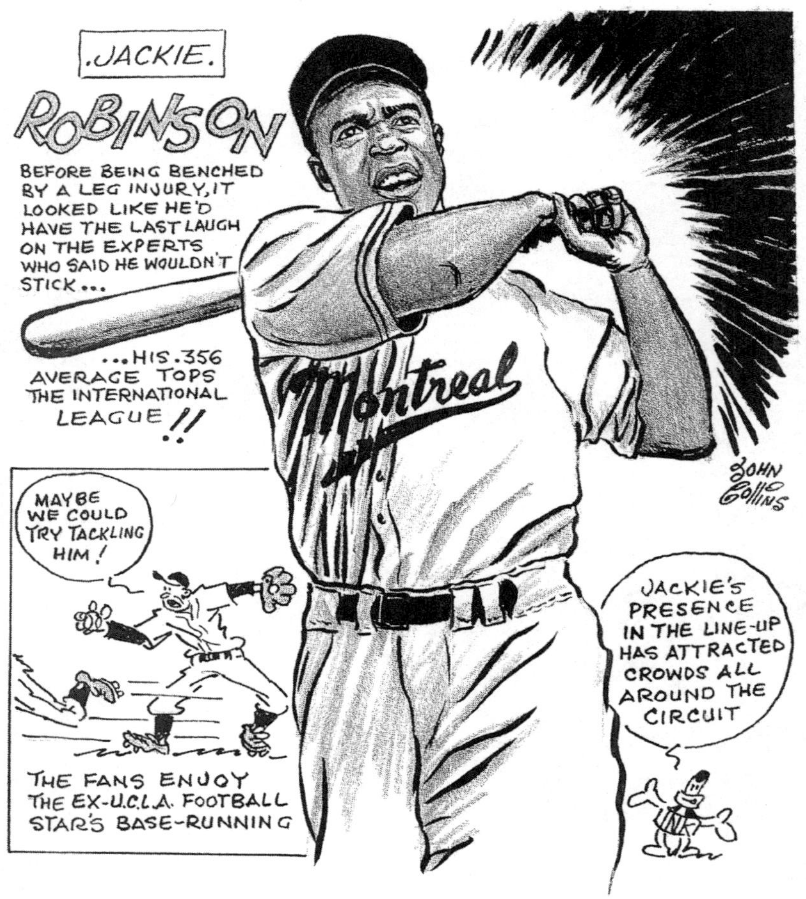

FIG. 8. John Collins cartoon for *The Gazette*, late 1946 season. McCord Stewart Museum (MSM).

FIG. 9. John Collins cartoon for *The Gazette*, after the conclusion of the 1946 season. MSM.

FIG. 10. Robinson signs the Golden Book at Montreal city hall on September 11, 1958. Standing (*left to right*): Mayor Sarto Fournier, unnamed official, Rachel Robinson, and Councilor Joseph-Marie Savignac. Archives de Montreal (AdM).

FIG. 11. Robinson takes a turn in net at the Expo 67 Sports Pavilion, September 1969. AdM.

FIG. 12. Terry Mosher, a.k.a. Aislin, cartoon for *The Gazette*, 1996. MSM.

FIG. 13. Robinson mural at Coco Rico. Author photo.

4

Settling In

Like plastic and penicillin, Robinson is here to stay.

—LLOYD McGOWAN, *Montreal Star*

It is easy for baseball fans to view the Minor Leagues as a stepping-stone to big league glory and overlook the many and considerable off-field hardships players face. Baseball is, after all, a sport where the very best hitters begin every at bat with all the odds stacked heavily in favor of failure. After the first-year player draft was instituted in 1965, some rough math indicates that only two-thirds of first-round picks would even play a single game in the Majors, a number that falls to just under half for second rounders and slides to about one tenth for eleventh- to twentieth-round draftees.[1] A AAA assignment would be the high-water mark for many professional baseball players.

From the dawn of organized baseball all the way through to the 2022 season, Minor Leaguers were left to their own devices when it came to finding housing during their temporary assignments. (MLB clubs now cover accommodations for about 90 percent of all of the players in their systems, the main exceptions mostly being those on Major League contracts and others earning over $100,000 in Minor League salary.) Back in the Dark Ages, the last thing any Minor League player who received a modest signing bonus and then an in-season salary that barely counted as a living wage wanted to do was to commit too much of his meager resources to rent. Getting locked into rental agreements carried another element of risk when players could only speculate on whether they would finish the season where they started it. Promotion to the big leagues was a good problem, but demotion was a catastrophe when it came with a salary cut on top of being left on the hook for a rental property in a city in which the player no longer lived. These issues were even more stressful for players with wives and families.

The Robinsons faced a couple of unique problems on the eve of their move to Montreal in the early spring of 1946. Jackie had been to the city just briefly the previous fall, and Rachel would be moving there sight unseen. Their house hunt came with the expectation that a color barrier would limit their rental options in the same manner they could have expected in any northern American city. Neither of them had much lead time to try to learn passable French, which also meant that they had to contend with a language barrier, given that they would likely be searching for a home in an outlying neighborhood where English was less prevalent than in the city center.

Writing in the late 1980s, Rachel Robinson remembered the trek north from Florida. "We left the South bruised, stimulated, and more contemplative than we arrived. A more resilient pair," she wrote. "But our totally opposite experience in Montreal later that year provided us with an excellent springboard into the majors."[2] Their experience began to turn around for them when their dreaded house hunt—which had been left to Rachel while Jackie was off playing baseball—defied their pessimistic expectations.

The Royals played at Delorimier Stadium at 2101 Rue Ontario Est in the heart of Sainte-Marie, not far from the banks of the Saint Lawrence River, and the Robinsons were hoping to find a home that was either walkable to the park or at least easily accessible by mass transit. The club gave them a lead on a furnished walk-up duplex at 8232 Avenue de Gaspé up in Villeray that was a little further out than they might have liked—nearly five miles to the north—but it was situated in a tranquil residential neighborhood just a few blocks from the future Montreal Expos' first home, Jarry Park. The unit itself was quintessentially Montreal, complete with the ubiquitous metal stairs that strike outsiders as unnecessarily hazardous for a city that receives more snowfall than nearly any major urban center on earth. There were certainly some pros to the location: a relatively short walk to the Marché du Nord in Little Italy (now the sprawling Jean-Talon Market, one of the biggest open-air food and produce markets in North America) and enough distance from the bustle of downtown to give Jackie faint hope of relative anonymity. It was a relatively easy ride down to the ballpark on a streetcar, a cheap and popular means of moving around the city in 1946.

The big unknown for the Robinsons was just how well they would fit in anywhere in Montreal, a city with a population that was just 2 percent Black. Villeray was a sleepy village of fewer than one thousand people a little over a generation earlier when it was annexed into the city of Montreal. It was still firmly working class, nearly all white and overwhelmingly francophone in 1946. (Today, its multicultural character, eclectic collection of boutiques and cafés, and vibrant public art earned it an eighteenth overall ranking on Time Out's 2021 coolest neighborhoods in the world list.)[3] Villeray was also a fairly long way, both culturally and by distance (four miles), from Little Burgundy, the gritty, beating heart of Black Montreal. How would two college-educated Californians get along as double outsiders, racial and linguistic, in this new environment?

Rachel approached her interview with her prospective landlady with justifiable trepidation. Remembering the encounter in a 2011 statement to mark a ceremony where Mayor Gérald Tremblay unveiled a historic plaque to celebrate the Robinson's former residence, she wrote, "On Avenue de Gaspé, we encountered nothing but kindness. The woman who owned the duplex we rented let me into her house the first day, served me tea, and insisted that we live in that apartment and use her things—the sheets, the dishes. No one spoke English, and we didn't speak French, but they treated us with respect."[4] One of the neighbors came by to translate, and Rachel and the landlady quickly agreed to terms for the rental. Jackie stopped in with Rachel later in the day after practice, and they put their signatures to a lease.[5] The landlady realized they were coming from the United States with just a couple of suitcases full of clothing, so she surprised Rachel further by offering to leave all the dishware and sheets to spare them the trouble of shopping for their own.[6]

The ease of it all left Rachel wondering, *How can a few miles, a mere border, make that much difference in people?* She fondly remembered that otherwise unremarkable little apartment at 8232 de Gaspé as their "honeymoon cottage," and it has since become one of many Robinson pilgrimage sites for diehard baseball fans passing through the city. She gushed that "Jack and I both fell in love with Montreal. Where the housing situation in Florida had been simply a nightmare, up in Montreal it was a delight."[7]

Rachel got celebrity treatment from neighborhood kids who would rush over to carry her groceries, later working up the courage to ask through her screen door, in heavily accented English, if they might have a piece of their favorite fruit. Many of them had gone years without seeing anything much more exotic than an apple, thanks to the war. The women of the neighborhood then started sharing meat coupons—Canada continued shipping out food aid to Britain through 1946 and maintained its wartime rationing policies longer than the United States—once they learned that Rachel was pregnant with her first child. She resisted, but they insisted. This was an incredibly generous sacrifice from neighbors of modest means who had been suffering through wartime shortages for nearly six years. Not only were they giving up food from their own tables, but this act also showed a willingness to forgo the money that could have been made selling surplus coupons to supplement their meager incomes. The neighborhood women also started popping by the apartment to help Rachel sew maternity gowns, another item in short supply off the rack in 1946—all this for a stranger.[8]

Robinson talked about his experience nearly two decades later during an interview with CBC television in 1964:

> I remember Montreal as a city that enabled me to go on to the Major Leagues. . . . The fans there were just fantastic, and my wife and I have nothing but the greatest of memories, especially as we'd go to the ballpark the Gaspé way out where the French Canadians [lived]. . . . Every morning going to the ballpark . . . somebody was making a racket because heads would pop out of each of the adjoining houses as we walked past, and the people were so friendly and nice that we shall never forget them.
>
> In one short year the fans in Montreal eliminated [fears of riots about me playing]. Their great warmth and love and the

> way that they treated us up there, I shall never forget this. I think it's one of the reasons why I was able to overcome many of the problems we had knowing full well that the only thing the people in Montreal were asking was that I do the best I possibly could for the Montreal ballclub.[9]

Toward the end of his life, when he looked back on the family's living conditions in Montreal during the 1946 season, Jackie noted ruefully that things took a decided step backward the following year when he was called up to Brooklyn. He, Rachel, and the baby, Jackie Jr., spent a miserable first year there cramped into a tiny room at the Hotel McAlpin in Midtown Manhattan. They were always surrounded by people in what was once New York's highest-occupancy hotel, but these were transient strangers rather than friendly neighbors like the ones they enjoyed in Villeray. The absence of any sense of community was all the more glaring in contrast.[10]

The Robinsons had another major source of worry about how things would go in Montreal—how would Jackie get on with his new manager, Clay Hopper, a part-time cotton broker from rural Mississippi?—but it had thankfully already resolved itself before their move north for the start of the regular season.

Hopper is the most famous son of Porterville, Mississippi, an unincorporated hamlet with a 2020 population of thirty-four people in the middle part of the state, just off the Alabama line. His birthplace is about as deep as the South gets, but he relocated to Greenwood, a pretty, little town in the northeast part of the state that then had around ten thousand people. It nonetheless produced an impressively long list of famous and infamous characters from twentieth century America. Among them were pre–World War I era Governor James K. Vardaman, also known as the "The Great White Chief" and an enthusiastic public advocate of lynching; Robert Leroy Johnson, a musician who according to legend sold his soul in a crossroads deal with the devil to become the world's greatest bluesman; Byron De La Beckwith, the assassin who murdered civil rights leader Medgar Evers in 1963; and Academy Award winner Morgan Freeman, who plausibly played the role of God in the 2003 film *Bruce Almighty*.

Hopper was a first baseman and outfielder with decent power and good plate discipline who toiled for sixteen Minor League seasons mostly in the St. Louis Cardinals system, never advancing beyond a very short stint in AA Rochester (then the highest Minor League level) during his age twenty-five season in 1928. He did not quite have the talent for a big league future as a player, but Hopper was recognized early on for his great baseball IQ and shifted into player-manager duties by age twenty-eight. He excelled in this new role.

Branch Rickey had known and respected Hopper for fifteen years while they were in the Cardinals' organization together, so the incoming Dodgers general manager decided to poach him as a new dugout boss for a Dodgers high Minors affiliate after the 1942 season. In 1945 Hopper established his managerial bona fides by leading the Dodger's new Southern Association affiliate, the Mobile Bears, to an improbable league championship after finishing the regular season 19.5 games back of the pennant-winning Atlanta Crackers. His stock was clearly on the rise.

Over the years, Hopper had shown more than enough brains and moxie to get on Branch Rickey's short list to move up to the Royals in 1946, the apex of the Dodgers' Minor League system. Hopper indeed landed the job in early December, but he was not brought on board until after Jackie Robinson was already signed in the fall of 1945 and it became clear that Montreal would almost certainly field an interracial roster during the upcoming season. By taking this position, Hopper had accepted a responsibility that would ultimately force him to either suppress or reverse every racial prejudice he had absorbed during his forty-three years in the Deep South if he wanted his team to succeed.

As with all his decisions, Rickey's pick was quite intentional. He thought that if he could convince the small-town Mississippian who managed the squad to acquiesce in the Great Experiment, all the other dominoes could be subsequently knocked over with relative ease. Rickey's calculation contained a good deal of risk.[11] In December 1945, Montreal *Gazette* reporter Baz O'Meara predicted tension between Hopper and Robinson on racial grounds, but Rickey felt he knew Hopper well enough to predict that he would ultimately come around for the sake of his team.[12]

This did not happen overnight. One of Hopper's first questions for Rickey was whether Robinson could be reassigned to another Dodgers affiliate instead of joining his squad in Montreal. "Please don't do this to me," he pleaded to Rickey. "I'm white and I've lived in Mississippi all my life. If you're going to do this, you're going to force me to move my family and home out of Mississippi." When spring training began, he did at least offer Robinson an unenthusiastic handshake on their first meeting, but his attitude remained unchanged. Within a few days he confided to a sportswriter that it was some relief his father had passed away, because "if he were alive, he would probably kill me for managing a black player."[13]

Ten years after the fact, Branch Rickey shared a story about Hopper from the Dodgers' 1946 spring training camp during a speech in Atlanta broadcast over the radio on AM WERD 860. During a practice game in Daytona Beach, "Jackie made one of those tremendous remarkable plays that very few people can make—went toward first base, made a slide, stabbed the ball, came with it in his left-hand glove and as he turned with the body control that's almost inconceivable and cut off the runner at second base on a force play. I took Clay and I put my hand on his shoulder and I said, 'Did you ever see a play to beat it?'" Rickey continued,

> Now this fellow comes from Greenwood, Mississippi. And he would forgive me, I am sure, because of the magnificent way that he came through on it. He took me and shook me and his face that far from me and he said, "Do you really think that a 'n——' is a human being, Mr. Rickey?" That's what he said. That's what that fellow said. I have never answered him until this minute.
>
> And six months later he came into my office after the year at Montreal when he was this boy's manager. He didn't want him to be sent to him. And he said to me, "I want to take back what I said to you last spring." He said, "I'm ashamed of it." "Now," he said, "you may have plans for him to be on your club"—and he was, "but," he said, "if you don't have plans to have him on the Brooklyn club," he said, "I would like to have him back in Montreal." And then he told me that he was not only a great ball

player good enough for Brooklyn, but he said that he was a fine gentleman. Proximity. Proximity, says [historian Frank] Tannenbaum, will solve this thing if you can have enough of it. But that is a limited thing, you see.[14]

How did Hopper go from probable villain to improbable hero in the Jackie Robinson story? A fundamentally decent man had absorbed indecent values that were prevalent in his time and place, but he later shook them off when they threatened his greatest priority: winning baseball games. Two more specific factors helped him do an about-face in the spring of 1946. The first was Robinson's character itself, and second was the attempt of various Florida municipal officials to keep him off the field, which had a rallying effect for the skipper and the rest of his team. An attack on one (or two, including Johnny Wright) quickly came to be viewed as an attack on all, as the Royals closed ranks under pressure. Hopper never made the loud public declarations Racine did that spring, but he had quickly and quietly come to the same conclusion: Robinson was with the Royals, and any community that tried to block him from playing would face a boycott from the entire team.

The Dodgers moved their spring training in 1947 down to Cuba to avoid a repeat of the Florida debacle from a year earlier. This time, Hopper gave Robinson a firm handshake when he heartily congratulated him on his promotion to the Dodgers for the upcoming season.

As regular-season play began, the 1946 Royals established a very simple path to victory: they utterly bludgeoned opponents to death, scoring on average over 6.6 runs a game, and got by on perfectly serviceable pitching. There was a dearth of home run power on the squad—no one player hit more than 17 on the year—but it did have incredibly patient hitters up and down the lineup, and men were always on base, translating into a feast of runs. The team collectively hit .288/.387/.431, and the lowest on-base average among the regulars was outfielder Red Durrett's perfectly respectable .353, while Robinson led the squad with a Bondsian mark of .468. There simply was not a weak spot anywhere in the lineup, and even the platoon players contributed in a major way.

They say in baseball that hitting is contagious, which may well be true when one of your starting pitchers, Steve Nagy, hits .265/.358/.482 with 3 home runs and two others hit over .300. In an era when the stolen base had reached record lows at the big league level, the Royals were burners who swiped 189 bags (the entire eight-team National League stole just 478 that year). Outfielder and leadoff man Marv "Rabbit" Rackley led the team with 65, Robinson stole 40 hitting out of the two hole, and number-five hitter Tommy Tatum added 28 more. The Royals' formula was getting on base at a high clip, running well, and trusting everyone down the lineup to do his part to cash them in.

Of all of these solid, overaged players, only one other than Robinson really enjoyed any success at the big league level, and that was Dixie Howell, a serviceable right-handed-hitting platoon catcher who got parts of eight seasons in the big leagues from 1947 to 1956. He had given up his peak seasons to the U.S. Army during World War II and then found his path to Brooklyn blocked by a young, competent, high on-base average catcher, Bruce Edwards, who was himself a placeholder for future Hall of Famer Roy Campanella. Howell did finally get the call from the Pirates at age twenty-seven in 1947, and he made sure to reach out to congratulate Robinson, his former Royals teammate, early in the season on his own promotion to Brooklyn. This was a small but meaningful gesture from a proud Louisvillian who bucked sectional attitudes of the era and wished nothing but the best for one of the most decent men with whom he had ever played.[15] They did reconnect briefly as big league teammates after Howell rejoined the Dodgers organization in 1953 and came up for a handful of games over three seasons before the team moved to Los Angeles.

The roster had other interesting players who were probably good enough for a few years of mostly full-time work at the big league level had they played for a less competitive organization. Undersized infielder Spider Jorgensen won the Dodgers' third base job in 1947 when veteran Hall of Famer Arky Vaughan went down to injury in spring training. Jorgensen's great moment came as a complete shock, and then embarrassment set in once he realized that he had been assigned to Brooklyn after all of his equipment was shipped to Syracuse, where the Royals were opening their 1947 season. Jorgensen ultimately made his big league debut using a second baseman's glove that Robinson loaned him, along with another player's cleats.[16]

Any other rookie on the 1947 Dodgers would be playing in Robinson's shadow, but Jorgensen put up a very serviceable .274/.360/.410 line (102 OPS+) over 506 plate appearances. This solid rookie showing at the dish could have translated into a permanent role on an excellent team, but Jorgensen badly damaged his throwing shoulder from the recoil of a hunting rifle in an offseason accident. His hitting was unaffected, but he had difficulty making good accurate throws across the diamond from third, and he had future Hall of Fame teammates at shortstop and second, Pee Wee Reese and Robinson, preventing a move to a less taxing position for his arm. Bad luck ultimately derailed a promising career, though Jorgensen did collect a World Series ring for part-time work with the 1951 New York Giants. He hung on in pro baseball until age forty and had a productive denouement back in Canada over three-plus seasons with the Pacific Coast League's Vancouver Mounties during the late 1950s before transitioning into coaching and scouting.

Speedy outfielder Rabbit Rackley found himself in a similar position. He won a spot on the 1948 Dodgers at age twenty-six and hit a robust .327/.370/.409 in 304 PA, but skipper Leo Durocher did not have his players run much, minimizing the best part of Rackley's game, and even his supporters recognized that his weak throwing arm was a liability. Rackley was squeezed out the following season despite continuing to hit well, as the Dodgers found themselves spoiled with an abundance of riches in the outfield. At age twenty-two, Duke Snider stole a full-time job, hitting .292/.361/.493, while productive veterans Gene Hermanski (.299/.431/.487) and Carl Furillo (.322/.368/.506) had their spots locked in. All three brought loud slugging to the lineup, casting Rackley's pop-gun approach in a less favorable light. He got in five more games after being sold to the Reds for the 1950 season, but was done as a big leaguer by age twenty-eight. Rackley was a South Carolinian, a Southerner like Howell, who similarly bucked expectations by giving his full support to Robinson when they played together on the Royals.

Al Campanis, Robinson's double-play partner and the only Greek-born player in MLB history, had the best season of his pro career with the Royals in 1946 (.294/.375/.393), but he never showed enough to earn another call-up after a seven-game wartime cup of coffee with the Dodgers in 1943. He hit well enough to displace the uberpopular, glove-first Québécois Stan Bréard at short, but this certainly did not at all endear him to Montreal fans, who were enraged when a local icon lost playing time. (Bréard was ultimately traded to the unaffiliated San Diego Padres of the Pacific Coast League, leading to a rare moment of consternation among the fan base during a season that was otherwise going perfectly.)[17]

Campanis had far more baseball success in the Dodgers' organization after he hung up his cleats. As a scout, he found both Roberto Clemente—lost to the Pirates in the 1954 Rule 5 Draft in an epic blunder that was not his fault—and Sandy Koufax, two of the greatest players of the 1960s, and then he had an incredibly long and successful run as a general manager. He took over the Dodgers in 1968 and put together a mid-to-late-1970s dynasty that really took off when the Big Red Machine in Cincinnati finally began to ebb, winning a World Series in 1981 in the Dodgers' fourth try in eight seasons. What had been a very fine career ended on a sour note with his resignation after almost twenty years as general manager just two games into the 1987 season.

Campanis was by all accounts one of the best Royals in early 1946 in terms of his welcome for Jackie Robinson, joining a cohort that included Lou Rochelli during spring training and then Dixie Howell and Marv Rackley during the regular season. He and Robinson roomed together, and Campanis made an extra effort to help get him familiar with his new position at second base. Years later when Campanis's son, Jimmy, wanted to do a show-and-tell assignment at school on Robinson, Campanis called in a favor and had Robinson—at the peak of his Dodgers stardom—shock the room by walking through the door to meet the entire class.[18] This certainly would not have happened if Robinson had any reason whatsoever to doubt their friendship.

Nearly all the goodwill that Campanis had built up over a long, successful career came undone in early 1987 during one of the most disastrous television interviews in American sports history. Ted Koppel brought Campanis on the popular ABC late-evening news staple, *Nightline*, on April 6 for a soft Opening Day piece on the fortieth anniversary season of Robinson's Dodgers debut. Parts of the segment with Rachel Robinson and some of Jackie's Dodgers teammates had been prerecorded, but Campanis was slated to appear live from the Astrodome in Houston, where the Dodgers were playing that night. Joining him on the panel was respected sports writer Roger Kahn, author of the 1972 classic *The Boys of Summer*.

The length of their appearance would be determined by the conclusion of the Marvin Hagler–Sugar Ray Leonard middleweight championship fight, which had been oddly scheduled for a Monday night in Las Vegas. *Nightline* wanted to break the result of one of the most important bouts of the year, so Koppel's plan was to keep Campanis talking until he could announce a winner. Everyone was hoping for flowery platitudes about "so much done, but so much more to do" on equal access in baseball.

Koppel had given many hard-hitting interviews over the years with heads of state both friend and foe to America, but he was not exactly pressing Campanis when he asked him if he could explain the dearth of Black managers and the complete absence of any Black general managers in Major League baseball. This was a completely fair question, given that Campanis had had major input in the decision over who would replace Walter Alston as dugout boss after the 1976 season, either boisterous third base coach Tommy Lasorda or first base coach Jim Gilliam, a long-time Dodgers player and former Rookie of the Year who had a baseball IQ that was widely seen as off the charts. Lasorda, who came to be known nationally as a lovable loudmouth who shilled for SlimFast weight-loss drinks on television, won the job in the end. In twenty-two seasons on the job, he won two World Series championships, but cumulatively led one of the best-resourced teams in all of American sport to a fairly modest .526 winning percentage.

Campanis was known for sometimes mangling his words and began his on-air appearance by questioning the leadership qualities of prospective Black candidates for these roles. He then delved into popular unscientific tropes about their swimming prowess and finished by doubling down on his initial point despite having a commercial break to consider how it might have been perceived by the audience. In one of the worst parts of the exchange, Campanis said, "Now, as far as having the background to become club presidents, or presidents of a bank, I don't know. But I do know when I look at a black ballplayer, I am looking at him physically and whether he has the mental approach to play in the big leagues."[19]

Those who knew him best in the Dodgers organization gave Campanis the benefit of the doubt; he was over seventy years old and in failing health, the interview was given very late at night, and he had never before shown outward signs of prejudice toward Black teammates or colleagues. His confession on *Nightline* did, however, confirm what many had long suspected: that soft prejudices continued to close doors for Black applicants for leadership and administrative jobs. Campanis was deeply embarrassed and publicly apologized the following day in a joint statement with team owner Peter O'Malley, then he chose to resign two days later to spare the Dodgers a lengthy pressure campaign for his ouster.

MLB followed up on the Campanis debacle two months later by hiring Harry Edwards, a widely respected former discus thrower at San Jose State turned civil rights activist and sociology professor at the University of California, Berkeley, to help open up coaching and front-office opportunities in baseball for nonwhite candidates. Campanis was finished in baseball by this point, but he surprised Edwards by reaching out to him immediately after the announcement to offer his help for the endeavor. He knew he had to go out on a better note, and Edwards welcomed the opportunity to collaborate with him.

The Royals' pitching staff had a solid front three of late twentysomethings Steve Nagy, their ace and only starter to throw two hundred innings; Cy Buker; and Glen Moulder, all of whom had ERAS comfortably in the 3.00–4.00 range. Still, none of their pitchers graduated to any notable Major League success. Jack Banta did throw 152.1 mostly good innings with a 3.37 ERA for the 1949 Dodgers, but this was the highwater mark for a staff made up mostly of older journeymen.

Eleven different pitchers started games for the Royals in 1946, a fairly high number for a team that had so much success, and the squad finished with a 100-54 record. Local favorite Jean-Pierre Roy struggled badly after overuse in 1945, throwing an ugly 5.59 ERA across 111 innings. Banta was just twenty-one and slightly overmatched by the competition, putting up a 5.04 ERA in 125 innings. Their woes created an opportunity for swingmen like Chet Kehn and John Gabbard, who both performed adequately as spot starters. Late-blooming Curt Davis was fighting to return to the bigs at the ripe old age of forty-two and finished sixth in the International League in ERA, but he pitched mostly out of the bullpen in the swansong of outlier career path that saw him put up an impressive 39.9 WAR despite not making his Phillies debut until he was thirty years old.

Robinson's spring training comrade in suffering, pitcher Johnny Wright, lasted just two games out of the Royals bullpen and returned to relative obscurity following a demotion to the Class-C Trois-Rivières Royals of the Canadian-American League (the rough equivalent to A ball today). Wright is typically viewed as a minor supporting character in the Robinson story, a player signed more to keep Robinson company in the trying early days in the Dodgers' organization rather than as a serious prospect, but he was a talented pitcher in his own right who, under different circumstances and with a little more grit, may well have earned himself a spot on a big league roster. He even spoke some Louisiana French, which should have made his transition to life in Québec a little bit easier.

Wright shone brightly for the powerhouse Homestead Grays of the Negro National League during the war years and had emerged as one of the best Black pitchers in the country by 1943 when he went 18-3 with a 2.54 ERA over 181 innings for the Negro World Series champions. His recipe for success was a mix of great fastball velocity, plus control, and a hard-breaking curve that got the better of most opposing hitters. Wright missed a good chunk of both the 1944 and 1945 seasons while he served stateside in the navy, but he did continue to pitch on competitive, integrated military teams, including a New York squad from Floyd Bennett Field Naval Air Base that held exhibition games with the Red Sox, Dodgers, and White Sox. His performance in these games was a bit of a mixed bag, but some of the scouts in attendance saw glimpses of promise. Wright (using the alias Leroy

Leftowich for his professional appearances while he was still in the navy to avoid getting caught for breaching service terms) also threw a dazzling six innings against a group of Major League stars in an October 1945 exhibition game at Ebbets Field that helped convince Rickey that he was worth a flyer.

The Dodgers got around to offering Wright, then twenty-nine years old, a Minor League contract in January 1946 in the aftermath of Robinson's signing with the Royals. He took the opportunity despite a gentlemen's agreement with Grays owner Cum Posey that he would return to Homestead once he got out of the navy. Posey was livid and trashed Wright's fielding and ability to hold baserunners in a profanity-laced interview with Sam Lacy of *The Chicago Defender*, but he was powerless to stop Wright from taking his chances in the Dodgers' organization.

Early on in spring training, Wright faced all the same pressure as Robinson, but he showed enough promise that the Québec press thought the Royals might have stumbled upon a new front-end starter for the 1946 season. By temperament, he was extremely reserved and surprised many by taking deeper offense at racial epithets than Robinson despite having grown up with a steady diet of them in the Jim Crow Deep South. As the weeks wore on, his trademark command mysteriously seemed to evaporate, and his plus stuff often deserted him as the stakes grew larger. He probably would not have been assigned to Montreal to start this season if not for Rickey's belief that he would provide valuable company for Robinson during the transition to integrated play in the International League.[20]

Wright stumbled and surrendered 4 earned runs in his Royals debut, the team's second game of the season on the road in Jersey City, and he did not appear again for a week when he was needed for mop-up duty. Hopper was simply not confident in him after a poor spring training and let him ride the bench until he was finally sent down in late May. To his credit, Wright concealed any bitter disappointment he may have felt over his demotion to Trois-Rivières, a paper-mill town of about forty-five thousand that may unfairly be seen mostly as a convenient stop for travelers who need to gas up their cars at the halfway point between Montreal and Québec City. He ate up a lot of innings for the shorter-season club, but the results were not good enough (a 4.15 ERA over 154 innings) to warrant a callup back to Montreal, where Robinson was making a strong case for an early big league promotion a tantalizingly close eighty miles away.

Wright's much-less-heralded former Grays teammate Roy Partlow, a two-way player who was too long in the tooth for even a remote chance at a future with the Dodgers, took his spot on the Montreal Royals roster. Hopper liked Partlow quite a bit better—he showed superior control than Wright in 1946, even when his secondary pitches deserted him—and ran him out for twenty-nine innings. Partlow struggled against higher-level competition, but after his demotion back down to Trois-Rivières he pitched well and helped propel the team to a Canadian-American League championship, winning playoff MVP honors. In the grander scheme of baseball history, the Nashua Dodgers with Roy Campanella and Don Newcombe get some deep insider credit for fielding one of the earliest successful, integrated Minor League teams, but Trois-Rivières did just the same with Wright and Partlow and have received virtually no recognition for it.

Both Wright and Partlow returned to the Negro Leagues the following year. Partlow was never seen as a legitimate prospect and did himself no favors by angrily refusing to accept his late July demotion back to Trois-Rivières at first, but the much more reserved Wright did start to perform much better once Partlow became his teammate down the home stretch. As the season wound down, Wright developed some hope that he would get a second chance in Montreal in 1947.

The general consensus on Wright was that he had the talent to pitch for Brooklyn if only he had more mental toughness. In the end, Robinson said that "John had all the ability in the world . . . but John couldn't stand the pressure of going up into this new league and being one of the first [Black players]." Partlow hung on in the low Minors—after two years in the Negro Leagues—until he was nearly forty (or over, depending on whether stories about a fudged birthdate are true), while Wright played itinerant baseball for a little while longer before returning to New Orleans and taking a steady but modest income as a railway porter. He had virtually nothing to say to the public in later years about his near brush with stardom.[21]

Royals fans had to wait nearly two long weeks before their super team finally came north for its home opener, a Wednesday, May 1, matinee that nonetheless drew over sixteen thousand fans. The attendance was the biggest Opening Day crowd since Delorimier Stadium opened in 1928, when a capacity twenty-thousand-person crowd turned out, setting a Canadian record for the highest-attended sporting event. Over the first third of the team's home games, Royals attendance had skyrocketed up 55,000—to 214,352—from the same period in 1945, largely thanks to Robinson's presence.

This was doubly notable for anyone familiar with the city's "spring" climate. The last snowfall for Montreal came unexpectedly early in 1946 on March 13, but the temperature stayed cool with a frost as late as May 3 and daytime highs in the fifty-to-sixty-degree Fahrenheit range well into the middle of the month. Every honest Canadian fan who has had the pleasure of attending AAA baseball while it lasted more recently in Ottawa, Calgary, or Edmonton would admit that Canada's climate is wholly unsuitable for a full season of outdoor pro baseball.

Populist Mayor Camillien Houde, a hero to Québécois nationalists who had been reelected to his old office in 1944 after a four-year stint in a World War II internment camp for vocally encouraging resistance to conscription, threw out the ceremonial first pitch on Opening Day. He then made sure to track down Robinson for a photo op before the playing of "God Save the King." Standing before a cheering crowd of Montrealers years earlier during a royal tour of the city, Houde is said to have leaned over to King George VI and remarked, "You know, Your Majesty, some of this is for you."[22] He certainly was not the type to turn down an opportunity to ride on the coattails of someone else's fame.

Everyone wanted to meet Jackie Robinson, the hottest name in town in 1946, not just self-serving politicians.[23] As Scott Simon writes, "The city received Jackie Robinson as if he were a black American expat jazz musician in the Latin Quarter." The biggest applause always came for Robinson, who needed a police escort to exit the stadium through a mob of fans who hoped to get a close-up glimpse of him. Rachel Robinson would often stand in and sign autographs so they would not come away from their trouble with nothing.[24]

The Royals came home in fourth place with a 7-7 record, but then they caught fire in early May and never looked back. A 9-1 homestand—which ultimately rolled into a 22-5 run over the next month—pushed them to the top of the International League, and Robinson's play was clearly elevating everyone around him. He came home hitting .370 and had scored 26 runs and swiped 13 bags through the team's first twenty-four games, becoming the undisputed lynchpin in a high-octane offense. The *Star* had seen enough to call him "one of the great athletes of our time, of any time, [with] all the tools to be a very good baseball player." *Le Canada* saw a player with a "big heart" unlike any they could recall in recent memory. *La Presse* gushed that he "continued to boost his popularity by emerging as a veritable batting artist" and that the 1945 Royals—International League champs—could not compare with the speed game on Robinson's squad.[25]

Robinson's home park, Delorimier Stadium, sometimes known as Delorimier Downs, was the envy of the International League when it opened in 1928 at 2101 Ontario Street in the city's east end. The stadium was a veritable delight for left-handed power hitters, thanks to a 293-foot right-field line, and a massive outfield expanse for doubles hitters, owing to deep twelve-foot walls in center, 441 feet from home plate, and a deep left-field pole at 341 feet. This rectangular configuration created dual-use possibilities, prompting the fledgling Montreal Alouettes football club to move into Delorimier for their inaugural season in 1946, in addition to setting up nicely for occasional high-profile soccer friendlies for visiting British clubs.

Fans mostly came to the park on foot or by streetcar, which was a cheap but typically overcrowded means of mass transit until the Montreal Metro finally opened in 1966 after nearly a half century of off-and-on progress. The club kept ticket prices low for its working class, mostly francophone fan base, charging just twenty-five cents for Sunday doubleheader bleacher tickets, roughly $4.50 in 2024 dollars, and the stadium had its own spit and sawdust tavern just as the Forum did for hockey crowds. A popular pregame spot was across Ontario Street from the park, Montreal Royals Restaurant, where early-bird fans would stop by in the hope of crossing paths with one of the players.[26] Sometimes these encounters could be heartbreaking.

One of them, Alvin Guttman, approached Royals players at a restaurant called the Chic-N-Coop and told them he was a huge Robinson fan only to hear in response, "Yeah, but it's a shame to take a job away from a white man."[27]

That 1946 home opener was a particularly raucous affair, in large part thanks to Robinson's presence on the field. The biggest round of applause of the day went to Robinson when he came up for his first at bat. Sam Lacy, now of the *Afro-American*, was on hand to cover it and reported that the team's victory was actually an "anti-climax . . . [for] the Montreal Royals' dead-in-earnest followers." All the attention went to Robinson, not hometown hero Stan Bréard or outfielder George Shuba, who was on some kind of tear with 7 home runs among his first 8 hits that season. After the game, "the big 'nine' was literally ripped from [Robinson's] back by youthful admirers who besieged him after the game. Jackie shared the spotlight with no one."[28]

The local press wrote months of early-season articles that always referred to Robinson's race before it started using cringe-worthy nicknames for Robinson—the "Dark Dasher" and "Colored Comet" were two of the most common—but the reporters were clearly behind a fan favorite and openly cheered on their underdog. For his part, Robinson came to enjoy being reminded of his popular outsider status and took great pleasure in how "the bilingual announcer at the park would introduce him with a Québécois accent [as] 'Yak-ee Rob-eenson.'"[29] He was clearly embracing life as a fish out of water.

A late-season fly-on-the-wall piece in *Le Front Ouvrier* offered a snapshot of life in the cheap seats at Delorimier Downs, where there was a considerable amount of small-money gambling and expected fan grumbling about shortstop Al Campanis's defensive liabilities compared to Stan Bréard's. The reporter intensely watched a group of Black Royals fans as they zeroed in on Robinson, elbows on their knees and hands on their chins in concentration, as he came up to bat. "For them, it's an honest joy to see one of their own shine in front of roughly nineteen thousand fans," wrote André Rufiange. After Robinson cracked a two-run double, "you should have seen [their] joy!" This was, to the writer, a very promising sign that baseball was helping facilitate better race relations.[30]

Ivan Livingstone, a bilingual, teenage Black Montrealer of Jamaican-Guyanese origins and Royals fan who may well have been among the group Rufiange observed, later noted, "As soon as you got near the park, you got the energy. There were not a lot of Black people in the stands, but we gained a level of respect. I remember people smiling at us, as if we were associated with Jackie, as if we had something to do with it! And the truth is, we kind of felt like we did have something to do with it. Like we were on the inside."[31]

Livingstone had many American scholarship opportunities and transferred from one of Canada's top universities, McGill, where he was barely tolerated by coaches and teammates on the football team, to the University of Dubuque in Iowa, where he went on to become the captain of the track and field team. He turned professional and played for seven Canadian Football League seasons from 1954 to 1960, including three with his hometown Alouettes, but he had a much longer career as an educator who taught chemistry and French as the first Black teacher in the Protestant School Board of Greater Montreal. He pressed on through decades of doubts from white colleagues who could not imagine a Black man excelling in a nontraditional role and later spent many years in Africa on government-funded aid projects or conducting research, but his success served as a testament for his students back in Verdun who hoped for more opportunities than their parents.[32]

However ephemeral the Robinson effect might have been on Montreal race relations during the 1946 season, it was real and noticeable in the moment. Robinson's teammate and Montreal native Jean-Pierre Roy noted, "Up in the [Royals] stands, no one dared insult Jackie. He was Black, but in their eyes and hearts the fans didn't see that. I heard obscenities thrown at him in the US. In Montreal, he was always respected as a baseball player."[33]

Robinson fever spilled over into other major professional sports in Montreal over the course of the 1946 season. It is so common today to hear the best Canadian players in the Major Leagues describe themselves as "failed hockey players" that it has almost become a cliche—Larry Walker and Justin Morneau immediately come to mind—but in the summer of 1946 the biggest and brightest star in the NHL was at least semiseriously entertaining his own baseball dreams.

The love for Robinson also came from other athletes beyond baseball. Sportswriter Dink Carroll christened Maurice Richard with one the best nicknames in hockey: The Rocket. (His younger brother, Henri, a fine center in his own right and a fellow Hall of Famer, got the hand-me-down tribute "Pocket Rocket.") Montreal born and raised, Richard was a diminutive right-winger charitably listed at 5 feet 10 inches and 180 pounds, who joined the Canadiens, hockey's equivalent to the New York Yankees, at age twenty-one during the 1942–43 season. It was an improbable rise to the NHL for the son of a modest railway carpenter, a pond-hockey and backyard-rink player who started organized play very late and seemed destined to follow his father into the building trades after quitting high school at sixteen to help support a family of ten.

Richard excelled as a prolific scorer with the Verdun Maple Leafs, a junior club for high school–aged players, for two seasons from 1938 to 1940 before he moved up to the Montreal Senior Canadiens to start the 1940–41 season and got his chance to play for a spot on the big club. He showed serious promise, but injuries threatened to derail his professional aspirations. He suffered a severe fracture to his ankle after crashing into the boards during his first game in 1940 and lost the remainder of the season. A wrist injury cost him a good chunk of the following year as well, but he scored 17 points in thirty-one games and had a solid playoff run. He tried to join the military in 1941, but was turned down for medical reasons and had to accept a call up to the Canadiens big club instead as his consolation. He suffered another broken ankle after just sixteen games that season and tried to enlist in the military once again, but he was turned down for a second time in 1942. He spent his summers before his big break working in a machine shop, which felt like his most viable career path when he was in his early twenties.

Richard nonetheless came through adversity and made the most of his wartime opportunity, emerging as a speedy goal scorer and perpetual All-Star. Immediately recognizable by his slicked back hair, intense focus, and steely eyes, he was part of the Habs prolific Punch Line of the mid-1940s, alongside center Elmer Lach and Toe Blake on left wing. They led the club back to Stanley Cup glory after an uncharacteristically lean decade during the Depression years. He finished his career with 544 goals, including an unprecedented 50 in fifty games in 1944–45, leading the league on five separate occasions. Such was his dominance that the NHL inaugurated the Richard Trophy in 1999 to honor the league's leading goal scorer. He was quite simply the greatest player of his generation, one of the finest to ever play the game, and an icon across his home province.

Sports Illustrated profiled Richard in March 1960 just weeks before he hung up his skates after the Habs swept their way to another Stanley Cup, their eighth of his eighteen-year tenure with the club:

> Richard is regarded in Canada as no athlete is in the United States. He is not only a sports idol, he is the national idol, particularly among the French-speaking people of Montreal and the province of Quebec. When Maurice Richard scores a goal in the Forum, even an insignificant goal in a meaningless game, it touches off a unique celebration. First, an astonishing, prolonged din of cheering and applause, then newspapers, programs, galoshes, hats are thrown onto the ice. Richard skates in abstracted, embarrassed, lonely circles through the heavy snow of objects. The game has to be stopped until the attendants clear the ice. But adulation sits on him like an uneasy crown.[34]

Richard was a man of few words who occasionally had trouble with English, but he was ferocious on the ice and never backed down from a fight. By the time he hit his mid-twenties, he was among the league leaders in penalty minutes because he was far quicker to throw down his gloves than one would expect from a top-tier goal scorer. Opposing teams threw their biggest pests at him, the best player on the league's best team, and the taunting that is known in the hockey world as *chirping* always crossed a line into what would be considered racist or xenophobic by twenty-first-century standards. He could not turn away from epithets like "French bastard" and "pea souper" (with hearty, rustic split yellow pea and carrot soup being a staple of Québécois cuisine), but what really angered him were the "where are your medals?" taunts that insinuated he had shirked his duty during war.

Richard's worst antagonists were often northern Ontarians who grew up close to the border with Québec in mixed or semimixed linguistic communities where French was often heard in public spaces. Ted Lindsay of the Detroit Red Wings was the worst of the bunch, but Leo Labine of the Boston Bruins deserved honorable mention. Richard once said, "When people spit on my race, the blood rushes to my head."[35] Donnybrooks began when he slashed the offender with his stick and then followed with a blur of punches, an enduring part of Canada's game that horrifies the more delicate sensibilities of most Old World players and fans. Richard took his penalties and postgame fines while anglophone league officials turned a blind eye to the precipitating causes of all of this violence on the ice.

Richard had already become a folk hero for his scoring prowess, but his physical defiance in the face of provocations from his English-speaking Canadian rivals unwittingly transformed him into a political avatar for Québécois nationalists. Canada had always been a tenuous political project, a forced coupling between two ancient European enemies with seemingly insurmountable linguistic and sectarian schisms. By the middle of the twentieth century, resentment was growing in francophone Québec, stemming from legitimate perceptions that the Québécois had been marginalized economically and politically within their own homeland.

In the years before a broadly organized separatist movement took root, Richard became the symbol of their national aspirations, with each successive Canadiens Stanley Cup testifying to their fighting spirit. Over 98 percent of the league was made up of Canadian players during the 1954–55 season, even though two-thirds of the NHL's original clubs were U.S.-based, which meant that Canada's internal politics and prejudices traveled everywhere the game was played. Unsurprisingly, Montreal fans took every attack on Richard as a direct attack on Québec itself.

Every rivalry in the old six-team NHL was heated, but Boston-Montreal was one of the most pronounced. Both clubs were jockeying for playoff spots with just a couple of games remaining in the regular season when they took to the ice at the Boston Garden on March 13. Richard took a savage high stick to the head from his former teammate Hal Laycoe and immediately set out to settle the score as soon as the play ended. Richard had almost certainly been concussed and was bleeding profusely from a gash that later took five stitches to close when he used his stick to hit Laycoe so hard he broke it in two. Two misdirected punches landed on linesman Cliff Thompson, who was trying to break up the fight and ended up getting knocked unconscious.

It is taken as gospel among Canadian historians that the decision of an anglophone NHL commissioner, Clarence Campbell, to suspend the Habs' star francophone player for the remainder of the season, playoffs included, in March of 1955 was a direct causal factor behind the rise of the Quiet Revolution in 1960 and the subsequent growth of the separatist movement. Campbell was a decorated World War II veteran turned prosecutor for the Canadian War Crimes investigative unit who helped secure a death sentence for a particularly savage former Waffen-SS general during the postwar Nuremburg Trials, but many hockey fans felt he had a selective interest in meting out justice when he returned to the NHL. Richard had indeed hit a linesman, but the Québécois on the street thought that the penalty was too harsh and clearly racially motivated. Richard would certainly lose his chance at his first scoring title, and, more important, running his suspension through the playoffs would severely diminish the Habs' Stanley Cup hopes. In Québec, a general feeling was that the penalty was retaliation for Richard calling Campbell a "dictator" after he imposed a severe punishment on Richard's francophone teammate Bernie "Boom Boom" Geoffrion for a similar incident the previous season. Meanwhile, the rest of the league thought Campbell let Richard off lightly for a career's worth of excessively violent play, with some even calling for a lifetime ban.

Campbell responded to the Boston incident by handing Richard the longest suspension he had ever issued and took death threats from enraged Habs fans as a result. He then made the incredibly ill-advised decision to walk into the Forum for the Habs next home game on the 17th, inflaming Montreal fans to the point that they launched what became known as the Richard Riot.

It all started when the crowd threw missiles at the commissioner at the end of the first period—mostly eggs and produce—then worsened when a fan who slipped by security feigned a handshake only to slap him and throw a punch. Someone then opened a tear gas canister near Campbell, prompting officials to order the building evacuated. Thousands of angry fans spilled out onto Saint Catherine Street only to join thousands more protesters. Together, they launched an orgy of violence and vandalism—$100,000 of property damage in a fifteen-block radius of the arena—and left sixty-seven police and demonstrators injured. The following day, Richard issued a short and contrite statement accepting his suspension and urging fans to do likewise for the sake of the team and the city, while Campbell insisted that he had been asserting his right as commissioner to attend any game he pleased, and he took no responsibility. Without Richard, the Habs suffered a heartbreaking Game Seven Stanley Cup Final defeat to the Detroit Red Wings.

Their circumstances were very different, but historian Benoît Melançon argues that Richard was to the Québécois what Jackie Robinson was to Black America: an athlete who played a bigger secondary role as a symbolic leader in his people's civil rights struggle.[36] In Montreal in 1946 their paths intersected.

It was little surprise that a twenty-four-year-old Richard was just as excited as everyone else in the city to see Robinson come to town for the first Royals homestand. It is nearly impossible today to imagine the biggest superstar in his country's most popular sport, fresh off a championship, sitting outside with all of the other hometown fans of a Minor League team in another sport—imagine Kansas City Chiefs quarterback Patrick Mahomes, recipient of a $450 million contract, hanging out at an early-season home game for the independent league Kansas City Monarchs as a contemporary parallel—but there Richard was in the stands, cheering wildly just like everyone else in the park.

The Rocket was treated that afternoon to a 12–9 slugfest victory over Jersey City highlighted by a Dixie Howell grand slam and some defensive wizardry at shortstop from local favorite Stan Bréard. Robinson took an ovation during his first at bat and had a relatively quiet day with just an RBI single at the dish and three plays in the field, but the crowd left happy after a defensively clean if poorly pitched affair.[37]

The Sporting News claimed that the fans were so riveted by the action on the field that Richard simply blended in with a crowd of thousands.

Deeper into the season, Richard got an unmissable opportunity to use his high-watt star power to engineer a meeting with his favorite Royal, using the occasion to give Robinson a very enthusiastic welcome into the city's sporting pantheon. Robinson was invited to join Richard and fellow Stanley Cup champion teammates Toe Blake, Elmer Lach, and Bill Durnan—all four of whom became hockey Hall of Famers and were established Canadian megastars that summer—for a goodwill visit to recuperating veterans at Military Hospital. Durnan and Lach were anglophones, the former Toronto-born and the latter a Saskatchewan farm kid, whereas Blake grew up in bilingual northern Ontario to an English-speaking father and a French-speaking mother. Together, they could have been mistaken for a stage-managed national unity panel.

Sam Maltin reported that the Habs players enthusiastically "took Robby under their wing on the trip through the hospital wards. It didn't take long for Robinson and the hockeyists to get to be friends. A Mutual Admiration Society (Montreal Branch) was soon formed, with Robby praising hockey while the pucksters raved about baseball—and it all ended up with Robby getting an invite to join a regular foursome for golf with some of the hockey champs."

At the time of the meeting, Robinson was nursing a hamstring injury that had cost him the better part of the month, and his new friends on the Habs were eager to share their advice. The NHL season then amounted to about one third as many games as full season pro baseball, but the level of physicality was unparalleled outside of American football. These men were always playing through one sort of ailment or another. They queried Robinson about which of the city's doctors he had seen and advised him against hurrying back onto the field before he had fully recovered. All the while, they moved room to room "signing autographs on service papers, pictures, medical certificates and other personal belongings," with the hockey players proudly showing off the newest member of their entourage. "In the background, Les Canadiens, Montreal's pride and joy of the sports world, had proud grins on their faces. They were proud of their charge."[38]

Richard, hockey star and baseball fan, relished the opportunity to see his new friend play on as many occasions as he could over the course of the season. His embrace was decidedly more full-hearted and genuine than that of Robinson's nearly all American-born Royals teammates or the first group of Dodgers he played with in 1947. This was not a simple one-time handshake; when Robinson made one of his many return visits to Montreal in late November 1966 to mark the twentieth anniversary of his championship season with the Royals, Richard came out in a black suit and tie for the gala to rekindle their friendship, and they were photographed beaming next to one another in the ballroom of the Mount Royal Hotel.[39]

Richard noted fifty years later, "With all the athletes of color who perhaps represent half of all active players in baseball's two major leagues, today we have trouble believing how difficult Robinson's debut with the Dodgers was. I remember him very well. I often went to see him play. In 1946 he even joined Canadiens players in softball games. Robinson was a real inspiration for black people and Branch Rickey, General Manager of the Dodgers in the 1940s, was right in sending this famous athlete to acquire his letters of nobility with the Montreal Royals."[40]

These two old acquaintances had long been lumped together in francophone Quebec's public consciousness as opposite sides of the same coin in a manner that may well feel like a stretch to some, but there was a genuine and mutual affection between them.[41]

Richard was far more than a casual baseball fan, and he actually crossed over onto the diamond to play for the Drummondville Cubs of the Provincial League during his 1947 offseason from the Canadiens. The Provincial League was then a quality independent circuit made up mostly of Québec-born players, some of whom would work their way up to the high Minors, and Richard would have charitably been described as a long shot for playing time.[42] There is plenty of reason to suspect that Drummondville added him to the roster simply to capitalize on his novelty value at the gate, but Richard seems to have brought the same competitive spirit he showed on the ice onto the diamond. There are no accurate season statistics, but Richard socked a 350-foot game-winning home run playing left field in a road game against the Saint Hyacinthe Saints on June 30. It appears as though he came off the bench as a defensive replacement at third base as late as the first of August.[43]

The Canadiens brought the experiment to a close after Richard reportedly broke his nose chasing a foul ball into the stands off the third-base line, indicating that he played the same tenacity he brought to the ice. The Habs obviously could not risk the club's best player for a summer lark on the diamond, but one suspects they waited until after Drummondville's championship hopes had been dashed before politely asking him to come back to Montreal and focus on the upcoming hockey season.[44] In any event, his presence did not propel the Cubs to greatness—they finished sixth in an eight-team league at 35-39—but this did not stop a group of local baseball fans from presenting Richard with "a magnificent trophy . . . on varnished wood . . . topped with a silver statuette representing a hockey player."[45]

Of all of the twentieth century's fine two-sport professional athletes, Richard did not exactly cover himself in glory like Jim Thorpe, Bo Jackson, or Deion Sanders, but something just might have been there had things unfolded differently. Richard may well have viewed his sojourn in Drummondville as a short-term opportunity to keep fit during the summer months when many Canadian hockey players usually softened up, thanks to many backyard barbecues and too much beer. But maybe he was so inspired by Robinson that he deliberately wanted to follow him onto the diamond, even if at the lowest level of organized play. In the summer of 2000, the Montreal Expos marked Richard's passing by adding No. 9 patches to their jerseys, an unusual cross-sport acknowledgment for someone who played an outsized role on Québec's sporting and cultural landscape.

It was not just the members of the Canadiens who were eager to associate themselves with Robinson back in 1946; Delorimier Downs had secured a new tenant, the fledgling Montreal Alouettes of the Interprovincial Rugby Football Union (the precursor to the Canadian Football League). Its ownership decided to make a pitch to Robinson after seeing how much he had electrified Royals fans. They put a bid in that could have kept him in the city through the fall as a two-sport star.

New Alouettes head coach Lew Hayman, a New York-born standout at Syracuse University during the early Great Depression years, was the driving force behind this improbable pursuit. Hayman came north to Canada straight out of college to coach first at the University of Toronto and then at the professional level for the Toronto Argonauts, a team he guided to three Grey Cup victories in eight seasons from 1933 to 1941 before joining the Royal Canadian Air Force during World War II. The Argos broke a gentlemen's agreement to hold Hayman's job open until after he returned from the war, pushing their former wunderkind coach to seek out his revenge in Montreal, Toronto's eternal rival in all matters sporting and otherwise. He joined fellow Torontonian Eric Cradock and the American-born Léo Dandurand, an owner, coach, and general manager of the Canadiens in the 1920s and 1930s, on the original team ownership group. His role was to do double duty as head coach. Showing the Argos up meant more to Hayman than just winning more games; he wanted the Alouettes to draw more fans and showcase even bigger stars to really let them have it.

Hayman, Cradock, and Dandurand were all outsiders—mostly, Dandurand was born and raised in Illinois, but had family roots in Québec—so they chose the Alouettes name as a deliberate nod to Québécois folklore. *Alouette* is French for "lark" or "song bird." Veterans of the American Expeditionary Forces in World War I had popularized the original lyrics of the traditional and progressively more gruesome colonial-era *coureur de bois* (rugged individuals who traded with Native people deep in the interior) rowing-turned-children's song, about plucking a lark's feathers, beak, and eyes, by singing it to the tune of "Frère Jacques."[46] There was a familiar, blue collar, and highly regional appeal to the team's name, but Hayman took a slightly risky approach to roster construction when he brought in an entirely anglophone squad supplemented by a handful of American imports. In year one, the Alouettes featured no local hero like Roland Gladu, Stan Bréard, or Jean-Pierre Roy of the Royals for home fans to cheer for, prompting Hayman to make his long-shot approach to the uberpopular Robinson as a consolation prize.

The Alouettes' courtship of Robinson could perhaps be regarded as a semiserious publicity stunt that, even if unsuccessful, would still help drum up interest for the new team during the preseason. There were perfectly legitimate athletic reasons for the pursuit, though. Robinson had been a fine football player at UCLA, and he could finally test himself against competition that was on par with that of the Pacific Coast Football League, his intended destination for the 1942 season had the Pearl Harbor attack not intervened. On a more practical level, Robinson was still after all a Minor League baseball player who would have to go on the off-season baseball barnstorming circuit to provide for his growing family. It was going to be one sport or the other rather than downtime for him that fall and winter. The Alouettes hoped that an offer of fair pay would tempt Robinson into delaying his move out of Montreal until after their season concluded, no later than early November. The IRFU also played on a relatively tight travel circuit that pitted the Alouettes against rivals just a relatively short distance away in Ottawa, Toronto, and Hamilton. This theoretically offered him the opportunity of continuing to work without having to endure the barnstormers' lot of living out of a suitcase in an endless string of hotels and motels for weeks at a time.

While Robinson was in Florida for spring training, the Los Angeles Rams had signed his former Bruins teammates Woody Strode and Kenny Washington, both of whom were likely to reintegrate the NFL, after an implied twelve-year ban, when the team took the field for its first regular-season game on September 29. The Rams had just relocated from Cleveland and would have faced serious local opposition if they attempted to field a segregated roster in the publicly funded LA Coliseum, so they opted to preempt controversy that spring with the Strode-Washington signings. If Robinson had accepted the Alouettes offer, he could have beaten them onto the field by three weeks and earned the distinction of first Black player in modern professional football in the post–World War II era. Whether this meant anything to him one will never know, but the Alouettes certainly could not have been blamed for trying.

Hayman made his initial approach no later than mid-May, just two weeks after Robinson played his first home game at Delorimier Stadium, telling the press that Robinson "would prove quite a sensation, as well as a good crowd pleaser," transitioning into the offense-oriented

Canadian game from the smaller fields of the NCAA. His presence on the roster would certainly help shore up interest in professional football throughout the city. *Le Droit* predicted "he would take Canadian football by storm."[47] Local sportswriters were aware that he had once been a far better football player than baseball player, raising expectations about what he could bring to the gridiron.

Robinson never seriously entertained the Alouettes' offer in the end, but Montreal's sports reporters did not hold it against him. *Le Samedi* chalked it up to his desire to "return to the sunny skies of California" before Montreal was enveloped by the grim, gray clouds and plunging temperatures of autumn.[48] The Alouettes went on to put up strong gate numbers during their inaugural season, drawing surprisingly well with a francophone audience that was more inclined to follow sports that featured native sons. In the end, the Robinsonless Alouettes finished in a first-place tie with the Argos, with both teams putting up 7-3-2 records even though Montreal was the superior unit on both offense and defense. Their Cinderella story was not to be, unfortunately, and the Argos advanced to the Grey Cup after taking an uncharacteristically low-scoring IRFU playoff game in Delorimier Stadium in front of roughly twenty-two thousand disappointed home fans on November 16.

There was one notable silver lining in the Alouettes' failed attempt to sign Robinson that spring: Hayman pivoted to another Black player, Herb Trawick, who did integrate the IRFU and Canadian professional football that 1946 season, along with teammate John Moody. Trawick was a stocky, hard-hitting, Pittsburgh-born All-American with surprisingly good speed for a lineman at the Kentucky State College for Negroes (now Kentucky State University), who was just coming out of a stint in the U.S. Army and looking for an opportunity to play before the NFL had been reintegrated. IRFU rosters had a cap of just five American-import players, but Hayman believed in Trawick's talent and knew that Alouettes fans would embrace him. These were, after all, the same people who spent their summer cheering on Robinson in the very park where the Alouettes would play their home games.

Moody returned to the United States after the season in an attempt to make an NFL squad, but Trawick opted to stick around with Alouettes for the long haul. When asked early in the season how he liked living in Montreal, he replied, "Everybody has been great to me here. And [they've] got to be because I got a sweetie in Kentucky and we are getting married around Christmas."[49]

Trawick became an instant fan favorite in Montreal and led the team to its first Grey Cup championship in 1949, picking up a fumble and running it in for a 34-yard touchdown in a game the Alouettes won, 28–15. *Maclean's*, Canada's equivalent to *Time* or *Newsweek*, dubbed him "the Gentle Bone Crusher of the Alouettes" in a glowing November 1956 profile. He never played for any other team and spent his entire twelve-year career as an Alouette as the accolades just kept rolling in. He racked up seven All-Star selections, became team captain in 1951, had his No. 46 retired by the team, and is widely acknowledged by CFL fans as one of the greatest linemen in the history of the league. Trawick became a Canadian citizen in 1953 and settled permanently in Montreal, where he took on a community-leader role in Little Burgundy.

The Dodgers had planned on using Johnny Wright and Roy Partlow as Robinson's companions for the 1946 season, but he developed an organic and genuine friendship with Trawick during the few months when they overlapped in Montreal. In the longer arc of Canadian sports history, not only did Robinson's presence on the Royals spark the initial integration of the precursor to the Canadian Football League, but perhaps more important it also led to a much deeper integration relative to the NFL in the first fifteen years after the war.

Woody Strode, friend and UCLA teammate of Jackie Robinson, joined the Calgary Stampeders in 1948 and picked up a Grey Cup championship after the Rams cut him loose for marrying a white woman. Quarterback Johnny Bright, a Heisman Trophy candidate at Drake University, suffered a broken jaw during an October 21, 1951, road game against Oklahoma A&M when Cowboys guard Wilbanks Smith delivered a savage, racially motivated uppercut that was clearly captured in multiple frames by photographers. The following year, Bright was selected by the Philadelphia Eagles in the first round of the NFL draft, but he opted instead to join the Edmonton Eskimos (renamed the Elks in 2021), where he won three Grey Cups and was selected for the Hall of Fame at the conclusion of a twelve-year career that saw him retire as the all-time leading rusher. He too took Canadian citizenship and continued to play a major role in the community life of his adopted city postretirement.[50]

Jackie Robinson's popularity in Montreal unwittingly opened the door to Herb Trawick, who in turn opened the door for a generation of Black football stars during the CFL's early years. There were of course pockets of resistance and rearguard acts of pettiness from some opposing players as well as a handful of hoteliers and landlords, but the CFL and its fan base were collectively far more enthusiastic about integration than their NFL counterparts as late as the 1960s.

The league later came to be known stateside as a haven for Americans who were temporarily exiled for being politically controversial (John Carlos, a sprinter famous for his Black-power salute at the 1968 Summer Olympics and briefly later an Alouette who was very happy in Montreal), eccentric college players (Raghib "Rocket" Ismail, a Notre Dame receiver who chased big money with the Argos in the early 1990s), and NFL stars who were sitting out drug suspensions that look quaint in retrospect (Ricky Williams, a Miami Dolphins running back who used cannabis to treat anxiety and did not at all feel punished by having to spend the 2006 season in Toronto with the Argos). The CFL's relatively progressive streak also meant the door was open to Colin Kaepernick, the former San Francisco 49ers quarterback who was effectively blacklisted after refusing to stand for the national anthem in a racial-justice protest during the 2016 season, though he seems to have been set on returning victoriously to the NFL rather than simply continuing his playing career anywhere that would take him.

Michael Sam, a Black Texan who starred for the University of Missouri, entered the 2014 NFL draft as the reigning SEC Defensive Player of the Year, and early projections saw him going as high as the third round. There were some legitimate concerns about whether he was big enough to play on the line or fast enough to succeed in the NFL as a linebacker, but many suspected that he fell all the way to the seventh round, where the St. Louis Rams selected him with their final pick, because of widespread reservations about bringing an openly gay player into such a testosterone-fueled sport. Sam played well during the preseason, but a Rams team that had been uncompetitive for a decade still cut him loose and then left him off their practice squad. His NFL dream came to an end when the Dallas Cowboys released him in late October 2014 after about six weeks with their practice squad.

Sam then followed the footsteps of so many other Black American athletes who could not find the right opportunity at home and came north in the spring of 2015 on a two-year contract with the Alouettes, becoming the first openly gay player in the CFL. The NFL had to wait on Carl Nassib to emerge as its own pioneer in 2021, because of deeply ingrained homophobia throughout the sport. Sam's CFL career was over after a single regular-season game as he spiraled into a mental-health crisis fueled by childhood trauma, rejection by his parents after he came out, the pressure of firstness, and the collapse of his NFL aspirations, but the Alouettes organization and the people of Montreal had done what they could to welcome him warmly rather than adding to his burdens.

Many in the media wanted to cast Sam as "the gay Jackie Robinson," but it simply was not meant to be because "Michael Sam did not have his Branch Rickey" in the NFL.[51] Alouettes Vice President and Director of Player Personnel Jim Popp very much wanted to honor a gay family member by playing the Rickey role, but whereas Montreal had been a stepping-stone for Robinson, it was a disappointing consolation prize for Sam.[52] Sam ultimately ended up taking relatively low-profile coaching assignments in Europe in the post-COVID era and may well someday find his way into the NFL holding a clipboard rather than being in uniform.

As the 1946 Royals entered their dog days of summer, a fear started to creep in that undercut the sheer joy fans had been taking from watching Robinson play all season long at Delorimier Stadium. The Dodgers were locked in a tough dogfight with the Cardinals, and their twenty-one-year-old first baseman, Ed Stevens, cooled off in July after a torrid June and then went colder than a Montreal winter through August and September. The Dodgers' offense was sputtering badly in the second half, leading to the very legitimate question of whether Rickey would break Royals fans' hearts by dipping into their roster and calling up Robinson to salvage the big club's pennant hopes. This was the nightmare that success bred.

Montreal's embrace of Jackie Robinson, underdog outsider, in 1946 fit a pattern that started when American jazz musicians first came to the city during the Roaring Twenties and fell under an established tradition of opening up to talented athletes and artists who had been at least partially rejected or blocked from fulfilling their dreams back home. The Royals had a prominent role in this, but so too did the Canadiens and the Alouettes, pack leaders all when it came to fairness and equity in the sporting world. Back on the diamond, the Royals had themselves a championship to win before the story of their epic season could be finally written.

5
Glory

In the last game in Montreal, my jersey was literally torn from my back. I guess that means they like me.

—JACKIE ROBINSON, *Michigan Chronicle*, December 10, 1946

Drive west from Montreal on the Trans-Canada Highway, then veer south on Highway 401 the length of Ontario for seven or eight hours all the way down to the Detroit border crossing, and you will pass through a series of towns and cities that look and feel virtually indistinguishable from one another. Offshoot 400-series highways go in all directions, but a sameness is everywhere from Kingston to Windsor, this band where nearly all the people in Canada's most populous province reside. These cities recycle the same street names—Queen Streets and Wellington Roads—and feature the same fast-food chain restaurants and big box stores, though some do have nicer waterfront views than others. Toronto, Canada's showpiece, can at times feel like the biggest version of these orderly and predictable communities rather than a departure from the pattern.

Montreal, by contrast, is a unique force unto itself, an intensely creative space that celebrates its artists and heroes through murals, statues, and plazas unlike any other Canadian city. It is out of step, in the most complimentary way, with both the province of Québec and the rest of the country.

The municipal political class has, however, spent over two decades grappling with whether or how to commemorate the city's best-known writer, Mordecai Richler, a novelist who chronicled the city's mid-century working-class Jewish experience in classics such as *The Apprenticeship of Duddy Kravitz* (1959). Later in life, Richler turned into a polemicist who spent his last decades inflaming Québécois nationalist opinion by mocking the province's increasingly restrictive language laws. He was already deep into his forties and paunchier, his trademark long, combed back hair graying, but he still held his ever-present cigarette. At that time, he found his antagonist in the Parti Québécois, a separatist movement that was first elected to power in 1976 and ran independence referendums in 1980 and 1995, the latter failing to dissolve Canada by just 0.6 percent of the vote at the culmination of an existential national crisis that hardly made the news south of the border.

In English-speaking Canada and abroad, Richler was a wildly entertaining storyteller whose work deservedly got the Hollywood treatment, while at home many francophones accused him of peddling damaging and backward stereotypes. In his 1992 work *Oh Canada! Oh Quebec! Requiem for a Divided Country* Richler launched a satirical attack on the consequences of Québec's French-only language laws on signage—to him, tanking the economy by driving anglophones and major businesses out of the province and making life more difficult on American tourists—and leveled a more serious accusation that the *pure laine* (pure wool, meaning of 100 percent French stock) strain of Québécois nationalism was tainted by deep-rooted and persistent anti-Semitism. Some Québec anglophones expressed discomfort about how his constant needling undermined Canada's extremely fragile national unity in the 1990s, while plenty of francophone cultural figures defended the principle of allowing him to write whatever was on his mind. Some separatists called for the book to be banned outright, but Richler may have had the last laugh when Parti Québécois Premier Jacques Parizeau, glass of red wine in hand, blamed his narrow defeat in the 1995 independence referendum on "money and ethnic votes," proving to many Richler's very point.

No wonder Richler never got a street posthumously named after him in his beloved and often infuriating hometown; no reelection-seeking francophone politician could call for some sort of public tribute to him without facing serious blowback from voters. The Richler family's consolation prize was "a dilapidated gazebo in a Montreal park now frequented by Sunday afternoon stoners and barefoot hippies who flock to Mount Royal's famous drum-ins"[1] until Mayor Denis

Coderre made a more fitting tribute by renaming Mile End Library in Richler's old neighborhood in his honor in 2015. Mural treatment followed at 19 Laurier Avenue West just off his old family home on Rue Saint-Urbain.

Long before he became an internationally known writer and hornets' nest–poking political commentator, Richler was a fifteen-year-old sports fanatic who was completely riveted by Jackie Robinson during the summer of 1946. Richler's fandom began during the lean war years, and one of the first lessons he and his friends learned about baseball was that farm teams like the Royals existed to feed their parent club. Rickey was the architect of Dodgers greatness, and whatever success came elsewhere in the system was an ancillary benefit for those looking down from the top of the pyramid.

"Before we had even reached the age of puberty, Ziggy, Yossel, and I had learned to love with caution," Richler wrote looking back in 1984. "If after the first death there is no other, an arguable notion, I do remember that each time one of our heroes abandoned us for Ebbets Field, it stung us badly. We hated Mr. Rickey for his voracious appetite." Losing one of the Royals' best hurt worse when his replacement was an injured or ineffective Dodger whom Brooklyn no longer wanted.

Richler continued, "In 1944 . . . the nefarious Branch Rickey bought the Royals outright, building it into the most profitable club in all of minor league baseball, its fans loyal but understandably resentful of the head office's appetite, praying that this summer the Dodgers wouldn't falter in the stretch, reaching down for fresh bats and strong arms, just when we needed them most."[2]

Richler believed the 1948 Royals to be the best team in club history, behind a bona fide ace in Don Newcombe, and, indeed, they pitched much better than the 1946 squad. The 1948 team's offense was nowhere near as balanced, however, and it lost its anchor once Rickey called up twenty-one-year-old Duke Snider, who had been hitting .327/.403/.644 with 17 home runs through seventy-seven games in Montreal. The Royals still won an International League pennant, charged through the playoffs, then took the Junior World Series (also known as the Little World Series, its official title until 1932, the ultimate faceoff between the champions of the International League and the

American Association) from the Saint Paul Saints in a flat five-game affair. The Royals handled Brooklyn's other AAA affiliate in what was considered a lesser-caliber league fairly easily even without Snider, but the Dodgers still finished a distant third in the National League race even after bringing him up.

The experience of coming through in 1948 despite having their wings clipped sat ill with Royals fans, but they did eventually get Snider back in 1973 when he returned in the dual role of Expos play-by-play announcer and occasional uniformed hitting coach. As great as Snider was, he was nowhere near the star Robinson had been two years earlier, and he lacked the same resonance. Snider was a very fine ballplayer, but Robinson was a cultural force who happened to play baseball well. As Richler writes, "Montreal adored him, as no other ball player who has been there before or since. No sooner did Robinson reach first base, on a hit or a walk, than the fans roared with joy and hope, our hearts going out to him as he danced up and down the base path, taunting the opposing pitcher with this astonishing speed."[3]

For perfectly understandable reasons, there was no bigger fear in the stands of Delorimier Stadium in the late summer of 1946 than the one posed from above in Brooklyn. Would Rickey rob the Royals of their greatest hero ever to save the Dodgers? How could he not?

No one in baseball ever discounts the possibility of an epic collapse (à la the 1978 Boston Red Sox of Bucky "Expletive Deleted" Dent lore) or an improbable comeback (think the 1951 New York Giants team that surmounted a thirteen-game mid-August deficit in part through an alleged elaborate sign-stealing scheme), but the Royals had all but wrapped up an International League pennant as play began on August 1 when they held a 71–36 record that put them fourteen games clear of second-place Syracuse. A day earlier, Robinson had doubled in a tenth inning game-winning RBI that gave the Royals a series victory over Newark in a four-game set on the road. Royals fans were becoming quite accustomed to his heroics and had no desire to share him with Brooklyn just yet.

By this point in the season, the Royals were coasting to an inevitable postseason berth, and some could even start looking forward to returning to the Junior World Series. Montreal had only once previously advanced to the biggest showdown of the two best teams of the highest level of the Minor Leagues, losing to the Columbus Red Birds of the American Association in six games back in 1941. The Royals had earlier won the International League pennant in 1935 by five games, but they did not advance to the Junior World Series after falling to the Syracuse Chiefs in the final of the newly introduced Shaughnessy playoffs that pitted the top four regular-season finishers against one another. The International League playoffs of 1945 had been full value for money, with Montreal taking its opening series in the seventh game then falling to Newark in the finale of a championship series that went the distance. The last Canada-based team to take home a Junior World Series title was the Toronto Maple Leafs all the way back in 1926.

The 1946 Royals had very legitimate hopes of winning the most elite prize in Minor League baseball, which meant that Rickey would have done considerable damage to his relationship with the club if he exercised his right to pluck Robinson away for the Dodgers' own playoff run. Would this be enough to resist temptation?

On August 10 the Dodgers traveling secretary Hal Parrott announced in Brooklyn that the Dodgers had made a final decision that Robinson would not come up to the big club in 1946.[4] This was nowhere near enough to satisfy the conspiratorially minded north of the border. Such a statement would have carried more weight coming from Rickey himself, or Rickey Jr., the Dodgers' farm director, rather than a potentially disavowable former sportswriter turned PR man. Further, would his position hold, say, a week later if a losing skid turned the Dodgers' two-and-a-half-game lead on the Cardinals into a two-and-a-half-game deficit? As the 1946 Royals entered their dog days of summer, a fear started to creep in that undercut the sheer joy fans had taken from watching Robinson sparkle all season long at Delorimier Stadium.

Up in the National League, the Dodgers were locked in a tough dogfight with the Cardinals and could count on solid production from their outfielders (Pete Reiser, Dixie Walker, and Carl Furillo—all of whom had a similar good average, high on-base average, and little home run power profiles) and their middle infielders (always-steady shortstop Pee Wee Reese and late-blooming second baseman Eddie

Stanky, the NL walks leader in both 1945 and 1946 who was firmly entrenched in the leadoff spot), but their twenty-one-year-old first baseman, Ed Stevens, was still ice cold. The Dodgers were also weak at third and could have used an upgrade across the diamond. Cookie Lavagetto had put up some fine seasons for the Dodgers at the hot corner since coming over from Pittsburgh in 1937, but age and the rust he had accumulated after four years of military service turned him into a diminished asset by the time he returned to the field in 1946.

Leo Durocher had been tinkering some in the hope of kickstarting the Dodgers' offense. Outfielder Augie Galan was an aging on-base-average machine who had played a little first base back in May, but he was getting to the twilight of an excellent career and had turned into a singles hitter who could no longer be thought of as an everyday player. He was not the answer. If Rickey was tempted to make a mechanical swap and send Stevens down, his Royals counterpart Lester Burge had been on a tear, finishing the year with a .285/.401/.493 line, but at twenty-nine he was not the sort of energy player who might spark the rest of the lineup.

The blindingly obvious solution for the Dodgers was to call up Jackie Robinson and move him over to first base with a few spot starts at third. Why did Rickey reject a roster move that probably would have changed the course of the Dodgers' season?

There might have been some legitimacy to concerns that having Robinson do a second positional shift in 1946, late in his first full season of professional baseball, might have been asking too much. By all accounts he had done just fine and taken well to coaching when he moved from short to the keystone back in the spring. He did, after all, play every single one of his 151 games at first base the following year when he won the National League Rookie of the Year Award and earned down-ballot MVP votes. Clay Hopper also had Robinson play some third base in September to increase his versatility, and the reporting was that this new exposure was all about 1947, but doubters would always speculate that this was a sign that the Dodgers might not keep their word about letting Robinson finish out the year with the Royals.[5]

Maybe too there was an unacceptable amount of injury risk in pushing Robinson into the brightest spotlight at the tail end of a season where he missed thirty games—nearly twenty percent of the schedule—due to various lower-body ailments. By mid-to-late summer he was feeling run-down and having difficulty sleeping, as he found himself in the midst of an uncharacteristic slump. So he went to see a doctor, who advised him to step away from baseball for ten days to calm his nerves. Rachel Robinson was delighted—she had had blissful visions of afternoon picnics in the park at Mount Royal and finally getting the chance to explore the city with her husband, but Jackie abided by his doctor's orders for just one day, during which he never stopped thinking about baseball, and then returned to the field.[6] If Robinson was pressing badly at a juncture when his Minor League team was coasting to a pennant, how then would he fare as a newcomer in a high-pressure pennant race in baseball's biggest market?

Rickey ultimately concluded that he had made too big of an investment in Robinson, as both a player and a broader change agent in American culture, to rush the Great Experiment, which had been planned and executed methodically up to this point. If Robinson were white, it is nearly unimaginable to think that he would not have gone up to Brooklyn mid-season. Reality being what it was, Royals fans could breathe easy, and Dodgers fans would have to wait for next year after finishing just two games back of the eventual World Series champion Cardinals.

When the International League season came to a close, Robinson finished with numbers that screamed, "Major League ready." He won the batting title with a .349 average, five points clear of the two next best hitters. His .468 on-base average led the league by a huge margin. He tied for the league lead in runs at 113 with an Oriole, Soup Campbell, who played in twenty-five more games. He stole 40 bases, second on his team to league leader Rabbit Rackley, but 10 more than the next-leading thief in the league. He was one of the most difficult hitters in the league to strike out—only 27 times in 553 plate appearances. He led his team and was fifth in the league in OPS, thanks to a home park that, even more so than Ebbets Field, suppressed righty power. The league MVP award went to a plodding first baseman on the third place Baltimore Orioles, Eddie Robinson (.318.405/.578 with 34 home runs and 123 RBI), who later bounced around some despite good success in the Majors. He was the safe pick for traditional voters who did not quite feel like sending a message to America about social change.

Sportswriter Sam Maltin drank all this in and took to his typewriter for a stinging riposte to Bob Feller, the Cleveland ace and Robinson doubter who had predicted failure for the Royals star before the season started. Maltin wrote for the *Montreal Herald* and *Star* as well as the *Pittsburgh Courier*, a Black paper that suddenly found itself in need of a Montreal-based sportswriter after Jackie Robinson signed with the Royals in 1945. Over the course of the season, Maltin took pleasure in telling his American readers that Royals fans yelled open threats of physical violence against opposing pitchers who dared throw at their favorite player. He wanted them to know a good number of Montrealers would not tolerate racism.[7]

Maltin was firmly rooted in Montreal's progressive Jewish community, which shared strong links with its counterpart in Brooklyn. In the years ahead, a sense of shared otherness and outsider status had pushed many New York Jews to rally hard around Robinson and all the other Black Dodgers stars who followed him into the big leagues.[8]

Before 1947 they had Hank Greenberg of the Tigers, and then briefly a Pirate for his final season, as their icon. Greenberg had directly expressed feelings of solidarity to Robinson from the moment they first met on the field, passing the torch from one hero of the Jewish sports fan community to the next. "Jackie had it tough, tougher than any ballplayer who ever lived. I happened to be a Jew, one of the few in baseball, but I was white," he wrote in his autobiography. "I identified with Jackie Robinson. I had feelings for him because they had treated me the same way. Not as bad, but they made remarks about my being a sheenie and a Jew all the time."[9]

Maltin did not have to wait until 1947 like his coreligionists in Brooklyn—he had access to Robinson a year earlier and became one of his biggest supporters in all of Montreal in 1946.

Maltin may have crossed an ethical line for journalists by becoming such a close personal friend of a player on whom he reported, but Sam and Jackie and their wives Belle and Rachel got on so fabulously that they all became regular dinner companions over the course of the 1946 season. The two wives were shopping partners out in all of the downtown department stores that were springing back to life a year after the war ended.

Much of the yearslong correspondence between the Maltins and the Robinsons can now be found at the Jewish Public Library in Montreal. Going through these personal letters shows that they had the sort of genuine couples friendship in which one party would write the other asking to borrow a photo negative to make a copy of a particular shot of the children playing together, so as to frame and mount on the wall. Jackie Robinson was particularly grateful for a handknit sweater Belle Maltin had mailed to him. This is largely why Maltin could not resist the temptation to publicly call out Bob Feller on something he had said almost a year earlier.

Feller the athlete was remarkable on so many levels—he not only debuted, but excelled as a seventeen-year-old strikeout machine with Cleveland in 1936, while a decade later he threw an AL-leading 371.1 innings, 36 complete games, and 10 shutouts but was not even the top vote-getting pitcher in the MVP race. (The Cy Young Award was introduced as a separate prize in 1956.) When exhausting seasons like this were over, he would immediately head out on the barnstorming circuit and throw even more over the fall and winter to earn extra cash for his family.

Feller the patriot responded to the Pearl Harbor attack by enlisting in the navy, the first high-profile American athlete to sign up for military service, then he insisted on a combat assignment. He served as a gun captain on the USS *Alabama*, an escort battleship that helped decisively turn the tide of the Pacific War during the American victory in the Battle of the Philippine Sea in June 1944. He stuck with the navy as an instructor at the Great Lakes Naval Training Station even after his tour ended in January 1945 and he was free to return to the big leagues. He waited until a week after V-J Day to return to civilian life. When asked years later whether he regretted missing out on the near certainty of winning 300 career games (he finished with 266) after giving over three-plus seasons in his prime to the military, his answer was always a firm and automatic no.

For all of Feller's martial bravery and athletic talent, years' worth of awkward takes on Robinson and then later his own teammate Larry

Doby revealed his enduring discomfort around Black athletes, at least through the middle years of his playing days. Perhaps growing up in Van Meter, Iowa, a lily-white heartland community of about four hundred people, did not prepare him well for interacting with other kinds of his fellow citizens.

More likely it was just him. During this author's Little League days in the early 1990s, he was very excited about the opportunity to hear a mid-seventies Feller regale a sportsmen's dinner audience with tales of Golden Era baseball glory as a guest speaker in Sarnia, Ontario, but instead Feller subjected a bewildered Canadian audience to an atonal political rant that weirdly previewed the Fox News era. All of the preteen attendees there found the 300-pound linemen from the Detroit Lions and various mullet-sporting, teeth-missing hockey players much more approachable than Feller during the mingling and autograph-seeking portion of the festivities.

Maltin certainly enjoyed his triumphalist revenge in his open letter to Feller, talking up Robinson's broad skill set and reeling off statistics about Robinson's fresh batting title and how his .349 average set a new Royals record. "As a pitcher, you must realize that your fellow hurlers must have tried various offerings on the gifted Robinson—including inside pitches," he wrote. "Seldom has Jackie failed to connect in some way. . . . He has them all."

Maltin then got a little personal, accusing Feller of hypocrisy. "You know of [Robinson's] attraction at the gate. He's the Ted Williams and Bobby Feller (you see, we recognize talent) of the International League. You know, because you asked him to join your barnstorming troupe of baseballers. He declined because he will be touring with his own stars, including two Royals, Al Campanis and Marvin Rackley."

Then Maltin reached the crescendo. "This may sound like showing off. Well, Jackie is not the type. And we in Montreal are very proud of him. The fans and sportswriters, even those who thought he wouldn't make good, are sure he'll make the grade in the majors. And if he doesn't a record crowd would be on hand at the ball park to welcome him back here."[10] Robinson never needed anyone to fight his battles for him, but it is hard to imagine he did not smile when he read this clipping from his friend.

Former Royals general manager turned International League president Frank Shaughnessy had been thoroughly Canadianized over the years and brought an NHL-style playoff format to Minor League baseball. By the 1940s the NHL was down to six teams, not enough to justify splitting into separate divisions. The bottom two finishers in the regular-season standings went home, then the first-place club faced the third and the second the fourth in two best-of-seven series that would determine who met up in the finals. The advantage of this new approach was that fans of trailing teams kept coming out for late-season games even if their club had little or no hope of overcoming its first-place rival. The regular season still mattered, but now seeding came into the equation as a new high-octane postseason competition began.

Shaughnessy had been working as an executive in both professional hockey and baseball, which led him to conclude that what had been pioneered in one sport would work just as well in the other. Baseball's Minor Leagues had previously handed their championships to the pennant winner, an inherently fair approach that valued the long haul over the unpredictable results of a short series, but the unintended consequence was that attendance cratered whenever a league had a runaway leader late in the season. This got International League owners willing to consider a new format that came to be known as the Shaughnessy System when it was first implemented in the eight-team International League in 1933, albeit with different ranked matchups than that of the NHL, which IL owners adjusted over the years.

Traditionalists howled at the calamity it brought that year when the lowly fourth-place, 82–85 Buffalo Bisons won the championship rather than the first-place, 102–62 Newark Bears. Unpredictability was the very point of the new system, and it did exactly as Shaughnessy argued, driving strong gate revenue for most teams despite the economic hardships of the Great Depression. Over the course of the 1930s, the Shaughnessy System was copied across other baseball Minor Leagues and eventually became the norm in most major team sports in North America.

By virtue of their 100–54 record and commanding eighteen-and-a-half-game lead over second-place Syracuse, the Royals first-round opponent in 1946 was a plucky fourth-place Newark Bears squad that was not to be underestimated in a seven-game series. The Bears, the top Yankees affiliate, were the defending champs, after all. Over their 154 games, the Bears' offense scored almost 300 runs fewer than the Royals, but it was powered by two A+ grade twenty-one-year-old prospects, Yogi Berra and Bobby Brown, who could turn the course of a game on their own. These odd-couple roommates—Berra was well known for his love of comic books, whereas Brown preferred medical textbooks—would both contribute to the Yankees' success when they won the World Series the following year.

Well before he became nationally known as a repeat October hero and one of the most likable players in the history of the game, Berra had held his own as an eighteen-year-old with the Class-B Norfolk Tars of the Piedmont League in 1943 before joining the navy, where he spent three years and fought as a machine gunner on a transport ship at Omaha Beach on D-Day. By 1946 he was back in professional baseball and quickly established himself as the International League's finest catcher. Over his seventy-seven games in Newark that year, he hit to a .314/.360/.534 line with 15 home runs over 297 plate appearances.

Brainy shortstop Bobby Brown out of Tulane seemed to be headed toward a career as a doctor before the Yankees signed him in early 1946 and gave him a challenging first professional assignment with their top affiliate. He finished just behind Jackie Robinson in the batting race with a .341 average and was a walk machine with a .431 on-base average. He and Berra both got cups of coffee in 1946 then came up for good in 1947. Brown told his future wife that when he was to meet her parents for the first time she should tell her mother he was studying to be a cardiologist and her father that he was the Yankees third baseman. Both statements were indeed true, but the message was tailored to its audience. Berra picked up a remarkable ten World Series rings and Brown a none-too-shabby four. Brown did later practice as a cardiologist down in Texas, but baseball lured him back, and he took on roles as interim Texas Rangers president in 1974 then later American League president from 1984 to 1994.

There were plenty of other competent hitters up and down the Bears lineup. Allie Clark later had a seven-year run as a utility man for four different big league teams; in 1946 he tied for second in the International League batting race with a .344 average, playing mostly at third base. Outfielder Ford Garrison and first baseman Buddy Hassett were by this time graybeards on the wrong side of thirty, but both were big league veterans who hit for decent average and took plenty of walks. Milt Byrnes, a twenty-nine-year-old outfielder, had hit well (.295/.396/.393) for the AL pennant-winning St. Louis Browns of 1944 and was hoping to claw his way back up to the bigs. London, Ontario–born outfielder Frank Colman, twenty-eight, was in the same boat after having spent the war years with the Pittsburgh Pirates, and he had just put up his best Minor League season yet, slashing .305/.400/.571 and tying Berra for the team home run lead with 15 in just 84 games. Later-blooming twenty-three-year-old first baseman and outfielder Joe Collins finally made his way up to the Yankees in 1948 and spent a good decade as a fairly productive big league platoon player.

None of the other regulars or semiregulars shone much, and the Bears lacked home run power and base-stealing speed, but their lineup offered an interesting mix of explosive young talent and veteran experience that could easily scratch out enough runs to win games. There were not many easy outs before the pitcher's spot.

On the bump, the Bears had a solid one-two punch with twenty-eight-year-old Herb Karpel (14–8 with a 2.41 ERA in 187 innings), a promising Yankees prospect before he joined the military, and twenty-three-year-old first-year professional Duane Pillette (11–10 with 3.66 ERA in 194 innings). If the Royals had a slight edge with Steve Nagy and Cy Buker, it was not by much. The rest of the Bears' staff was fairly pedestrian, but a few of their arms did later graduate to the big leagues. The paper matchup overall heavily favored the Royals' more balanced roster, but the Bears were not to be taken lightly.

There is a reason they play the games, the adage goes. The Royals took the first two games at home, 7–5 and 2–1, respectively, on the 11th and 12th of September, but neither were particularly convincing wins. A hair over fifteen thousand fans came out for the Thursday-night opener at Delorimier Stadium, where they "shivered in the Stadium, first from the nippy weather and then from the Royals jittery finish."[11] The home team lit up Karpel, who was chased from game in the fifth, while staff ace Steve Nagy had been dealing. A southpaw was exactly what the doctor ordered to shut down a Bears lineup where all the best hitters were lefties. The visitors had managed some vaguely threatening traffic at various times, but Nagy was helped out by three timely double plays, and the Royals went into the ninth up 7–0 before the wheels nearly fell off.

Hopper waited until after Nagy lost his command before going to the bullpen, leaving his fading ace out on the mound despite a walk, a hit batter, a Berra double, another walk, and then a single. The Royals lead shrunk to 7–3 with two men on base. The call to the bullpen went to Chet Kehn, a swingman who had the manager's trust despite being walk prone and not particularly effective over the regular season. Kehn immediately walked Garrison, loading the bases, then outfielder Earl Naylor dropped an easy fly ball, leading to another run while the bases were still full for the dangerous Bobby Brown. Kehn finally settled down and preserved the 7–5 win with a knee-buckling 3-2 curveball to Allie Clark, the Bears' best hitter, for the third out. This was how a laugher turned into a nail-biter. Robinson, meanwhile, had 3 hits, 3 RBI, and 1 run.

The temperature plunged to pitcher-friendly the following day—a high of 57°F falling to just 38°F at night—and a thinner crowd of 12,570 Royals faithful got a different sort of squeaker. Glenn Moulder, the Royals' third-best starter over the course of the year, faced off against Pillette, and both were on their weather-assisted A games. Robinson walked in the first and advanced on a fielder's choice, but he was thrown out at the plate when he tried to score on a Les Burge single that cashed in the lead runner, Rabbit Rackley. It was an otherwise uneventful day for Robinson. The Bears equalized in the second when Berra doubled and was singled in, then the pitchers took the reins. The score was still knotted at one when the Royals came up in the bottom of ninth, but Pillette was running out of gas and loaded the bases.

The prelude to the Royals' walk-off went Burge double, walk, walk, call to the bullpen, and force out at the plate on a ground out. Batting from the left side with the bases drunk, switch-hitting shortstop Al Campanis came up with one out and dropped a picture-perfect squeeze bunt down the first base line on veteran reliever Alex Mustaikis, who threw home but not in time to stop Red Durrett from scoring the game-winning run.[12]

With the Royals comfortably up 2-0 in the series, Montreal's Sunday papers started looking ahead not only to the Royals' potential opponent in the Governors' Cup, the final of the International League Playoffs, but also to their most likely Junior World Series matchup.[13] As if on cue, the Royals high-octane offense went completely flat on the road when the series moved to Newark on the 14th following an off day. The inevitability of glory came into question as the baseball gods struck the Royals down 4–0 in Game Three, then 3–2 in Game Four to knot the series up at two games apiece with one more to play in Newark before play returned to Montreal.

Game Five was a closely fought affair, and Robinson played a pivotal role in the Royals' 2–1 victory. This one was another pitchers' duel between Game Two starter Glenn Moulder, filling in after Nagy begged out with a sore arm, and Vic Raschi, one of the Yankees' best pitching prospects and a rotation mainstay from 1947 through 1953 who was called up from the Single A Binghamton Triplets very near the end of the season to help the Bears out in the playoffs. Raschi was big league ready and had immediate success with the Yankees when he went up for good the following season. Raschi basically shut down the Royals' lineup, surrendering his first run of the game in the second inning only after a hit by pitch and a stolen base in which a Berra throwing error allowed Red Durrett to advance to third before Campanis singled him in. It was Robinson who ripped a line drive single in the fifth to knock in the go-ahead and eventual game-winning run.

Moulder was even better, though, allowing just a single run that came in during the first inning when, per Dink Carroll's vivid recap, "smoke from burning rubbish in a dump behind centre field blew over the diamond. It was so thick that you couldn't see the outfielders from the press box." Outfielder Earl Naylor lost a fly ball in the smoke that went for a triple, prompting the umpires to call a game delay until the air cleared.[14]

The players should have felt some relief up 3-2 as they headed out Montreal-bound, but Hopper was riddled with a summer cold so bad he had veteran reliever Curt Davis manage the game in his place while he tried to recover in his hotel. Part of the illness must have been driven by stress. Carroll told *Gazette* readers, “Hopper is worried by the team’s feeble showing at the plate. The fielding has been adequate, as good or better than it was over the regular schedule. But the hitters stopped hitting a couple of weeks before the playoffs started, a fact which did not escape Skipper Hopper’s observation. ‘If we hit we’ll win,’ he said at least a week ago.”[15]

Regaining home-field advantage was huge for the Royals, who had a full house of 19,322 howling fans come out to watch them attempt to put away the Bears with a game to spare. Hopper’s rotation was in flux, though, and he was forced to go to newcomer Frank Laga for the start. Laga had breezed through AA with Mobile (7-2 with a 2.07 ERA in 74 innings), but he, like Raschi, had been plucked off a noncompetitive lower-tier club at the last minute as playoff depth. Hopper was not entirely rewarded for his act of faith, as Laga kept the Bears hitless and off the scoreboard through four, then quickly unraveled in the fifth when a string of singles, a double, and a Robinson error put the Bears on the scoreboard. Laga finally got the hook after surrendering 4 runs, 3 earned, in just 4.2 innings before Kehn was called in to relieve him. Robinson helped the Royals chip away, scoring one of the team’s two runs in the bottom of the fifth and doubling in their third in the seventh. Tensions were high as the Royals still found themselves down 4–3 heading into the “thriller-diller” bottom of the ninth that “played like a symphony of thrills up and down the spines of . . . customers who would have been glad to pay twice as much for the kind of action provided.”[16]

The Royals were down to their final out and Herb Karpel, in for relief of starter Duane Pillette in an all-hands-on-deck approach from Newark, was on the cusp of locking down the win when Les Burge took him to a 2-2 count. The Bears bench erupted in fury at home plate umpire Artie Gore when he called the next pitch a ball, leading to the seeming baseball inevitability of a home run immediately following a critical blown call. Burge’s heroics allowed the Royals to draw even and a spit-flecked Karpel then engineered his own removal by charging at Gore and attempting to fight him. By the time the dust settled and ejections had been processed, the Bears lost Karpel, fellow pitcher John Moore, infielder Jack Phillips, and manager George Selkirk.

Alex Mustaikis, one of the best primary relievers in the International League that year, came in hoping to preserve the tie. Two batters later, it became clear that the umpires had turned on the Bears after their collective display of unsportsmanlike behavior earlier in the inning. Fleet-footed Tom Tatum singled into left, and up came Herman Franks, a left-handed-hitting catcher who had been dining on Delorimier's short right-field wall all season long. He proceeded to smash a line drive into the fence in right, and Hopper, doubling as third base coach and feeling lucky, went full windmill on Tatum, who was bearing down on him from first knowing well that Frank Colman, the Bears' right fielder, had a cannon for an arm and had already thrown out a baserunner at home in the seventh inning. The throw home was on target, and the play at the plate was very close, but most with a good eye on it thought Berra had tagged Tatum before he touched home. Whether motivated by revenge or genuinely having blown it, Gore ruled that Berra missed the tag and Tatum was safe with the game-winning run.

Ever-colorful sportswriter Dink Carroll described the ensuing action as a riot in which "umpire Artie Gore nearly lost his life," a vivid but hyperbolic description of the game's denouement. This time an irate Berra seemed to be on the verge of throwing a punch at Gore as all the players and a healthy contingent of Royals fans poured onto the diamond to help beat back the Bears if needed, but police wisely intervened to get Gore off the field safely, and the combatants slowly dissipated.[17]

If there was a silver lining to the Bears early playoff exit, it was that Berra and Brown both got to play out the final week of the season up with the Yankees. Years later, Berra recalled, "We lost the series, and I lost my head against the plate umpire, Artie Gore, on a close play at the plate. I got fined because all hell broke loose after the play, and if I had actually hit him, I might've gotten thrown out of baseball. I was lucky, and fortunate, too, since the Yankees actually paid my $500 fine. I also learned a big lesson. If you're a catcher, you better get along with umpires."[18] His fine was actually reported as $100 (about $1,600 in 2024 money), but Berra's restraint in the heat of the moment was baseball's gain for the next fifteen years of his remarkable career.[19]

This deciding game might not have been clean, but it certainly was electrifying for all but the road fans who traveled north only to see their team eliminated. Robinson had factored into the victory, doubling and scoring two of the Royals' five runs, but one of the bigger lessons he drew was the extent to which Royals fans were willing to insert themselves as an active part of the team's championship run. He had never before seen passion like this from the stands, and it was certainly going to come in handy in the weeks ahead. The two teams that matched up in the other semifinal, the Syracuse Chiefs and Baltimore Orioles, had earned notoriety for having the International League's most racist fans and players who resorted to dirty tricks in an attempt to injure Robinson and knock him off the field before he could beat them.

There was no rest at all for the Royals, who proceeded immediately from this high adrenaline clincher to the first game of the Governors' Cup final at home the following evening. Their bats went completely silent in the opener, which they dropped, 5–0, to Syracuse Chiefs, the very distant runner-up in the International League pennant race. Royals fans rained boos down on reliever Jean-Pierre Roy, the hometown hero and 25-game winner for the pennant-winning squad of a year earlier, when he came in to relieve Cy Buker in the ninth and promptly surrendered 3 runs to put a comeback out of reach. What a difference a year makes. Dink Carroll suggested management might have "put the whammy on them" by presenting each Royals player with a gold watch before the game to commemorate their pennant-winning season.[20]

The Chiefs' lineup was dominated by players who would be considered old even by 1946 standards when veterans flooded back into professional baseball after years in the military. Their best hitter was twenty-nine-year-old Hank Sauer, a power-hitting outfielder who finished the 1945 season with the Cincinnati Reds after mustering out of the Coast Guard. He actually hit better than any of their primary outfielders that year but blew out his tendons in a bad slide at third base and permanently lost footspeed for the rest of his career.

The Reds' brass thought Sauer could add power if he switched to a heavier bat, and he proved them right by hitting 21 home runs for Syracuse. He was then left to overbake at AAA the following year when he hit a ridiculous .336/.428/.668 with 50 home runs in one of the most impressive seasons ever for an International League hitter. The Reds were very bad and had two unproductive corner outfielders and a thirty-five-year-old in center, but they still talked themselves into believing that Sauer's diminished baserunning ability was a liability and did not call him up at any point in 1947. He finally came up for good at age thirty-one in 1948 and reeled off six 30 home run seasons over the next seven years, winning an MVP award with the Cubs in 1952. He remained a productive pinch hitter and bench player during a journeyman stage that lasted into his early forties. The gaudy power numbers he put up past thirty lead one to wonder if he might have earned a spot in the Hall of Fame had the Reds not so thoroughly botched his development when he was in his twenties.

Fellow outfielder Dutch Mele was stuck in his fifth-straight season in Syracuse—where he spent eight and change in total—and at thirty-one was never going to get another chance to go up to the Reds despite regularly putting up .400 on-base averages and showing some home run power. Catcher Dick West had been a backup in Cincinnati during the early war years but was not able to reclaim his job when he came home from the military and became another competent Syracuse lifer. Utility infielder Kermit Wahl had the advantage of youth and would later collect parts of five big league seasons with Cincinnati and the Philadelphia Athletics, but he had little power and was not much of an offensive threat. Infielder Chuck Kress had a similar profile and the same future in front of him. In sum, the Chiefs offered a workmanlike if not particularly threatening offense. If the Royals could hold Sauer at bay, they would likely have little trouble outscoring the Chiefs.

Syracuse did have a promising stable of young starting pitchers, with three workhorses—Earl Harrist, Jim Prendergast, and Dixie Howell—who all posted sub-4.00 ERAS in 190 innings or more. This front three was complemented by a very competent swing man, Mike Shultz, and a bunch of effective southpaws to throw at the Royals' left-handed power hitters. The Royals' offense had been sputtering by its own lofty regular-season standards, scoring just 18 runs in the six-game series with the Bears, and the Chiefs staff had the potential to cause headaches.

Coming off the Game One letdown, Game Two opened with an unmitigated disaster, as the Chiefs lit up Glenn Moulder, who had been excellent in the Bears series, tagging him with 10 runs over four innings. The Royals were down by a disheartening score of 10–2, but they started chipping away immediately with a 6-run fourth, highlighted by a Lew Riggs grand slam. Then they blew the doors off with a 5-run eighth to take a 14–10 lead, before surrendering 2 in the top of the ninth just to keep everyone in the park on edge. Along the way, there was a hard and possibly dirty slide from Campanis and a rhubarb that forced police intervention to keep Mele from landing a punch on Hopper in a three-and-a-half-hour game "that had everything . . . but a bingo game."[21]

This 14-run outburst reactivated the fearsome Royals offense, and the team got back to what it did best, trouncing the Chiefs in their home park 11–1, 7–4, and 7–1 to take the series in a tidy if anticlimactic five games. The Royals were Junior World Series–bound.

Their opponent was a Louisville Colonels team that offered a very different profile than any they had seen in the International League that year—a formidable pitching staff coupled with a run-and-gun offense. For the first time in nine years, the best teams from both leagues by record and by the eye test had advanced to the Junior World Series in what promised to be an excellent matchup. The Colonels were making their third-consecutive appearance and deserved plenty of respect as the reigning champions. Adding to the fun, there had been no real advance scouting as we understand it today, and both teams would be facing each other sight unseen with very limited information on one another. The Royals were furnished with some reports from Saint Paul Saints manager Ray Blades, who admitted over the phone to Hopper, "I haven't done too well against them" following his team's feeble American Association semifinal exit at Louisville's hands.[22]

Kentucky's great metropolis looks out at Indiana from the south bank of the Ohio River, which until 1865 was the border between the free Midwest and unfree Dixie. Tens of thousands of visitors have been flooding into Churchill Downs in sports jackets or flowery hats every May since 1875 for the Kentucky Derby, said to be the most exciting two minutes in all of sport, and horse racing enthusiasts have another excellent, must-visit race course, Keeneland, just seventy miles east outside of Lexington. One sport dominates them all in the Bluegrass State, however: men's college basketball. Good Louisvillians are supposed to follow the University of Louisville Cardinals, but Kentucky as a whole tilts in favor of the University of Kentucky Wildcats, winners of eight NCAA tournament championships to the Cards' still-impressive three. In addition to rarely ever losing at home, the Cats regularly draw better than all but the top-three NBA teams.

Meanwhile, bat maker Louisville Slugger is baseball's most iconic brand, and fans in Northern Kentucky today can follow two fine college baseball programs, again UK and UofL, in addition to the AAA Louisville Bats, a Cincinnati Reds affiliate that plays in one of the nicest parks in the International League, Louisville Slugger Field, which is replete with the appropriately named in-stadium Against the Grain Brewery. These days, America's pastime does, however, feel much more niche and tucked away than it should be in Kentucky's sporting landscape. It remains a very distant third or maybe fourth to hoops and horses, then possibly football.

In the late nineteenth century, Louisville was an important railway juncture, a bourbon-manufacturing powerhouse, and most definitely a baseball town. It was twice home to Major League teams—first the Louisville Grays, a charter member of the National League that folded after most of its players were found to have thrown games for money in a massive gambling scandal in 1877, then the American Association's Louisville Eclipse from 1882 to 1884, rebranded the Louisville Colonels from 1885 to 1899. The Colonels were new members of the National League from 1892—and were twice lost under tragic circumstances. Cincinnati was a similar type of city and just a two hours' drive away, but luck was on its side rather than Louisville's. The Reds are now approaching their 150th season, whereas Louisville has been relegated to Minor League status or been left without any professional team at all for brief windows since the turn of the twentieth century.

The American Association sent teams to face the National League champs in a proto–World Series in the 1880s, but baseball was in flux during this period, and the balance of money and power favored the Senior Circuit. Association teams were usually located in river cities, which was late nineteenth-century code for towns where prostitution, drunkenness, gambling, and other forms of vice ran rampant. Many of the teams were owned by breweries and distilleries that offered cheaper tickets than National League clubs, knowing they would make their money back in alcohol sales. There was no prohibition on Sunday baseball either; why leave that easy money on the table? Overly lubricated crowds in American Association cities like Louisville were far more boisterous than those of the more civilized (and dry) National League.

It all started to come apart in the late 1880s, as the National League began poaching clubs from the American Association, which came under new pressure from the upstart new Players' League in 1890. The 1889 Colonels were one of the most awful teams in Major League history (27-111-2) and cycled through a revolving door of harried managers with first-class baseball names from Dude Esterbrook to Chicken Wolf, all of whom were completely unable to contain the drunken carousing of their players. At the end of the year, the Colonels cut ties with their star player, native son Pete Browning, also known as "The Louisville Slugger," who treated a near-crippling case of mastoiditis with copious amounts of sweet Kentucky bourbon and was one of the most misunderstood players of the nineteenth century. He went on to have the best season of his career with the Cleveland Infants of the Players' League, but all of the other hitters on the Colonels roster picked up the slack, and their young pitchers dominated the competition. The Colonels won the association pennant in a Cinderella season that took them all the way to the World Series, which they tied 3-3-1 with the Brooklyn Bridegrooms, the forerunner of the Brooklyn Dodgers.

The home fans were sorry to see ol' Pietro go, but they were delighted with the progress the team made in 1890. This was undoubtedly the absolute pinnacle of professional baseball in Louisville. One might call the Colonels co–World Series champions, but technically there was no winner that year. There was very much a play-it-by-ear approach to the postseason during this era, and both the Louisville and Brooklyn managers had agreed that Game Seven would be the final one for 1890 due to inclement weather. The clubs planned to meet up the following spring for a winner-take-all game, but in typically hard luck Louisville style it was never actually played because the two leagues could not agree that winter on an equitable distribution of players from the rival Players' League, which had drawn considerable star talent and was considered Major League quality but folded after just one season. Their cooperation agreement fell apart, and there was no more AA-NL World Series in the offing heading into 1891. This dispute also meant that there could be no delayed Game Eight to decide the 1890 playoffs, and no fairytale moment of mass pandemonium at 28th and Elliot in West Louisville as the Colonels finally hoisted their trophy.

The baseball gods turned fickle, and the Colonels returned to their losing ways in 1891. Then the AA collapsed entirely. The Colonels were fortunate to join the National League in 1892, but they did not fare well in their audition to become a permanent member of what was then the only Major League. The club worked its way up from atrocious to just barely below .500 by the end of the decade, but the Colonels were one of the worst-attended teams on a regular basis, despite having lucked their way into bringing a young infielder and outfielder named Honus Wagner onto the roster. The Colonels' owner, a thirty-five-year-old German immigrant named Barney Dreyfuss, saw the writing on the wall and seized an opportunity to buy a half share in the Pittsburgh Pirates, a middle-of-the-pack team with a much more loyal fan base. Having full ownership in the Colonels and half stake in the Pirates simultaneously, he then proceeded to trade all of Louisville's best players—including future Hall of Famers Honus Wagner, at shortstop; Fred Clarke, in the outfield; and Rube Waddell, from the starting rotation, along with extremely solid players Tommy Leach, at third, and starter Deacon Phillipe—to his new team.

This move to basically consolidate the best players from two rosters turbocharged the Pirates to the top of the National League and turned them into one of the best teams in baseball all the way into the World War I era. The Colonels had been raided, discarded, and then contracted when the National League dropped four of its twelve teams heading into the 1900 season. When the American League was founded in 1901, it included new or resurrected teams in three cities that hosted and then lost National League teams in the 1890s: Baltimore, Cleveland, and Washington. But Louisville alone was not invited to join the fledgling circuit. Louisville's Major League dreams died then and there. The Colonels, meanwhile, chugged along mostly at the highest level of the Minor Leagues, with only occasional interruptions, up until 1972.

All peoples and places thrive on myths, and mid-century Kentucky was no different, though its two primary ones were as audacious as they were comforting to the state's white population. There was the original myth about "the dark and bloody ground," the idea that in the eighteenth century, savage Indians had existed in a state of constant and ferocious warfare to the point that none could establish any permanent settlements in what became Kentucky before the white man and his enslaved peoples arrived to civilize this wondrous and fertile blank slate. No one needed pushing out because everything just fell into their laps. This was guilt-free American expansion.

The second was that although Kentuckians indeed practiced slavery, it was a much more benign form of it than in cruel places like Mississippi or Alabama. They believed that their ancestors were paternalistic enslavers who cared for the enslaved as one would a dear family pet. And yet the origin of the phrase "sell someone up the river" came from the practice of sending an enslaved person from the massive human chattel market in Louisville to the Deep South by boat along the Ohio and Mississippi Rivers.[23] After Congress banned the international slave trade in 1808, Kentucky stepped forward as a breeding ground that produced humans for the domestic market. Conditions further south were universally understood to be so violent and oppressive that they amounted to a virtual death sentence. Kentucky nice in the nineteenth century meant holding out the threat of dispatching any enslaved person who staged a work slowdown or was otherwise noncompliant up the river to a miserable new home in the Deep South.

Beneath all the outward mid-twentieth-century charm of the mint juleps, bow ties, and rolling horse farms out in its hinterland, Louisville was a hard place to live for its Black residents. Proximity to the North did not at all mean Jim Crow was any more relaxed there than in the old Confederacy. This was a place where 1946 might as well have been 1926 or 1906 so far as the social order was concerned. Rigidly enforced segregation in education, businesses, and virtually every public space had sharpened the city's most famous son, Cassius Clay until he took the name Muhammad Ali on his conversion to Islam in 1964, into a razor during his childhood in the 1940s and '50s. Once his talents in the boxing ring became apparent, in came the white predators from the city's business community who wanted to exploit him via sponsorship deals that tilted heavily in their favor. It took him years to shake off those who felt they had the right to control him as if little had changed since the days of the overseers.

But Louisville was roughly 20 percent Black in the World War II era, a population that was almost entirely concentrated in the city's West End. This Black Louisville on West Walnut Street from 6th to 13th Streets of Ali's youth had blocks and blocks with 150 successful businesses of every sort—restaurants, banks, theaters, and more—that took all the market share of a demographic white ones did not want.[24] A tough-minded, hard-working entrepreneur could get ahead in this environment, and plenty of aspirational middle-class Black Louisvillians in 1946 had walking-around money to spend on various forms of entertainment, including baseball.

Louisville was in a good geographical position to field a team in the Negro American League, which coming out the war had a team in nearby Cincinnati (a time-share club that played some in equally convenient Indianapolis), along with others in not overly remote locales, including Cleveland, Memphis, and Chicago, but professional Black baseball had a spotty track record in Kentucky. Heading into 1946 there had been many ephemeral clubs in Louisville—first the Unions, then the White Caps, the White Sox, the Black Caps and others—that all folded within a season or two. The Louisville Black Colonels, a local semipro club that dated back to 1930, only joined the Negro American League, which was severely diminished in quality by integration, in 1954.

The result was that the all-white Colonels still drew a fairly large contingent of Black Louisvillians, despite corralling them through a separate entrance and limiting them to segregated seating in the least desirable corner of the stands at Parkway Field. It might be proper to think of these folks as baseball fans first rather than Colonels supporters, and there was an understandable desire here to see Jackie Robinson lead the integrated Royals into their home park. History was being made in their very own city at a time when local civil rights leaders were struggling to break down barriers.

The Colonels' management had a dilemma before the first home date in the Junior World Series: take advantage of Robinson's star power and sell the park out by accommodating all the Black fans who wanted to see him, or close the doors to a local demographic that would most likely be cheering heavily for the road team and undermine the team's gate revenue.

For too many of the city's white fans, the very notion of a Black man taking the field was a complete affront to the established social order. If they had to accept the inevitability that Robinson would play in their park, they could still do everything in their power to make his stay in the city as miserable as possible. The first three games of the seven-game series were slated for Parkway Field, and the mixture of excitement and dread across the city was palpable.

This time, the Royals at least had an off day to decompress on the train en route to Louisville from Syracuse for the start of their next playoff series on September 28. There was also some enthusiasm that the trek South offered the prospect of playing a few more games in "baseball weather" rather than the dreary, autumnal north. Crossing the Mason-Dixon line, however, meant that Robinson would not be allowed to stay in the same hotel as the rest of the team in a disheartening repeat of spring training down in Florida. It was small comfort when Wendell Smith reported just before Game One that the Dodgers were moving their 1947 spring training down to Havana so Robinson, Campanella, Newcombe, and others would be spared the indignities of Florida.[25]

Parkway Field had been configured into one of the most offense-suppressing environments in all of professional baseball, and the Colonels built their roster to take full advantage. The left-field line was 329 feet, with a Green Monster–style outfield scoreboard wall advertising war bonds and Cream of Kentucky bourbon. The right-field line spanned 345 feet, where there would be no wall-scraping home runs for the Royals left-handed power hitters. The wall in dead center was a diabolical 485 feet away, after the fence had been moved in from 507 feet just a couple of years earlier. Seen from above, the entire field looked like a nearly symmetrical diamond encased in an L-shaped stand with its short arm wrapped around the third base line. There were no outfield bleachers because of the wall obstruction in left and the need for anyone who would sit beyond the right-field wall to use binoculars to see home plate. The city sits in a wide valley at an elevation of six hundred to seven hundred feet, so altitude would not help balls carry. Foul territory was expansive, like the Oakland County Coliseum, and many balls that would have fallen harmlessly into the stands elsewhere turned into outs.

The park itself was a concrete and steel structure that had been cheaply and quickly built in 1923 on the ruins of the burned-down Eclipse Park at 7th and Kentucky Streets in the city's west end, next to the University of Louisville campus. It was, by 1946, closer to the end of its life as a professional baseball venue than the beginning, though the Cardinals continued using it for NCAA games into the 1990s. Seating capacity was 13,496, fair by AAA standards and an upgrade from the original 8,500, but still much smaller than that of Delorimier Stadium.

Winners tailor their roster to the quirks and advantages of their home park, which is exactly what the Colonels did in 1946. They did not exactly run away with the pennant, finishing with a 92–61 record that put them four games up on the second-place Indianapolis Indians, but they were peaking by the time the American Association playoffs began. It took them just five games to dispatch the Saints, then they humiliated the Indians in a four-game sweep. The Colonels ranked dead last in home runs in the American Association with just 44 over a 154-game season, and the team leader was Al Flair with a paltry 7, but they made up for it by piling on with speedy hitters who stole plenty of bases and legged out more triples than any other competitor. None of their hitters graduated or returned to any notable big league success aside from Sam Mele, a first baseman and outfielder who went on to play nearly full time in seven of his ten seasons in the Major Leagues. The result was a middle-of-the-pack offense that still found a way to score 4.72 runs per game despite its complete lack of slugging power.

On the mound, the Colonels were absolutely lethal. No other team in their high-scoring league allowed fewer than 4 runs per game, and they were the runaway leaders with a collective 3.85 ERA. They had three young, bona fide aces in twenty-one-year-old Al Widmar and twenty-four-year-olds Jim Wilson and Fritz Dorish, all three of whom later went up to the bigs. Wilson and Dorish had success as Major Leaguers—Wilson's was all the more remarkable after he was nearly killed when he took a Hank Greenberg line drive to the skull in a 1945 game with the Red Sox[26]—but Widmar struggled some in parts of five seasons with the Red Sox, Browns, and White Sox before later finding his calling as a pitching coach and Minor League coordinator. He capped his career by picking up two World Series rings as a Toronto Blue Jays executive in the 1990s.

These three anchors were joined by a big cohort of more experienced, rock-steady starters and swingmen. Otey Clark was effective for the Bosox in 1945 but found himself the odd man out in 1946 and dominated in Louisville the following year. Mel Deutsch had four excellent seasons with the Colonels from 1942 to 1946, sandwiched around his military service, but Boston never gave him much of a look that season, which was Louisville's gain. Lefty Joe Ostrowski later collected three World Series rings as a reliever for the 1950 through 1952 Yankees. A host of other hurlers might well have earned more big league service time if the parent Red Sox were not so flush with great pitching themselves on their way to an American League–leading 104-win season.

The greater travel distance between Louisville and Montreal meant that the two-three-two home-road split of the league playoffs was abandoned in favor of three in Louisville then up to four in Montreal if the series went a full seven games. This put the Royals at the serious disadvantage of having to face by far the toughest pitching staff they had seen that year in a park with dimensions that negated most of their hitters' best attributes. Also, a bigger issue was at play: the Colonels' home park was full of hostile racists who were determined to make life hell on the Royals' star player, Jackie Robinson, for three games before the series shifted to Montreal. The Royals were generally considered the slight favorites going into the series, but conditions were such that the Colonels might have put them in a stranglehold before they even got in a single play in front of their own fans.

The Colonels president, Bruce Dudley, had vaguely promised the Black press in advance that "no race questions will arise" when the Royals came to Louisville, but this sentiment apparently did not trickle all the way down throughout the organizational depth chart. MLB Commissioner Happy Chandler, a native son who had moved the league offices from New York to Cincinnati so he could look out on his beloved Kentucky across the Ohio River, had already warned Dudley that "the colored boy has every right to play." Still, the Colonels could try to undermine Robinson in other ways. The ticket office set a minimal quota on a small Black section, turning away hundreds of Black ticket buyers, while white Louisvillians were free to come up to the wicket and buy good seats at will. The excuse was that the club did this for the Black fans' own good. If the park had something resembling a more equal racial split, the thinking went, rowdier elements on either side might provoke fighting in the stands.[27]

Parkway Field had been used for Negro League, American Association, and collegiate play for years, but this was the first time it would host a mostly white professional team with a Black player. The club restricted all of the best seats in the house behind home plate and first and third bases, while Black fans were left with one option: the furthest seats from home that were barely under the stands down the first base line. The effect was that every time Robinson came to the plate, the Black cheers were far less audible than the white boos. Twenty-five years later, Robinson still remembered the taunts of "Hey, black boy, go on back to Canada—and stay."[28]

In one of the most shameless examples of revisionist folklore, some of those who had booed Robinson the hardest later claimed that it had nothing to do with race but rather with a perception that he was gunning for Pee Wee Reese's job in Brooklyn. Reese, the incumbent Dodgers' shortstop, was a Kentucky native who grew up in Louisville, after all, so the crowd had to look out for one of its own, this way of thinking went. Colonels center fielder George Bennington told a francophone Royals reporter days later on the train to Montreal, "If I were in his place, I would have thrown my glove on the ground and left the field and baseball altogether. Robinson is truly extraordinary."[29]

Two Colonels players tried to curry favor with the majority of the home fans with vicious and blatant attempts to spike Robinson. The first came from catcher and Mississippian Fred Walters on a spikes-up slide into second in Game One, while the second was courtesy of Texan third baseman Frank "Strick" Shofner, who came far off the baseline to kick at Robinson in a bid to break up a double play. Sam Lacy wrote that "Shofner's attempt was so obvious it was amateurish."[30] The lustiest cheers went out for Jim Wilson when he threw an inside brushback pitch that knocked Robinson to the ground.

Robinson was playing well in the field and hitting the ball squarely even if nothing fell in—he was just 1 for 11 in these first three road games—despite the inhospitable reception and opposing players' repeated attempts to injure him. The Royals' beat writers and the home fans following the series on the radio back in Montreal, however, were enraged by the repeated unsportsmanlike play of the Colonels and the appalling behavior of their fans. The home fans, down to every last man, woman, and child, vowed a ferocious revenge once the series shifted north. As Dink Carroll wrote, "Robinson was established as a genuine local hero. People felt that if you insulted Jack you were insulting Montreal. That was one point on which the Quebecois and the Anglos stood together. And the Jewish fans of Montreal felt the same way."[31]

Robinson was a complete nonfactor in Game One, going hitless in 5 plate appearances, but Colonels starter Jim Wilson was not sharp, and slugging first baseman Les Burge took him deep twice, as the "lusty clubbing" Royals took a 7–2 lead into the bottom of the ninth. Royals starter Chet Kehn did not have his good stuff and was constantly falling behind hitters, but Clay Hopper stubbornly refused to make a call to the bullpen until he really got in trouble in the final frame. The Colonels did their pesky best to make it dicey by cutting the lead to two, but the Royals bullpen held on for a 7–5 win that was never as close as the final score made it look.

The Colonels left the park feeling aggrieved after umpire Max Felerski had called hulking catcher Fred Walters out for interference when he collided with Royals shortstop Al Campanis on a sixth inning play that could have brought in two runs and turned the game around. Despite having to be restrained from assaulting Felerski by his manager, Walters was back out on the field for Game Two. That night, Fritz Dorish brought his A-game sinker and curveball, completely silencing the Royals' bats. Robinson took a walk, but no Royal aside from Rabbit Rackley was able to get a hit off Dorish. Carroll reported that the rest of the Royals' hitters "might just as well have been carrying toothpicks up to the plate." The Colonels won easily, 3–0.[32]

The final game of the series on the 30th was an unmitigated disaster made worse by the fact that Branch Rickey came down from Brooklyn so he could see the game in person. The Royals' players should not necessarily have been flattered; the Dodgers and Cardinals had finished in a tie for first with 96–58 records, which precipitated a best-of-three series for the National League pennant. The first game was to be played on October 1 in St. Louis, so Louisville was a logical way station for Rickey, as he was on his way back to his old stomping grounds. After watching the Royals get trounced, Rickey watched his Robinsonless Dodgers lose, 4–2, at Sportsman's Park, then get blown out at home, 8–4, two days later. The general manager was not much of a good luck charm in 1946.

The Royals jumped out to a 2–0 lead in the top of the first with Robinson walking and later scoring, but the ailing and usually dependable Steve Nagy immediately gave 3 runs back in the bottom of the inning, thanks to a throwing error and a couple of walks. He just could not find the zone and was chased from the game by the third. The Royals clawed back to 6–4, but every one of Hopper's calls to the bullpen brought more misery. Robinson finally collected his first hit of the series and scored a pair of runs, but the Royals' pitching was completely abysmal, and the Colonels took Game Three, 15–6.

Both teams hastily made their way to the train station immediately after the game, boarding the same special train the Canadian National Railway provided for them. There was a separate car for the commissioner, sleeper cars for the players, a well-stocked dining car for those who felt like celebrating, and ample room for about one hundred happy members of the Colonels entourage. Royals players had a lot to mull over on the route north to the Sarnia border crossing, most of it negative, during the nearly twenty-four-hour journey way up north to Montreal. Robinson hopped off in Detroit to negotiate the purchase of a new car with his playoff earnings then grabbed the night train separately, left alone with just his own thoughts for company for a half-day ride.[33]

There was one big saving grace, however: the Royals boisterous fans would finally get a chance to assert themselves at Delorimier Stadium and provide a tenth-man boost to the team. No Royal needed one more than Robinson, and no one had to tell him his team would be in a precarious position if it fell behind 3-1 in the series. The script called for heroics, and he stepped up to deliver.

A little early October pregame snow and a game-time temperature just barely above freezing could not deter the 14,685 faithful who came out in the hope of watching the Royals equalize the series. Visitors from Kentucky would have thought the locals were dressed more for very late season football weather than for baseball weather, but adapting to the cold was just part of life. No prior Montreal-Louisville sporting, political, or cultural rivalry of any type whatsoever existed up to this point, but the crowd had some awareness that Alouettes star Herb Trawick had been corralled into Kentucky State College for Negroes because prevailing Jim Crow laws limited his college options. And there was a hell of a lot of anger at the way Robinson had been treated as a guest in the road leg of the Junior World Series. Some in the crowd took to wearing the *ceinture fléchée*, a colorful wool Huron-Wendat Nation belt knotted to one side that had been adopted by the Québécois and carried strong nationalist overtones.[34] There was no state of war just yet, but it felt like one could break out very quickly.

Robinson remembered how the pressure of needing to win three of the next four games melted once he got back home:

> When we arrived in that city, we discovered that the Canadians were up in arms over the way I had been treated. Greeting us warmly, they let us know how they felt. They displayed their

> resentment against Louisville and their loyalty to us on the first day of our return to play the final games by letting loose an avalanche of boos against the Louisville players the minute they came on the field. All through the first game, they booed every time a Louisville player came out of the dugout. It was difficult to be sure how I felt. I didn't approve of this kind of retaliation, but I felt a jubilant sense of gratitude for the way the Canadians expressed their feelings. When fans go to bat for you like that, you feel it would be easy to play for them forever.[35]

One of the visiting American reporters asked his counterpart from Montreal whether it was customary for the home fans to boo opposing players. The Montrealer responded, "They booed Jackie in Louisville, didn't they?"[36]

Game Four was a see-saw affair, with the Colonels looking to secure a decisive advantage and the Royals fighting hard to shift the momentum back in their favor. Glen Moulder was on the bump for the Royals, and he did not have his good stuff, as he gave up 4 runs on 8 hits before turning the ball over to fresh-faced Frank Laga, the late-season hotshot callup from Mobile. The rookie stabilized the game over 3.2 innings, but he gave up an add-on run. So the Royals were trailing late, down 4–1 after five and then 5–3 as the game headed into the bottom of the ninth. None of the Louisville runs were particularly loud; they were the product of walks, singles, timely bunting, and hits with runners in scoring position.

The bottom of the ninth got off to an inauspicious start, as Colonels righty Otey Clark got Campanis for a quick out. On-base average machine Herman Franks came in to pinch-hit for Laga and did what he had done 72 times in part-time play in the regular season—he walked. In came Red Durrett to pinch-run as the lineup rolled over to lead-off man Rabbit Rackley, who forced him over to second as Robinson came up with two outs, representing the tying run. Clark wanted nothing to do with him and issued an intentional walk, then another to righty Tom Tatum to set up a lefty-lefty matchup for reliable Colonels southpaw Joe Ostrowski against slugging Les Burge with two outs and the bases loaded.

This high-risk approach went wrong, but not the way one might expect. Ostrowski had shown good control all year, but Burge worked him for a walk, an unintentional one this time, and the Royals were down just one with the bases still loaded and two out. After sabotaging himself, Ostrowski was then sabotaged by his catcher, Frank Walters, who gambled poorly when he tried to end the game with a snap pickoff of Tom Tatum at second base. His throw missed the mark, the ball scooted away, and in came Robinson with the tying run. Chet Kehn, who had apparently just had $1,600 worth of personal effects stolen on the train ride, was completely dialed in and shut the Colonels out in the top of the tenth. The pendulum had swung back in the Royals' favor.

The first Royals' hitter in the bottom of the tenth, Dixie Howell, who had homered earlier in the game, reached on an error by Ostrowski, who could feel the game slipping away. The next batter, Earl Naylor, dropped a bunt toward the mound and Ostrowski tried for the lead man rather than take the sure out, but Howell beat his throw to second. Another defensive gamble backfired for the Colonels. Ostrowski got the hook, and Mel Deutsch came in to try to shut down the Royals' rally. Campanis dropped yet another bunt to move the runners over to second and third with one out, and the pitcher, Kehn, was left to hit for himself. Kehn had proven himself as a very respectable hitter, slashing .333/.443/.392 in 66 regular-season plate appearances, but Hopper wanted a quick victory and took the bat out of his hands. Kehn got a solid squeeze bunt down, but Walters redeemed his earlier misplay by blocking the plate and getting a quick tag on Howell before he could touch home. This time the Colonels intentionally walked their way into a final two-out showdown with Jackie Robinson.

Everyone from the press box through the stands saw the dramatic game-winning single he roped over the Colonels' shortstop's head very much as "revenge for the hard ride he got from the crowd in Louisville."[37] Two hits, a run, and a game-winning RBI—Jackie Robinson was very much back in his element, and the home fans could not have been happier.

The skipper was in good spirits and not just because of the Royals' crucial Game Four win on his birthday. The Dodgers had given him a vote of confidence by having Hector Racine, the Royals' president, make a pregame announcement in front of a packed house that Hopper's contract had been extended through the 1947 season. Taking the mound for the Colonels in Game Five on October 4 was Jim Wilson, who had been battered in the series opener, while the Royals countered with their ace, Steve Nagy. Royals fans were reasonably confident that their team could bring home a victory and set up a clincher the following evening.

Montrealers were overjoyed to see the start of a week's worth of Indian summer temperatures during the day of the 4th, but the city had cooled off by the late 8:00 p.m. first pitch, and it felt like fans were in for a relatively low-scoring affair so long as both teams played good defense. The crowd had swelled to 17,658, a near full house. The Royals chipped away with single runs in the first three innings to take an early lead, and Nagy found a way to work out of trouble and keep the Colonels off the scoreboard until the fifth, when he surrendered just 1 run. As per managerial practice of the day, Hopper rode his horse too long and left Nagy in through the seventh, giving the Colonels the opportunity to come back and tie the game at three all. He returned for the eighth and immediately walked a batter before hot-hand Chet Kehn came in to relieve him.

Colonels manager Nemo Leibold had plenty of solid relievers to go to, but he also left his starter in longer than he should have, and the Royals retook the lead in the bottom of the seventh after Robinson smashed a triple to left center to lead off the inning. Wilson got the next two hitters on meek infield fly balls, but Lew Riggs was the hero who knocked Robinson in with a screaming double all the way to the right-field wall. The Royals added one more in the eighth on a walk, sacrifice bunt, and groundout to advance the runner to third, followed by a shocking two-out bunt single from Robinson to push across an insurance run.[38] The Colonels had not seen any player in the American Association with the audacity to try a move like this and were taken completely by surprise. Robbie was by this point on fire, going 3 for 5 on a double, triple, and bunt single, scoring a run and knocking in another. On the defensive side, he was in peak form on three key double plays that bailed Nagy out of jams. The Royals were a win away from taking the first Junior World Series title in franchise history.

The clinching Game Six was tightly fought, but at the same time a somewhat anticlimactic affair in which the Royals manufactured 2 runs in the second while everyone in the park spent the rest of the game wondering if this slim lead would hold. It did. Curt Davis, just a month past his forty-third birthday and a season removed from the last of his twelve full big league seasons, bid adieu to Montreal with a flourish, throwing a complete-game shutout. His opponent, Fritz Dorish, was nearly as good, but took a complete-game loss.[39]

Roughly nineteen thousand euphoric Royals fans never would have gone home had the grounds crew not shut off the stadium lights about a half-hour after the final out. Robinson had been in peak form over the past three home games, going 7 for 14 at the plate and playing some of his sharpest defense of the year. The Royals' star was a key factor in all three of these thrilling home wins. He, of course, got the loudest cheers of all as the fans thrust him up on their shoulders for a victory lap while the francophones belted out, "Il a gagné ses épaulettes, maluron, malurette!" which translated is "He earned his stripes," followed by rhyming sing-song folksy gibberish. The anglophones chipped in, "We want Robinson!"

Robinson had no intention of stealing attention from Curt Davis or Hopper, but the ushers had to come into the clubhouse to politely ask him to come out onto the field so the fans could serenade him one last time. It was clear that this was the only way anyone was going home, and they could finally shut down the park for the season, so he worked his way back toward the field after changing into his street clothes. As Robinson pushed through the throng of well-wishers, the team mascot, Little Frenchy, told him he hoped these people would never see him at Delorimier Stadium again. Needless to say, they all expected bigger and better things for him in Brooklyn.[40]

The foremost historians of the Royals' franchise, William Brown and Scott Terry, described the scene: "Tears streamed down Robinson's face as he was paraded around the field. Rachel Robinson was so caught up in the emotional tribute to her husband, she waded into the adoring crowd, even though she was eight months pregnant.

Fifty years after her husband's debut, she still lists the Royals victory over Louisville as the most exciting end to a baseball season that she ever saw."[41]

Sam Maltin was no impartial observer whenever his friend was involved; nevertheless, he anointed Robinson "the most popular athlete ever to wear a Montreal athletic uniform" based on what he saw in the park after the game. Maurice Richard himself likely would not have quibbled had he been able to break away from training for an imminent puck drop on the Canadiens Stanley Cup defense and join the Royals' throng. This outpouring of emotion was mostly driven by an understanding from fans that their time with Robinson, as a player at least, had come to an end and they were unlikely to ever see another like him. Matlin continued, "They want him back, but it was 'goodbye.' He's strictly Brooklyn. He never belonged to this league, despite its Class AAA rating, after the first month of the season."

Even after Robinson effusively thanked the crowd, promised to return, and shook every hand he could before pleading that he would miss his flight to Detroit, still two hundred or so fans wanted more and blocked the tunnel between the Royals clubhouse and the street. Every other player but Robinson had already escaped, and it was clear he was not going anywhere without an assist from all the ushers and police as well as a little old-school gridiron rushing.

Maltin had the call as he rounded out his best and final Royals column of the season. "It was a demonstration seldom seen here. Again, the crowd started hugging and kissing him, while . . . Robbie dragged and pushed through the crowd until he broke away and started running under the grandstand, where an usher had a door open for him."

Bedlam poured out onto the street. Maltin continued:

> Jackie ran out, with the mob running after him. Down the street he went, chased by an additional five hundred fans who were waiting for him outside. . . . For three blocks they chased him, until a car drew up and someone shouted, "jump in, Jackie." That he did and sat down—plunk on a lady's lap. They brought him safely to the hotel.

> Men, three times the age of Robinson, oldtimers in the local sports scene, men who saw some of the greatest Canadian athletes in action, failed to recall an ovation that matched that given to Robinson. It wasn't an organized reception, but was as spontaneous as the booing aimed at every Louisville player that stepped up to the plate here, an answer to the jeering given Jackie in the Kentucky city.
>
> To the large group of Louisville fans who came here with their team, it may be a lesson of goodwill among men. That it's the man and not his color, race or creed. They couldn't fail to tell others down South of the 'riots,' the chasing of a Negro—not because of hate but because of love.[42]

Robinson made his flight to Detroit after all. Alone, up in the sky, he finally had a moment to reflect. "As my plane roared skyward and the lights of Montreal twinkled and winked in the distance, I took one last look at this great city where I had found so much happiness. 'I don't care if I never get to the Majors,' I told myself. 'This is the city for me. This is paradise.'"[43]

Jackie Robinson's tenure with the Royals had come to a close, despite the fiction of reporting to Dodgers camp as a Minor Leaguer the following spring. Robinson was not finished with either Montreal or Louisville, though, and retraced his steps from the 1946 playoffs later in life.

Robinson came back to Louisville one more time as a player, this time as a veteran in a Dodgers uniform, for a preseason game against the Milwaukee Braves on April 9, 1956. The *Lexington Herald* ran a photo of him shivering in the Parkway Field dugout on a forty-four-degree day and the furrowed expression on his face seemed to presage his retirement at the end of the season. He held no ill will toward Louisville or Kentucky, though, and offered local sports reporters a solid one-liner: "Now I know why they call it bluegrass. It's frozen!"[44]

The weather was no better during his next and final trip to Kentucky on March 5, 1964, but this time the stakes were much more important than anything that had ever happened on a baseball field. That day, ten thousand civil rights protestors descended on the state capitol building in Frankfort in a bid to pressure Democratic Governor Ned Breathitt to take decisive action to sweep Jim Crow out of Kentucky for good. The state's leading civil rights figures were joined for moral support by Reverend Martin Luther King Jr., Reverend Ralph Abernathy, and a host of other nationally known activists. Members of the crowd were mostly bundled up in warm coats over their business suits and fine dresses, while marchers carried signs demanding "Equal Rights Now!" or simply declaring the allegiance of smaller cities and towns like Madisonville or Horse Cave.

In the second line of the vanguard was a rapidly aging Jackie Robinson, moving with more difficulty and sporting hair flecked with growing white patches. He was one of the day's main speakers, the only athlete to add his star power to the march.

The governor was one of Kentucky's finest of the twentieth century, a good-hearted man who wanted to set a positive example the rest of the South could follow. He had just been elected a year earlier at the age of thirty-nine at a time of widespread discrimination against Black Kentuckians in jobs, accommodation, and even the right to use public spaces or patronize many businesses. There was a fierce and ongoing debate among the political class over whether the state government should act against racial discrimination and, if so, just how much action it should take. Breathitt was convinced that the best path forward was a strong civil rights bill that had won the support of the state legislature rather than executive action. His political rivals within the Democratic Party, chiefly Happy Chandler, former governor and MLB commissioner when Robinson broke with the Dodgers in 1947, and Lieutenant Governor Harry Lee Waterfield, schemed with anti–civil rights Republicans to kill two moderate bills in a self-serving bid to undermine Breathitt.

Plenty of white faces were among the marchers, including Breathitt's thirteen-year-old daughter Mary Frances and his minister from Hopkinsville. They marched together near the front of the crowd. Breathitt stayed in the governor's office during the demonstration, but he did meet its organizers afterward. Dr. King pressed him on HB 197, but Breathitt offered only a weak promise that he would do what he could. At the same time, a group of thirty-two protestors launched a week-long hunger strike in the House gallery, but none of these efforts convinced state legislators to move the bill forward.

The governor shifted gears the following year, sharpening his knife for an attack on fellow Democrats who had been sabotaging his civil rights agenda. His faction picked up enough seats to form a working majority in the legislature, and they spent months working on the Kentucky Civil Rights Act that Breathitt signed on January 27, 1966. This act codified the federal Civil Rights Act of 1964 into Kentucky law and in many areas went even further, but in the grander picture it stood out as the first state civil rights bill passed in the South and a profound starting point for a new Kentucky. Dr. King hailed the act as "a milestone for a southern state . . . a great step forward for any state . . . [that] will serve as a great beacon of light for all men of goodwill . . . and hopefully inspire other states to follow suit."[45]

On that March 1964 day when it all began, Robinson joined a new team and helped it win a second victory over every single one of the spectators who had savagely booed him in Louisville during the 1946 Junior World Series. The biggest victory of all belonged in part to him.

6

Homecomings

Everything about Montreal is pretty dope.

—LAURENCE W. HOLMES, Instagram, outside Coco Rico on August 31, 2021

The unjust post-Reconstruction status quo for Black America rapidly began to crumble almost immediately after Jackie Robinson became a household name. In retrospect, he was the accelerant for long overdue social change, and his debut as a Major Leaguer in 1947 was the first of many big dominoes to fall in the terminal stage of the history of the civil rights movement. President Harry Truman desegregated the military in 1948 through Executive Order 9981. The Supreme Court ruled in 1954 that separate but equal in education was an unconstitutional violation of the Fourteenth Amendment. In the early 1960s lunch counter sit-inners, freedom riders, and demonstrators in Birmingham brought the indefensible ugliness of Jim Crow to newspapers and television screens in such detail that white America could no longer turn away from it. Then, the president and legislators followed with the landmark Civil Rights Act of 1964 and the Voting Rights Act of 1965. Each of these successive battles was part of a grand but incomplete victory.

There were still, however, plenty of major baseball-specific hurdles for Robinson and Rickey to overcome during the opening months of 1947. Both Rickey and Commissioner Happy Chandler recalled an owners meeting at the Waldorf Astoria in New York in January during which integration came up for a vote. Fifteen of the sixteen rejected it, Rickey being the sole exception. Neither Chandler, who had earlier surprised many by expressing prointegration sentiment to the Black press on the grounds that "if a Black boy can make it on Okinawa and

Guadalcanal, hell, he can make it in baseball,"[1] nor Rickey felt they had to abide by the vote and did not let it derail Robinson's debut. Rickey had apparently visited Chandler at his cabin in Kentucky in late 1946 in a bid to win his support for integration—more likely to deliver a flattering pitch to convince Chandler that he could be part of history by simply allowing Rickey to proceed with plans he had hatched on his own—and they appeared to have reached a consensus well before speaking with other owners. There is no known documentation of the 15–1 vote, and Larry MacPhail of the Yankees, Bob Carpenter of the Phillies, and Clark Griffith of the Senators all denied that it played out the way Rickey and Chandler had described.[2]

Robinson reported to Dodgers spring training in Havana as a member of the Royals on a $4,000 AAA contract so modest that most who reported on it found it insulting. Still, Robinson outwardly said all of the right things to avoid creating a rift with Rickey or undermining his chances of breaking camp with Brooklyn instead of heading back north for an unnecessary victory lap. Given what he had just accomplished on the field the year before and what was to come after, it was incredibly quaint in hindsight when he said, "I do not resent being with Montreal. I can understand that a lot of people might feel my showing in my first year was that of a flash in the pan. If I don't show well, I'll continue to play with Montreal and hope for the best."[3]

Robinson knew that he could count on the enthusiastic support of his new skipper, Leo Durocher, who was effusive in his praise and expected him to deliver an immediate contribution to the Dodgers' lineup. There was one big problem, though: Leo the Lip's days as the Dodgers' manager were severely numbered.

Durocher was known around baseball as a hard-nosed winner on the field and far too indiscreet off it insofar as his social life was concerned for the delicate mores of the 1940s. He had openly defied Chandler's warning to steer clear of his gambler and mafiosi friends, but it was news of his affair with Laraine Day, a married Hollywood starlet fifteen years his junior, that ultimately did him in as a Dodger. Influential Catholic groups in Brooklyn threatened to boycott the Dodgers unless Durocher was fired, an action Rickey refused to take despite pressure from co-owner Walter O'Malley to capitulate; for all of his faults, Durocher had always been a solid supporter of integration and was the right man to handle Robinson's rookie season.

Chandler took great delight in suspending Durocher for the entire season for "conduct detrimental to baseball" less than a week from Opening Day, throwing a major last-minute hitch into Rickey's plan for the upcoming season. None of this particular bit of late spring training drama ultimately came to much regarding Jackie Robinson, though. Rickey brought in an aging Dodgers scout, Burt Shotton, to take over from Durocher at the last minute, and his even-keeled approach made life easier for everyone over the course of a historic season. As for Durocher, he landed on his feet and suffered no lasting damage to his reputation. He and Day married later that year, and he returned to baseball as the new Giants manager in 1948. Deserved Hall of Fame honors came posthumously.[4]

Back at the beginning of camp, Robinson was, however, completely irate when he learned that he, Roy Campanella, and Roy Partlow would not be staying at the swanky Hotel Nacional with the rest of the team, but rather in the decidedly less impressive Hotel Boston in Old Havana. There was no local ordinance forcing Rickey to keep his players apart this time, but he did correctly anticipate trouble ahead from disgruntled white Dodgers who would at some point try to take a stand against the Great Experiment. Separate accommodations, Rickey thought, might give the ringleaders some time to consider just how far they were willing to take their protest. The Black players in camp were already plenty used to indignities such as this and could be left to grumble through the arrangement until Rickey found a solution to this bigger problem.[5]

The rebellion was spearheaded by Dixie Walker, a Georgia-born outfielder and fan favorite who had been one of the Dodgers' best players for years. He was the 1944 National League batting champion and an All-Star every year from 1943 through 1947 (except in 1945 when no All-Star Game was held, though the Associated Press selected him as an All-Star for its theoretical team). Joining him on sectional grounds were fellow Georgian and relief ace Hugh Casey and backup catcher Bobby Bragan from Alabama, just back with the club after spending 1945 and 1946 in the military. Both were veteran players.

Sophomore outfielder Carl Furillo of Pennsylvania got caught up in the excitement and threw his lot in with them as well. Together, they began circulating a petition demanding that Rickey leave Robinson off the Dodgers' roster or face the consequences.

Walker had been the unquestioned team leader and had major influence in the clubhouse, but Pee Wee Reese was about to succeed him in that role and refused to go along with the plot, a move that surprised some who assumed place of birth was the ultimate determinant on one's views on race. Rookie Gil Hodges, a future Hall of Famer who later took on a significant leadership role through the Dodgers' glory years, similarly resisted, as did outfielder Pete Reiser. In one of his final and most significant acts as Dodgers manager, a livid Durocher reamed the Walker gang out once he learned of their boycott campaign. Years later, he reflected, "I told them what they could do with their petition, and I don't think I got much back talk on it. I told the players that Robinson was going to open the season with us come hell or high water, and if they didn't like it they could leave now and we'd trade them or get rid of them some other way. Nobody moved."[6]

Rickey was better prepared for turbulence like this and responded to the ultimatum by delivering one of his own face-to-face with each of the mutineers: any player who could not abide Robinson's presence would be shown the door. Would they really choose exile from a team that was a pennant favorite, risking the loss of rich playoff bonuses? As Rickey had predicted, they all backed down to a man and went on to play out the season without further incident. Furillo felt more like a follower than a leader, and he alone of the petitioners had any long-term future with the club.

Fifty years later, Bragan admitted to having acted out of blind racism and made his final statement on the matter: "In the twentieth century, Billy Graham did the most for humanity. But Jackie Robinson and Branch Rickey have to rate pretty high."[7] Walker expressed much deeper late-life regrets, telling Roger Kahn in the 1970s that his anti-Robinson campaign was the "stupidest thing he'd ever done," pleading with the author to get his mea culpa in print someday. It was Kahn's conclusion that Walker was motivated primarily by fear that his off-season wholesale business in Birmingham would suffer badly unless he showed some resistance to integration for the benefit of the white folks back home. Rachel Robinson acknowledged his apology as a possible sign of growth without quite accepting it, while Jackie never forgave Walker even after he tried to make amends by praising Robinson to the media later in the 1947 season. Whenever Walker homered with Robinson in the on-deck circle that year, Robinson pointedly refused to shake his hand when he touched home. Who could blame him?[8]

Robinson's first regular-season game with the Dodgers was nowhere near as dramatic as his Royals opener in Jersey City, but there he was playing first base and hitting out of the familiar two hole against the Boston Braves. His first three plate appearances amounted to a double play, a grounder to short, and a weak fly to left, but he reached into the tool bag with Dodgers down 3–2 in the seventh inning. Stanky walked as he always seemed to do, then Robinson executed a perfect bunt that first baseman Earl Torgeson badly misplayed. His hurried throw to the bag ricocheted off Robinson's leg, and the ball skipped into right field as the runners advanced to second and third. A Pete Reiser double scored them both, then Reiser came in on a sacrifice fly for an insurance run. The box score indicated that it had been a pedestrian effort, but Robinson still made a decisive contribution exactly when it was needed.

Back in Québec, Robinson was long gone but very clearly not forgotten on the sports pages. His photo ran in the game recap in *The Gazette*. *Le Canada* made his rapid, "masterful" transition to first base part of the lede. *Le Devoir* and *Montreal-Matin* played up the significance of his very presence on the diamond. But *La Presse* had the headline of the day with "Brooklyn Debuts with a Win—the Royal Is the Victor." Meanwhile, *The New York Times* was understated, calling his debut "uneventful" and describing Robinson as a "muscular Negro . . . who speaks quietly and intelligently when spoken to." One of his unnamed teammates was quoted saying, "Having Jackie on the team is a little strange, just like anything else that's new. We just don't know how to act with him. But he'll be accepted in time. You can be sure of that."[9] And so it began.

The last apparent rearguard action allegedly came out of St. Louis two weeks into the season when some Cardinals reportedly planned to walk off the field in a protest against integration when they faced the Dodgers on May 6. Regardless of whether an actual plan was in place or just a bunch of ugly locker-room talk that was whispered all the way up to the office of National League President Ford Frick, Stanley Woodward of the *New York Herald Tribune* convinced much of the baseball world that the Cardinals were a gang of knuckle-dragging troglodytes. Players and team executives protested in vain that a bit of isolated venting had been completely blown out of proportion, but the main consequence of the whole episode was that it transformed indifference toward the Great Experiment in much of the white press into open support. The epithets from fans on the road, spikes-up slides from opposing players, and death-threat letters never stopped that year, but when sportswriters eventually came around on a great underdog story, many of their readers started to change their tune as well.[10]

The single-most moving early-career public defense of Robinson allegedly came in mid-May when he was taking heaps of abuse from Reds fans in Crosley Field. It was then, the story goes, that Pee Wee Reese, native son of nearby Kentucky, walked over and put his arm around Robinson and stood with him for a moment, signaling to everyone in the crowd that Robinson was a full-fledged Dodger. This moment was immortalized in a statue at MCU Park at Coney Island and became a key scene late in the film *42*. In the perfect cinematic version, Reese reassures Robinson, "They can say all they want. We're just here to play ball," to which Robinson replies, "It's just a bunch of crackpots. Still fighting the Civil War." Reese follows with a bad joke about how the South would have won if it had not run out of ammunition, then he thanks Robinson, who responds by asking why. "I got family up there from Louisville. I need them to know who I am," he replies. As the umpire breaks up the conversation, Reese has the last thought. "Maybe tomorrow we'll all wear 42. That way they won't tell us apart."

One can hardly blame a screenwriter for leaning in on a touching moment of vulnerability for dramatic effect, but Ken Burns and leading baseball historians doubt that this actually happened, at least not during that May 13 game in Cincinnati. Robinson did describe something similar occurring the following year in Boston in his autobiography.[11] How or even if it played out, he and Reese were fast friends for life and had an amazing decade-long run together during which the Dodgers went to the World Series six times.

There was incredible team and personal glory for Robinson in 1947. The Dodgers rebounded from their heartbreaking loss to the Cardinals in the National League pennant playoff the previous year and returned to the World Series for the first time since 1941. It was a thrilling seven-game series against the Yankees; three games were decided by only a run and two more by just two runs. The Bronx Bombers got one of those legend-making playoff moments from reliever Joe Page, who came out in relief in the fourth and took it home with five shutdown innings in Game Seven. With Robinson hitting in the two hole, the offense scored 73 more runs than it had during the previous year, as its on-base average model showed real dividends. All the pieces were in place for a very long run of Dodgers success.

Robinson got off to a bit of a slow start and was hitting just .227/.346/.341 after his first two weeks as a big leaguer, but he picked up the pace in May, got blistering hot in June, flagged a bit over an exhausting thirty-four games in July, then steadied the ship over a great run from August through to season's end. Cumulatively, it all amounted to a .297/.383/.427 season in which he led the National League in both stolen bases and sacrifice bunts, collecting 175 hits and scoring an eye-watering 125 runs. Three times he stole home that year, to many the most dangerous and exciting play in baseball. What this impressive line does not show is just how much his disruptive presence on the basepaths threw off opposing pitchers to the advantage of teammates further down the lineup. His fielding over 151 games at first base, a brand-new position, was just marginally subaverage according to advanced metrics, but he was by no means a liability there. Adding him to the lineup in place of 1946 incumbent Ed Stevens had an enormous net benefit to the team. When Robinson shifted back to second base in 1948, he graded out as a plus to excellent defender back in a more natural position.

Just before the end of the season, Robinson's smiling face appeared on the cover of *Time* magazine with a sea of oversized baseballs as the backdrop. "He and the boss took a chance," the tag line to the biggest sports story of the year read.[12] Taylor Spink had long been throwing cold water on the idea of integration for years and cast preseason doubt on Robinson's ability to make it as a Major Leaguer, but he ate crow for readers of *The Sporting News* at season's end. "Jackie Robinson has done it all, in his first year as a major leaguer. What more could anyone ask?" he wrote.[13] Robinson was the Major League Rookie of the Year by a clear margin and even picked up a first-place vote in the MVP race.[14]

In spite of his late start, Jackie Robinson spent a full decade with the Dodgers, the lynchpin of a National League dynasty that finally got over the hurdle in 1955 and won its first World Series. This moment was doubly satisfying for Bums fans, coming as it did at the hands of the Yankees, who had denied them glory in 1947, 1949, 1952, 1953, then once more for good measure in 1956, Robinson's final season.

Robinson accumulated roughly 60 WAR over this period. He won a batting title and an MVP Award in an epic 1949 campaign, played in six All-Star Games, and finished with an excellent .313/.410/.477 career line. He selflessly moved around the diamond from first to second to third to left field as per team needs at the moment. There was some injury concern at the start given how he had broken down a little late in his Royals season, but he proved to be a very durable player right up to the end. So far as the sport itself was concerned, he made stolen bases exciting again, encouraging Willie Mays to show off his wheels in a pair of 30-30 seasons during the middle of a six-year 20-20 run and paving the way for 1960s burners like Maury Wills, Lou Brock, and Bert Campaneris. The game as a result started to become more multidimensional as a more exciting Negro Leagues style of play swept into the American and National Leagues.

No one in the baseball world ever really had to wonder how much gaudier his career stats would have been had Robinson broken with the Dodgers at twenty-two or twenty-three instead of twenty-eight; it was already clear that he was one of the greatest to ever play the game over his limited time.

By 1955 the Dodgers moved Robinson around to third and left in a bid to find playing time for Jim "Junior" Gilliam, a superior defender at second base. Future Hall of Famer Gil Hodges had been entrenched at first since 1948 and there was no going back, as Robinson was reduced to a platoon plus role over his final two seasons. He was by no means played off the field and had a productive 4 WAR, .275/.382/.412 final season in 1956. But sometimes his legs felt like concrete, and the dynamism of his early years eluded him. At thirty-seven, he was getting old, and he knew it. He had just cleared certain sentimental milestones—1,500 hits and 200 stolen bases—that year, and he already had his World Series ring. Really nothing was left to prove to anyone, and the time came to look for new opportunities beyond the game.

The Dodgers' front office tried to make Robinson look like a heel for opting for retirement over accepting a December 13, 1956, trade to the Giants and claimed he hid his plans to walk away from the game. Robinson had no love at all for Walter O'Malley, the Dodgers' owner who squeezed Branch Rickey out in a hostile takeover in 1950, and he had in any event signed a $50,000 contract with *Look* magazine that paid him to write occasional columns. He was contractually obliged by this deal, which exceeded his annual salary from the Dodgers, to break the news of his retirement in an exclusive for their readers. Fulfilling the terms of that lucrative deal meant keeping his cards as close to his chest as long as possible, so he quietly emptied his locker at Ebbets Field just after New Year's Day in 1957 and effectively broke off communication with the front office. O'Malley could read about his retirement in the Saturday papers on the 5th of January, just like every other sports fan, for all he cared.

Robinson deserved to walk out the door with more dignity than this, and the Montreal papers reflexively had his back. To Bert Souiliere at *Le Devoir*, Robinson was "a very courageous player, a natural athlete, [who] has taken no time in asserting itself under the big tent." If his heart was no longer in playing, he would not have to wait long before another opportunity came along. The payday from *Look* was obviously too tempting to pass on, and the deal would be a mere footnote someday.[15] Charlie Daoust at *Le Droit* thought general manager Buzzie Bavasi was a fool if he did not foresee a nearly thirty-eight-year-old Robinson choosing retirement over reporting to the Giants—more much ado about nothing from Brooklyn. Jean Chartier at *La Tribune* got to the real heart of the tragedy insofar as locals were concerned, lamenting that this acrimonious breakup probably ended the prospect of Robinson coming back to Montreal to manage the Royals, something he had previously expressed interest in and a dream for the fans.[16] There was more of the same from columnists for *Le Soleil* and elsewhere.

Nobody thought Robinson was completely finished with baseball, though, and Montrealers were encouraged by his repeat visits to the city to the point that some even wondered whether he might be open for a more permanent reunion. Robinson returned in 1957, his first year of retirement, then again in early November 1958 with Rachel to add his signature to the Golden Book at city hall, beaming for the cameras with Mayor Sarto Fournier. This was and is a high honor for those who have made great contributions to the city's civil, sporting, and cultural life, but it was also an opportunity to reconnect with old friends from his days with the Royals.

Later in life, there were other visits in 1969 to tour the new Sporting Pavilion and then in December 1971 to speak as the guest of honor at the city's annual celebrity dinner. Homecomings like this created an opportunity to catch up with his fellow Montreal No. 9, Rocket Richard, albeit in tuxedos rather than the more comfortable summer leisurewear from their first encounter in 1946.[17] No other Hall of Fame–bound Golden Age baseball superstars who took repeated victory laps in their old Minor League cities with such frequency and joy jumps to mind.

Robinson was the first of three successive Black superstars for the Royals, who kept smashing their own regular-season attendance records in 1947 behind Roy Campanella and again in 1948 with Don Newcombe. This run of excellence brought Montreal into the conversation as a very real candidate city for a big league promotion, at least for a fleeting moment in September 1953. The great Royals teams of this golden era drew between roughly 5,300 to 6,200 fans per regular-season game, and it was easy to see growth potential in the city for a big league club. Montreal, after all, had a population that was half a million or more greater than Boston or St. Louis, baseball-mad big league cities that split their fan market, albeit unevenly, between two franchises.

Major League Baseball was incredibly slow to expand after the war, even though air travel opened up the possibility of breaking into new markets far from the historic East Coast–Midwest circuit. The American League was founded with eight teams in 1901 and still held steady at eight half a century later, despite the United States having doubled in population. Relocation of an existing franchise was the only path forward for Montreal before the business logic of creating expansion franchises became overwhelming in the early 1960s. One blindingly obvious candidate could be sent off to a better home: the eternally hapless St. Louis Browns.

The Browns had already been relocated once after just a single abysmal season as the Milwaukee Brewers in the fledgling American League. They arrived in St. Louis in 1902 and took the team name that the original Browns of the National League gave up when they rebranded as the Cardinals for the 1901 season. The two clubs shared Sportsman's Park and spent their first two decades of cohabitation competing to see which one of them could disappoint St. Louis baseball fans more; each had just four winning seasons from 1902 to 1921.

Their destinies disentangled as Branch Rickey started executing brilliant new strategies that turned the Cardinals into the class of the National League. Two decades of Cardinals success and Browns futility almost led to the latter's relocation to Los Angeles as the first major West Coast sports franchise. (The Cardinals were in the awkward position of being the Browns' tenant at Sportsman's Park, so they were willing to generously subsidize the Browns' exit to gain full control of a robust local market.) The owners' vote to approve the move never took place, though; it was scheduled for Monday, December 8, 1941, a day that would not live in baseball lore as the day after a date of infamy.[18]

Confined to barracks because of the Japanese attack on Pearl Harbor, the Browns did enjoy their only sustained run of winning during World War II when their competitors' rosters had been hollowed out as players reported for military service. They did win their only AL pennant in 1944, a summer when most Americans were much more interested in following the Allies' growing bulge in Normandy than a bunch of seriously diminished teams fighting for a pennant. It was not a season that deserved an asterisk, but no one in baseball outside of St. Louis took their greatest accomplishment all that seriously. The Cardinals denied them World Series glory in the end anyway.

Coming out of the war, the Browns were so bad for a decade they simply had to be given a fresh start. There were noncompetitive teams during this era that still put up decent gate numbers, but the fans in St. Louis simply would not come out for a loser when they had the alternative of supporting the Cardinals. The most memorable Browns highlight for general baseball fans from this dark time in club history came in the second game of an August 19, 1951, doubleheader at home against the Tigers when they sent out a 3-foot-7 dwarf, Eddie Gaedel, to pinch-hit, wearing a uniform with No. ⅛ on his back. Gaedel took a four-pitch walk and was immediately pulled for a pinch runner in his only at bat, but no amount of Bill Veeck stunts or relief appearances from a fifty-something-year-old Satchel Paige could save this team. It became clear that the Browns would have to go after their 1953 season, their seventh-consecutive ninety-loss campaign. Attendance had fallen under four thousand per game on average.

Baltimore was the safe pick as the one-time home of the Orioles of the American League, a franchise that relocated to New York and became the Highlanders in 1903, then the Yankees in 1913. The city also had a perfectly suitable home park in Municipal Stadium, and it could be expanded to forty-eight thousand seats for baseball. There was one problem, though: three other American League teams were expected to oppose effectively sharing a local market with another big league team (Washington) or having another one close enough that it might peel off some of their potential ticket buyers (Philadelphia, more so than New York). This created some space for both Montreal and Toronto—successful clubs in markets that were close but not too close and clearly too big for the International League—to garner some real consideration.[19]

Relocating the Browns to Montreal, however, meant pushing the Royals out of town, a proposition that would have inevitably drawn opposition from the Dodgers. Their owner, Walter O'Malley, was still a few years away from executing his own relocation to sunny Los Angeles, where the team could play in a much bigger park in an untapped market. The Royals limped on for three seasons after the Dodgers headed west for the 1958 season, but this long-distance relationship grew increasingly untenable, and the Royals played their last game on September 7, 1960. The timing just was not quite right for big league baseball in Montreal in 1954. Baltimore won out in the battle for the Browns, and the Orioles were reborn in the American League.

New York was the center of the baseball universe in the 1950s with three excellent clubs divvying up a huge market, but the shocking exits of the Dodgers and Giants for California for the 1958 season left the Big Apple suddenly badly underserved with no National League club. Mayor Robert Wagner intervened by appointing power broker lawyer William Shea as point man for efforts to bring a new team into the city. Shea's original plan was to sweet-talk an existing small-market National League club like the Pirates or Reds into upping sticks, but he was surprised to find little interest there in breaking with their devoted, baseball-loving communities. Shea was not accustomed to being denied what he wanted, but he was at an impasse until an ever-cagey, late-seventies Branch Rickey, effectively retired after rebuilding the Pittsburgh Pirates, saw one last opportunity to do something revolutionary for baseball. His final scheme had potentially huge implications for both the city of Montreal and Jackie Robinson.

Shortly after Opening Day in 1958 Rickey made a public call via Taylor Spink at *The Sporting News* for the creation of a third Major League. "It should be the creation of the present two leagues," he said, and "it should be formed with their cooperation." Of particular interest to readers outside the United States, he also believed the new league could and should be fully internationalized. "Cities like Havana, Toronto, Montreal, Vancouver and those in our country like Miami, Houston, Dallas, Fort Worth, Atlanta, Minneapolis–St. Paul, Denver and even San Diego, Oakland and Seattle want, and should get, big league ball," he argued. Fidel Castro's revolution took Cuba off the table, and Vancouver still remains a long shot as a future expansion site, but every other one of these markets did get big league clubs eventually.

Rickey claimed that it would be easier to add a new eight-team league than add extra franchises to the existing eight-team American and National Leagues. There would inevitably be a talent gap in the beginning, but Rickey thought fans in these new markets would be so overjoyed by the arrival of Major League baseball that they could tolerate a few years of growing pains. He saw deep, patient scouting in Latin America as the path to eventual parity. Insofar as he was concerned, New York absolutely had to be on the list of host cities for the new league after losing the Dodgers and Giants. When Spink tried to shift gears and ask about the "most exciting event of his long and memorable career," Rickey replied, "It hasn't happened yet."[20]

By this point, Rickey walked with a cane and delivered his speeches seated per doctor's orders, but when he spoke, baseball listened. William Shea was certainly interested in this seeming alignment of interests, but so too were investors in Montreal who could envision joining in on the project if only the city and provincial governments would chip in to help subsidize a new, Major League–quality park in the city.[21]

Rickey had another grand vision, and Shea knew money men who could help turn it into a reality. Shea formally announced the creation of the Continental Baseball League on July 27, 1959, with five confirmed members in New York, Houston, the Twin Cities, Denver, and Toronto. Eleven more strong candidates rounded it out. All these new franchises had the backing of heavyweights from local business, politics, or both. Then Shea dropped his bombshell on representatives from the American and National Leagues in an August 18 meeting by introducing the formidable Rickey as the league's new president. Up until this point, the established leagues had at least entertained the notion of a slow-rolled expansion under strict conditions, but they had to take Shea's impatience much more seriously once Rickey formally attached himself to the project.

Every prospective Continental League owner to a man would have preferred to bring a new franchise into either of the existing leagues—this was, by far, a much safer bet than attempting a start-up league—but it was abundantly clear that the Major Leagues did not share Shea and Rickey's sense of urgency. The Continental League continued planning over the winter of 1959–60 for a 1961 launch, naming Dallas–Fort Worth, Atlanta, and Buffalo as the remaining three franchises. American and National League executives were left scrambling in a bid to stall just long enough to keep antitrust crusaders in Congress from resolving the standoff through legislation.[22] Montreal was not on this list of eight finalists, but everything was still in flux, and there was always the possibility of subbing in for one of the weaker candidates, say Buffalo, if more money and firmer support was in place.

But what did any of this have to do with Jackie Robinson? The first serious talk of Robinson graduating into a managerial role came just before the start of 1951 season when he was just thirty-two and still had plenty of good seasons as a player in front of him. After collecting Rookie of the Year honors in 1947 and an MVP Award in 1949, he had established himself as one of the most intuitive players in the Major Leagues. Black players had proven their physical talent on the diamond, but it remained to be seen how long ancient prejudices would keep them from showing off their intellect from the dugout.

It broke in the papers that Walter O'Malley had approached Robinson during spring training about taking over as Royals manager when his playing days were through. There was no comment from Robinson himself, but O'Malley claimed that Robinson "would be both delighted and honored to tackle this managerial post." He would be assigned to Montreal to start out for the obvious reason that the Royals' fans absolutely loved him and he "always had a warm spot in his heart" for them. This was a very preliminary discussion rather than a formal offer attached to a specific salary.[23] The thinking behind a Robinson-Montreal reunion was animated by all the same factors that Branch Rickey had considered in 1945.

Flash forward five years from the initial talk of a manager's job in the Dodgers system to 1956, and Robinson had finally collected an elusive World Series ring. He had also begun to lose a step on the field, as evidenced by two consecutive seasons of a sub-.300 average and declining stolen base totals. The postplaying career O'Malley had pointed to in 1951 was then fast approaching.

At the time, no one knew for sure that Game Seven of the 1956 World Series on October 10 would be Robinson's final big league game, but that very day a columnist at *Le Devoir* published a rumor that he would join the Royals' coaching staff the following year. His ultimate role was a little more complicated, given that manager Greg

Mulleavy was still under contract for one more year and was just a season removed from guiding the Royals to another International League pennant. Would Robinson be interested in taking a lesser role with Montreal while he waited for the manager's job to open up? Would the Dodgers risk stoking tensions with southern-born white players by appointing him to the role? No doubt the Royals and their fans wanted Robinson back in any capacity, but there was plenty of uncertainty over whether the parent club would ultimately sign off and Robinson would be content to bide his time.[24]

Three days later, it broke that the rumors were true and the Dodgers had extended Robinson a $25,000 player-manager contract to take over the Royals. This salary was a king's ransom for a Minor League assignment, but it amounted to a $6,500 per year pay cut from the $31,500 he earned in his final season as a Dodger. There was also no guarantee here that he could someday move up to the big leagues.[25] Though it was not reported at the time, this post did not come with the historic honor of becoming the first Black Minor League manager; that had already been claimed elsewhere in Québec by Sam Bankhead, a former Negro Leaguer turned player-manager of the Class-C Farnham Pirates back in 1951. In any event, Robinson was in no rush to decide and wanted to take some time to decompress after the World Series. He did join the Dodgers on an exhausting month-long but well-paid postseason barnstorming tour of Hawaii and Japan immediately after the World Series while he considered his options.[26]

O'Malley withdrew the Royals' offer before Robinson had a chance to definitively answer it. Robinson's enthusiasm for playing was badly waning before the shocking news on December 13, 1956, that he had been traded to the crosstown rival Giants for an ineffective reliever and $30,000 in cash. The Giants had little talent beyond Willie Mays and were coming off a 67-87 season that offered little hope for growth in 1957, while manager Leo Durocher, a strong early Robinson backer during the 1940s, had already been ushered out the door after the 1955 season. To many, going along with this trade would have amounted to an ignominious end for a Dodgers legend; Robinson took little flack when he opted to retire instead of reporting to the Giants.

There's no mention in Robinson's second and final autobiography, *I Never Had It Made* from 1972, of how seriously he entertained the notion of joining the Royals' coaching staff for 1957. What we do know is that he was still a young man of thirty-seven with three children under age twelve and that staying in the New York area would be infinitely less disruptive for his family. Staying put would also open up more lucrative job opportunities as well as enabling Robinson to fully participate in civil rights campaigns and political life, two of his biggest post-baseball priorities. The trade imbroglio had also poisoned his relationship with O'Malley for years to come, and he had no interest in continuing to work with the Dodgers organization in any capacity. Royals fans were the unfortunate victims of circumstances completely beyond their control.

Robinson indeed put on a new uniform in late 1957: the sharp, tailored business suit of the Mad Men era. The Chock full o'Nuts company was a New York staple, evolving from a Roaring Twenties nut seller to a ubiquitous coffee shop and lunch counter that offered hearty sandwiches for a great value during the Depression years. Its Jewish founder, William Black (originally Schwartz), had a very progressive track record on hiring Black staff for his franchises, and he approached Robinson with an offer to become the company's vice president for personnel. His business was in the process of expanding to over eighty stores across New York and had also rolled out its signature coffee in area supermarkets. Robinson's star power would elevate the Chock Full o'Nuts brand, while he stood to earn handsomely and become one of the leading Black business executives in the country. He dismissed criticism from those who said Black was just using him to undercut unionization efforts and genuinely believed he could help make working conditions better for the company's Black employees. This offer got an easy yes.

However satisfying his new corporate role was, there was no clean break between Robinson and baseball, and it seemed entirely possible that he could be tempted back onto the field under the right conditions—namely, a big league opportunity rather than a Minor League assignment and serious money that was comparable to what he earned with Chock Full o'Nuts. Baseball executives in Québec never gave up hope that someday he might be lured back into the dugout.

News broke in early September 1959 that a Montreal consortium led by construction tycoon Hy Richman had made an official bid for a Continental League franchise. More intriguingly, they approached Robinson about joining the endeavor as the new club's manager, and he had given a qualified yes. His condition was that he was in so long as he could also join the new ownership group, lining him up to mark two more historic firsts in postintegration baseball. Richman indicated that he would consider the request as he tried to line up other investors who could pool together a league-mandated $1.25 million for startup fees. The other crucial aspect of the project was securing municipal and provincial funding for the construction of a new twenty-five-thousand-seat stadium with ample parking.[27] Optimists believed the Richman group might ultimately put together a better package than, say, Buffalo and join the Continental League's founding eight franchises.

The potential implications of these ongoing negotiations were revolutionary: Jackie Robinson had a serious opportunity to go from the first Black player in the reintegrated Major Leagues to the first Black Major League manager *and* first Black owner outside the Negro Leagues. As Rickey and other ownership groups around North America certainly knew, the Continental League's prospects for success would be much improved if a superstar like Robinson threw his support behind it. The more hype he and the owners could generate, the more viable the project would become.[28]

For a second time, Montrealers were left disappointed, as a potential reunion with Robinson fell through in the late planning stages. Rickey's supporters in Congress came fairly close to passing a bill that would have eliminated baseball's antitrust exemption, a failed effort that nonetheless warned American and National League owners that there could well be an imposed political solution if they continued to stall on measures to bring Major League baseball to growing new markets. They had little choice but to negotiate with would-be members of the Continental League and called them in for talks in Chicago on August 2, 1960, just eight months out from the start of the new league's inaugural season.

There was plenty of bluster from both sides before Lou Perini of the Milwaukee Braves got to mutually agreeable terms: the existing Major Leagues would eventually take on eight new teams, four in the short term and four more in due course. There was no promise then as to which candidate sites would come first and no firm timeline for expansion, but the Continental League group accepted these terms on the spot, and everyone walked away from Rickey's dream of creating a third Major League. Opting for the surer-seeming long-term bet rather than building something new and uncertain from the ground up produced winners and losers; it took all the way to 1969 for the American and National Leagues to finally add the last of the eight expansion teams they had promised. Less time elapsed between John F. Kennedy's pledge that a man would walk on the moon and Neil Armstrong's "giant leap for mankind."

The National League expansion committee announced new teams for the 1962 season, William Shea's New York Mets and the oil-money-fueled Houston Colt .45s (renamed the Astros in 1965), during the 1960 World Series. The American League waited longer to announce its own expansion, but then moved much faster during the Winter Meetings with a complicated sleight of hand. In October 1960, the Washington Senators announced they would be moving to the Twin Cities for 1961, and then a new ownership group was granted an expansion franchise Washington Senators 2.0 that would be built up from scratch. The second Senators franchise ultimately relocated to Dallas and became the Texas Rangers in 1972. Actor Gene Autry, the Singing Cowboy, negotiated the purchase of the expansion Los Angeles Angels, the second new American League team for 1961.

But what of the promise to add four more new teams in a second wave of expansion? There was good news and bad news for Montreal's baseball fans as the 1960s approached their close. The amazing announcement, anticipated for a generation, finally dropped in May 1968 that they were going to get their own Major League team the following year, along with the San Diego Padres. But by this point the window for a formal Robinson reunion had most definitely closed. He had been insulin-dependent for years, possibly as early as the later stages of his playing career, while he suffered through constant leg pain and hypertension. His eyesight was also deteriorating to the point that driving had become difficult. All of these symptoms would have been exacerbated by frequent air travel.

Robinson's rapid physical decline through his forties was widely known around baseball, and the Expos never even considered offering him the manager's job for their inaugural 1969 season despite all of the sentimental appeal. He had spent years writing newspaper columns and making public appearances calling for Black participation in baseball management but had to watch from the sidelines as Gene Mauch took a job that would likely have been his years earlier if not for the impatience of Continental League owners back in 1960.[29] It took until the final week of the 1974 season before future Hall of Fame slugger Frank Robinson assumed player-manager duties for Cleveland, earning the distinction of becoming the first Black manager in the American or National League.

There was a consolation prize, though. Robinson had joined ABC's *Game of the Week* team in 1965 as an analyst, becoming the first Black former player on any broadcast team on American television. Despite badly failing health, he later joined the Expos television broadcast team in a part-time capacity for the 1972 season, giving what he could to his fans in Montreal, with the little time he had left.

There was plenty of making-do all around in the club's early years. It took a lot of charity to describe the Expos first home, Jarry Park Stadium, as Major League quality, and the team had little offense behind their first star player, Rusty "Le Grand Orange" Staub. On the business side, the Expos had enormous difficulty getting potentially lucrative English-language TV broadcasts out to a national audience in a country that was roughly three-quarters anglophone, a challenge that left the team perpetually underfunded right up until a cash crunch finally killed it in 2004. But the lemons turned into lemonade that summer of 1972 for fans of a team that had limited talent and was seven more years from finishing above .500 for the first time. Robinson was joined in the revolving door of TV color commentators by his old double play partner, Pee Wee Reese, and Yankees great Mickey Mantle, who had also been dabbling in baseball broadcasting for NBC.[30]

In the pressroom before Robinson's first game from Jarry Park that summer, one of the Expos reporters moved toward him with purpose to say, "Welcome home, Mr. Robinson," a deliberate sentiment that was shared throughout the room.[31] They were grateful to be working in his presence once again, even if the experience was years overdue and not in the capacity many locals had hoped for back in 1956 or 1959. Still, it was something, and it happened just in the nick of time.

Robinson made one final public appearance at Riverfront Stadium in Cincinnati to throw out the first pitch before Game Two of the 1972 Reds-Athletics World Series. He was fully gray, badly hobbled by a 1968 heart attack, and visually impaired to the point that he did not recognize a well-wisher in the tunnel to the field until Pee Wee Reese landed a big hug on him.[32] Robinson had initially declined MLB's offer to mark the silver anniversary of his Dodgers debut at the World Series as a protest against the lack of progress in desegregation of baseball's front offices. He was right to be frustrated as the game had reached a strange and infuriating crossroads; the Pirates had in 1971 featured a game with an all–Black and Latino lineup, yet still not a single Black manager or general manager was in any of MLB's twenty-four front offices.

In the end, Robinson decided not to pass up the opportunity to make a direct and meaningful statement to a television audience in the tens of millions. Commissioner Bowie Kuhn was standing next to him at the time as he thanked the late Branch Rickey for his vision, Pee Wee Reese for his friendship, and his family for their support. He did not speak long, closing by saying, "I am extremely proud and pleased to be here this afternoon, but must admit that I am going to be tremendously more pleased and more proud when I look at that third-base coaching line one day and see a Black face managing in baseball. Thank you very much."[33]

Robinson did not live to see that day. After the game he retreated home to Stamford, Connecticut, where he collapsed and then passed away from another heart attack just over a week later at only fifty-three years old. The end was foreseeable to those close to him, but the baseball world was nevertheless devastated, no fan base more so than in Montreal.

Québec newspapers ran the sad news above the fold on page one, while businesses took out in-memoriams and columnists took a final trip down memory lane with Robinson and the '46 Royals. *Montreal-Matin* immediately called on city hall to find a street or park to name in Robinson's honor then gave a full two-page photo spread of mourners at his funeral in a Brooklyn church. *La Presse* reported that well-known shoe shiner Tiger Jack would mark the passing of his idol by closing his business for three hours while Robinson was laid to rest in Brooklyn on the 27th. Other papers carried the official condolence message from Mayor Jean Drapeau to the Robinsons, reminding them that Montrealers had been following his post-Royals career with "pride and affection" for twenty-six years.[34]

Roland Sabourin at *Le Soleil* noted wistfully that Robinson appeared to have aged terribly when he appeared on television during the World Series, but no one thought at the time that he would be gone so soon. He argued that the best posthumous honor would be for baseball to heed Robinson's final call and open the door to a Black manager. The Expos had an excellent candidate on hand in Larry Doby, the first Black player in the American league and the Expos' hitting coach under Gene Mauch. Ernie Banks, Maury Wills, and Willie Mays also deserved consideration, too, as eventually would Frank Robinson. Sabourin pushed him to the bottom of his list because he still had a few more productive years as a player left in him, but it was indeed Frank Robinson who got the nod in the end from Cleveland in 1974.[35]

After his short Negro Leagues stint with Kansas City, Robinson played in just one organization and the lead in celebrating his on-field legacy most certainly belonged to the Dodgers. That did not mean, however, that the newborn Expos felt as though they had to completely defer to them; the Royals were cut loose by the Dodgers then folded, which created a fair opening for the Expos to step forward as the guardians of the Robinson-Montreal baseball-integration story. Over the next three decades, a scrappy, chronically underfunded organization did everything it could to promote the local memory of Jackie Robinson. The pattern was to celebrate him in partnership with the Dodgers when possible or on its own if need be.

Grand celebrations usually fall in anniversary years, but sometimes circumstances force one's hand, as they did for the Expos in 1982.

Regardless of whichever rank baseball has fallen to in national sports popularity standings, most of the best traditions began there and were later copied by upstarts in football, basketball, and elsewhere. These include the Hall of Fame, a hallowed and sacred ground, and the All-Star Game, the Midsummer Classic, which began in 1933 as a best-on-best showcase that pitted the two leagues against each other after days of pomp and ceremony.

Jarry Park's days were numbered from the moment it opened in 1969, but everyone understood it was just a temporary placeholder. Montreal experienced a great building boom in the 1960s in preparation for host duties of Expo 67, a massive, half-yearlong World's Fair coinciding with Canada's centennial anniversary. All told, Expo 67 drew over fifty million paying spectators in the biggest tourism bonanza the city had ever seen. This remarkably successful collaboration between the municipal, provincial, and federal governments, along with the job growth and tax revenues it generated, got many thinking in 1970 about making another big bid to host the Summer Olympics, then the crown jewel of international sporting events.

The 1976 Olympic games themselves are mostly remembered positively. For Canadians, it was their first opportunity to host—summer or winter—on home soil and a brief window to imagine that there was a semblance of national unity in the wake of high-profile kidnappings and bombings at the hands of Front de libération du Québec (FLQ) terrorists earlier in the decade and the imminent fall election of the separatist Parti Québécois. From a security perspective, it went off without a hitch, unlike the absolute debacle in Munich four years earlier when eleven members of the Israeli team were killed in an Olympic Village kidnapping by Palestinian militants, which was followed by a botched rescue attempt from West German security services. For actual sports fans, fourteen-year-old Romanian Nadia Comaneci stole the show as the first gymnast to record a perfect 10.0 score, and an American boxing team loaded with talented athletes like Sugar Ray Leonard and Leon Spinks shredded all of the competition.

And yet from a financial perspective, the games were a sheer and utter catastrophe that have served as a half-century-long cautionary tale for prospective host sites, particularly those in democracies where those who flagrantly waste public dollars will be held accountable by both the voters and prosecutors. Bread-not-circuses campaigners against Olympic bids often begin with "Remember Montreal."

Mayor Jean Drapeau promised at the outset of the bid process that "the Olympics can no more run a deficit than a man can have a baby," but Montreal became globally synonymous with corruption after running up a bill that was thirteen times the original estimate. The showpiece of all its infrastructure projects was going to be an enormous seventy-six-thousand seat stadium with a design that local sports writer Jack Todd described as "space-age fascist." Unions went on strike as their leaders solicited bribes to pick up the pace of work. Contractors built secret luxury properties for politicians who decided who got which piece of the pie. Oil crisis–induced inflation drove building costs to the moon. Honest accounting agents in the government had no hope of overseeing this firehose of cash on a project that was so much bigger than anything the province had ever attempted before.

The final bill came to a staggering C$1.6 billion (almost $9 billion in 2024 U.S. dollars), C$1.1 billion of which went to the ghastly stadium alone. It was meant to be called Olympic Stadium, or the Big O for short. The Big Owe it came to be known instead, as the city struggled for thirty years to pay off the debt it accrued to build it.[36] Every dollar that went to service this debt was one that did not go to roads, schools, or anything else that would have served Montrealers far better.

This white elephant became the new home of the luckless Expos, a small-market team that moved from a glorified Minor League park to a fifty-six-thousand-seat cavern that was too big even for a potential World Series crowd. At least the stadium was new and modern, right up until the mid-1980s when terrifyingly large parts of the tower and the concrete facade started raining down onto the field or the concourse around the field from time to time. Home runs from left center to right center fell not into the laps of eager fans in the bleachers but into a seemingly endless black expanse of a lower concourse. The team could never afford the renovations necessary to make the stadium feel safe, much less like an actual ballpark, because Canada's primary Ontario-based English-language sports broadcaster was willing to pay no more than C$5,000 per game in television fees, just five percent of what they gave the Toronto Blue Jays.[37]

The Expos began life eight years earlier, but the fix was in during the battle to become Canada's Team. And so the Expos played out the string until 2004 on mismatched, discolored, and rotting patches of Astroturf, in front of crowds smaller than the AAA Royals drew a half century earlier, as their park slowly crumbled around them like some Cold War relic from the wrong side of the Iron Curtain. They and their fans deserved so much better.

Back in 1982, however, the Expos' future was still full of possibilities. Their financial limits had forced the team to draft and develop as though their lives depended on it, a strategy that worked well for over two decades from the mid-1970s through the 1990s. They made their first playoff appearance during the strike-shortened 1981 season and then took their division series matchup from the Phillies before falling to the Dodgers in a tight NLCS that went the full five games. If not for a ninth inning home run from Rick Monday, they would have punched their ticket to the World Series.

Plenty of homegrown star power was on the roster, including future Hall of Famers Andre "The Hawk" Dawson, Tim "Rock" Raines, and Gary "Kid" Carter, who endeared himself to the home fans unlike any baseball player since Jackie Robinson. Carter, who spent twelve years with the Expos, helped one of the francophone ball boys with his homework in exchange for some tutoring with his own French skills. Carter was an uninhibited language learner, the absolute best kind, and he was always happy to chat with francophone fans in their native tongue. He stood out as the only Expos player who would agree to record French-language television ads.[38]

The 1980s were the last decade of the Astroturf era, before bespoke baseball-only parks returned to favor again in the 1990s and embarrassing municipal stadiums got embargoed for host duties for high-profile events. MLB awarded the 1982 All-Star Game to Montreal, and, better still, fans had voted in three Expos position players as National League starters. This was the first time the game had traveled outside the United States, and the Expos were determined to make the most of their time under the international spotlight in their newish park.

Few people would have looked more out of place at a high-profile team sporting event than brainy, balding intellectual Prime Minister Pierre Trudeau, brilliant mischief always lurking behind his eyes. But there he was sitting behind home plate with Commissioner Kuhn and Commissioner Emeritus Happy Chandler, wearing a sharp white blazer and his trademark red rose pinned to his lapel. Trudeau did have a legitimate connection to the game as the son of a former Royals owner, though it took him some courage to watch from the stands rather than the safety of a private box. The prime minister's poll numbers were tanking badly, and his appearance at an event such as this might have evoked a bit of feel-good popular recollection of Expo 67. At worst, it was an opportunity to come back to his hometown for a few days and watch a ballgame. He was coming to the end of a very long and extremely polarizing career, anyway. Whether using the carrot—enshrining French-language rights into the Canadian Constitution and aggressively opening up the civil service to francophones—or the stick—invoking the War Measures Act in October 1970 to send soldiers into the streets after the FLQ kidnapped British Trade Consul James Cross and then Québec Labour Minister Pierre Laporte—he was never one to waver. The question of whether Québec could find its way to a reasonable accommodation to life within Canada was left to the post-Trudeau generation of federalists and separatists to resolve.

American viewers, at least those who were not hockey fans, were pleasantly bewildered by PA announcements in both of Canada's official languages, the custom for professional sports in both Montreal and Ottawa. Old Mordecai Richler had used a column in the Sunday *New York Times* to prepare visiting Americans for doom and gloom in a hellscape version of his home town, painting a dramatic picture of bank robberies galore, astronomical taxes, gas prices so high it looked like the Oil Shock of 1973 had never ended, tourists forced to try to use the first language of most of the city's residents, and even the once glorious Canadiens in the doldrums; were it not for the Expos, Montrealers would simply have nothing to live for![39]

And yet it was another All-Star Game that looked like pretty much all the others. The playing field was festooned with colorful red, white, and blue bunting; the game was delayed by overly long player introductions; and the fans were drenched in heaping doses of nostalgia. Despite Richler's warnings, somehow there were zero tourist casualties. American visitors all got what they paid for: a pleasant mid-week vacation to one of Canada's great gems of a city for a wonderful carnival of baseball.

It had been a decade since Jackie Robinson last took to a ball field and thirty-six years since he had debuted with the Royals, but the Expos decided that he had to go front and center during the pregame ceremony. Legendary ABC sportscaster Howard Cosell conducted a pregame interview with Rachel Robinson, who was smiling in a pretty violet dress and taking a pleasant trip down memory lane about her time with Jackie in the city. In her minute on air, she told over thirty-five million American TV viewers the story about how easily she had negotiated a deal for their apartment on de Gaspé. "It was my first encounter with an atmosphere where there was no discrimination, where we were totally supported warmly, and the love that we took from Montreal really sustained us in more difficult days when we didn't have that kind of support," she said. "And so coming home to Montreal to me is coming back to really the birthplace of my belief in brotherhood. I really believe it can happen."[40] She was ushered back out on the field alongside Pee Wee Reese for a hearty mid-game round of applause from the Expos faithful.

The Expos had proudly staked Montreal's claim to a big part of Jackie Robinson's legacy, and they never looked back. During the professional-baseball interregnum from the Royals' demise at the end of the 1960 season and the Expos' arrival in 1969, the short-lived Montreal Beavers of the Continental Football League (not to be confused with the Canadian Football League, the other CFL, but an American upstart that played by standard four-down rules) had grabbed the torch in the fall of 1966 by proclaiming the original Jackie Robinson Day with the intention of fundraising for scholarships for the city's ten thousand Black youth. This happened to be the twentieth anniversary year of Robinson's debut with the Royals, and many Montreal-based athletes from various sports were eager to come out and mark it.

Buzzie Bavasi of the Los Angeles Dodgers had signed off on the project, and Robinson himself offered his support, but one of the driving forces appears to have been Herb Trawick, Robinson's old friend and former Alouettes star, who had stayed behind in Montreal and was serving as a line coach for the Beavers by this point. Robinson had bought a stake in his own Continental Football League team, the Brooklyn Dodgers (no relation to the baseball Dodgers), and their upcoming road game against the Beavers had sparked the original idea to collaborate on a civic-minded project. Everyone in Montreal was looking forward to seeing Robinson again—in fact, the game was the Beavers' first sellout—and it seemed only fitting to mark the occasion.[41] And so in a strange twist, the proto–Jackie Robinson Day commemoration actually took place on the gridiron, in Montreal, rather than on a baseball field somewhere in his home country.

Events such as these were ephemeral, though, and fan momentum in Montreal grew for something more permanent. In 1977 the Expos added an easily missed bronze relief of Robinson in a Royals cap on a pillar next to Olympic Stadium's 200-level beer garden, but they guarded it with stanchions and potted plants that screamed, "Keep away!" to passersby.[42] In any event, this modest marker only told a known baseball story to people who were for the most part already baseball fans and had heard it before. Something was lacking to this installation, and many fans wanted the club to do better.

By the mid-1980s Montreal's baseball fans began leaning in harder on efforts to incorporate Robinson into their own story. As spring training began in 1985, *La Presse* marked the fortieth anniversary of Robinson's decision to sign with the Royals by reprinting some of its October 1945 reporting on the surprising announcement, along with spring 1946 wire stories on his travails in Florida and his triumphant debut game on the road in Jersey City. This helped remind readers that it was time to do something bigger and permanent to mark Montreal's important role in baseball integration.

All the way back in 1984, Councilor Abe Limonchik, the son of Ukrainian immigrants and head of the Montreal Citizens Movement faction, pushed city hall to vote on commemorating Jackie Robinson somewhere in the city. Some had floated the idea of erecting a statue in front of the francophone high school that had been built where the old Delorimier Stadium once stood, but for the moment Limonchik was more inclined to put Robinson's name on a sporting complex and build a Jackie Robinson Museum somewhere in the city.

For those behind the effort, this was as much of a declaration of Montreal's progressive values as a tribute to a single unforgettable player.[43] Limonchik was a chemist by trade who got involved in municipal politics during the dirty, Wild West early 1970s lead-up to the 1976 Summer Olympics. He dedicated the next quarter century to transparency, good government, and, most important, bridge-building between the city's anglophone and francophone communities. He also happened to be a rabid Royals fan who had seen Robinson play at Delorimier Stadium on many occasions during his boyhood.[44]

Petty politics stood in the way of Limonchik's proposal, which was met with nearly universal enthusiasm around the city. The aging mayor, Jean Drapeau, had done many wonderful things for Montreal—building its metro and hosting Expo 67 above all—but he had also been one of the primary authors of the Olympic fiasco. He kept getting reelected, albeit by severely diminished margins in each successive race, and was growing increasingly rigid as he approached the end of his final term in office. Drapeau could be described as either a hands-on or dictatorial municipal boss, but either way he had no tolerance for dissent and demanded total control over the script. Limonchik headed up a municipal opposition faction that was pushing for cleaner government, so the mayor refused to let council vote on Limonchik's Robinson motion on the grounds that the majority had no obligation to take it up.[45] The sportsplex and museum motion would have easily sailed through council if not for this self-serving obstructionism.

As the backbiting ensued, Drapeau claimed that he had blocked Limonchik's proposal because city council already had something for Robinson in the works without elaborating what or where. Drapeau also claimed that it was inappropriate to give Royals fans like Limonchik implied credit for Robinson's future success and that any future commemoration would have to focus more narrowly on the player himself. This flew in the face of Jackie Robinson's own public statements of gratitude to Royals fans and everything Limonchik and thousands of others had seen with their own eyes back in 1946, but the focus had already shifted beyond baseball or civil rights to a personality conflict in city hall. Limonchik told reporters, "[The mayor] just could not raise himself to acknowledge that anybody else has played any sort of role in the history of this city."[46]

Palace intrigue did not permanently derail a Robinson tribute, but it badly undermined the civic-awareness campaign to mark the fortieth anniversary of Robinson's Royals debut. The Expos and city officials were able to cobble something together late in 1986 with just weeks remaining in the regular season, unveiling plans for a future Robinson memorial on the site of the former Delorimier Stadium during a press conference on August 11. (By the time it was actually built, however, the Expos biggest Black star who had come out for the plan unveiling ceremony had moved on to the Cubs as a free agent.) They also invited Rachel Robinson up for a formal, in-stadium commemoration during a September 3 home game against the Dodgers, their final road appearance at Olympic Stadium that year. The mayor's office promised that a model of the Delorimier-site monument would be ready to show the public before the game, while the Expos pledged to turn over part of their gate receipts from the 3rd to help finance the project.[47]

This game was actually the worst-attended of the midweek three-game set, as just 8,668 fans came out to see a pair of sub-.500 teams that had long fallen out of their respective playoff races. Many Expos fans might have legitimately wondered why they were being asked to pick up part of the relatively small tab for a memorial the club and the city should have been able to easily cover on their own. Others would have sighed at all the Drapeau-friendly media coverage in papers like *Le Journal de Montreal* that wanted to give the mayor sole credit for coming up with the idea of a monument. A worthy project got started with a whiff of poverty and desperation that felt a little bush-league to some.

The slapdash nature of this whole effort is best illustrated by a misunderstanding within the local Friends of Jackie Robinson fund-raising group. Apparently, it had not invited Rachel Robinson to a September 4 working lunch at the Montefiore Club, and when questioned about this gross oversight the unattributable excuses started flying in the press. One was that some in the group did not want her to "steal" credit for their efforts. Another, slightly more defensible claim was that she had a mid-afternoon flight to catch back to New York. Why then the meeting could not have been pushed forward to breakfast was a question that will never be answered. But the single worst excuse of all from some in the group was a perception—denied after the fact by the proprietors—that Rachel Robinson would not have been permitted to enter the Montefiore, a private, men's only establishment.[48] Imagine how good the food must have been to convince organizers of a meal to honor a hero pioneer in a venue that would not even have served his widow.

In any event, something, somewhere, was going to happen. There were two primary options for a new outdoor commemorative site, either in the formerly mixed, working-class, docklands-adjacent neighborhoods—not necessarily in Little Burgundy, home to Montreal's Black community, but not far from it—or on the former site of Delorimier Stadium in a less multicultural setting, albeit with a much more direct tie to the Royals. The latter won out.

Delorimier Stadium had been razed back in 1965, replaced in 1971 with École Polyvalante Pierre-Dupuy, a francophone high school, and a pair of soccer fields. Baseball was no longer played here, but this was a completely logical choice for a Robinson-Royals marker—theoretically, at least.

The Delorimier-site monument was unveiled on May 16, 1987, featuring the second statue of Robinson in North America. (Robinson's alma mater, UCLA, had beaten the Expos by two years.) The Expos held off on the unveiling for a month after what is now accepted as Jackie Robinson Day, April 15, so they could sync it up with another visit from the Dodgers and invite Rachel Robinson back yet again to throw out the ceremonial first pitch.

What currently stands at the Delorimier site is a home plate–shaped bronze plaque, lengthened beyond standard dimensions to accommodate French-only text and elevated to belt height on a gray plinth. It sits at second in a small infield with bases and baselines painted white, while red-gray bricks stand in for infield grass. A walkway separates the infield from a grass crescent bordering all around with more bricks meant to represent the outfield. The backdrop to this monument is layers of chain-link fence, red from the backstop that is part of the installation and galvanized silver on the school fencing just behind it that is not, then parking lots, sports fields, and Pierre-Dupuy itself. The plaque reads as follows:

> This commemorative plaque honors Jackie Robinson's stay with the Royals team and marks the former location of De Lorimier Stadium.
>
> While playing for the Royals, Jackie Robinson became the first player of color to play in the professional leagues. Jackie Robinson bequeathed his glory to his family and to all of baseball and earned an important place among the immortals of this sport.
>
> In the minds of Montrealers, Jackie Robinson will always remain a symbol of excellence, courage and perseverance.

As currently constituted, this now statueless installation leaves visitors with a powerfully underwhelming impression, as though the project is unfinished or was abandoned part way through construction. Those in the building trades would attest that a small crew of Laborers' International Union of North America (LIUNA) volunteers could have built the entire thing on a Saturday, raising the question of why it took so long to accomplish something so modest.

Mayor Drapeau had gotten his way, but he missed what real baseball fans had wanted and embarrassed himself for posterity when he described his memories of 1946 on the day of the plan's unveiling. "I was thirty years old when Robinson joined the Royals, yet I never witnessed any hostile gestures around immigrants. The Chinese who starched our shirts, the Italian who repaired our shoes and the Black who served us on the train were fellow citizens," he told reporters.[49]

This was not exactly the message of progressive inclusiveness that Limonchik and his supporters in the Friends of Jackie Robinson fundraising association had wanted to project, but it was the one the city got from a geriatric mayor who stuck around long past his best-before date. Robinson, Montreal fans, and the Expos all deserved another at bat.

The biggest problem with the Delorimier-site monument, aside from its amateurish design, was that few Robinson pilgrims would end up seeing it in what had become an almost entirely residential neighborhood. It originally featured a striking bronze Robinson statue (albeit with no plinth or descriptive plaque) as part of a $50,000 investment from Expos owner Charles Bronfman, the Expos, the Dodgers, and the city. Years of complaints that the statue was hidden from public view at Delorimier and that poor maintenance of the trash-strewn minipark that surrounded it was a disgrace led the city to quietly relocate the statue to Olympic Stadium itself, an entirely more appropriate location that allowed it to shine as a piece of public art even if Robinson had never set foot there. In the spring of 1989, Montrealers finally got the proper Jackie Robinson memorial they wanted.

The statue was a relatively early work from Jules Lasalle, a Montreal native who had trained some in France after graduating from the Université de Québec à Montreal (UQAM) in 1979. His first major work of public art, on the waterfront in René Lévesque Park in Lachine, Montreal, titled *Monica*, is a giant sculpted head of a woman in three separate pieces that evokes Easter Island. He then created *Forces*, a closed white fist made of concrete, marble, and silica holding three stainless steel cables anchored to the surrounding grass. This piece was installed in 1986 at the Lachine Canal as a tribute to the workers and engineers who had built this impressive piece of transportation infrastructure. Both are quite striking, and Lasalle would clearly have been the best local candidate to tackle the Jackie Robinson statue in the mid-1980s. Guatemala-born architect Carlos Martinez worked with Lasalle on sketching out a design that incorporated children, a request of the statue committee.

The statue features a uniformed Robinson smiling down on two children, one Black and one white, who appear to be roughly five to eight years old. Robinson is hatless, which slightly deemphasizes his role as an athlete and elevates the sociocultural aspect of his time in the city.

Lasalle made an interesting but understandable decision to use the road jersey with *Montreal* written in cursive script rather than the home version that read *Royals*. The road gray versus home white colors would not show in bronze, so Lasalle gave himself a bit of creative license to explicitly localize the tableau. Both boys are staring up at Robinson with expressions of joy and awe, the far one, the Black boy, with his left hand on the other's shoulder and the near one, the white boy, holding his hand out, palm up, as Robinson puts a baseball into it as part of a moving handshake. Direct physical contact between all three emphasizes Robinson's close connection to both his fans and the community across racial lines.

The ashy gray concrete of Olympic Stadium itself is the grand backdrop to the statue, but over the years the city has added pleasant landscaping upgrades around its base, with pops of yellow sunflowers and purple barberry bushes spring through fall. There are now spotlights on the statue as well. The block-lettered French text on the bronze plaque mounted to the concrete plinth underneath the sculpture reads as follows:

> Jackie Robinson. 1919–1972. In the minds of Montrealers, Jackie Robinson will forever remain a symbol of excellence, courage and perseverance. The first coloured player to play in the major leagues, he bestowed his glory to his own and to all of baseball and earned an important place among baseball's immortals. This monument was inaugurated on May 16, 1987, by Mrs Rachel Robinson, widow of Jackie Robinson, in the presence of municipal authorities from the city of Montreal and of the Expos Ltd baseball club.

Some of this text was directly recycled on a new plaque added at the Delorimier site, which many thought lacked context even when it did feature the statue. More important, though, the messaging here differs slightly by making no mention of the defunct Royals club or its former park, choosing instead to dedicate its limited word count to something more durable: the connection between a special player and the fan community that stood behind him.

So far as tourists and baseball fans are concerned, the city of Montreal's Robinson statue at Olympic Stadium was a clear win, so much so that Jules Lasalle was selected to create another statue of Maurice Richard outside the Bell Centre in 2001, a year after the Rocket's passing. A near carbon copy of the Robinson statue went up 1990 in Daytona Beach at the ballpark where he played his first spring training game as a Dodger in 1946, since rechristened Jackie Robinson Ballpark. The primary difference here is that Robinson is wearing a home Royals jersey, unlike the original, and the accompanying plaque text began from scratch with a locally appropriate story about his City Island Ballpark debut.

Christopher Stride, Ffion Thomas, and Maureen M. Smith, academics who have explored Robinson statutory, claim that Lasalle's pieces use "a motif of racial integration between Robinson, players and fans . . . [that] speaks not only of a city in which sport is integrated but one where the roots of society are founded on racially integrated principles, a culture that Robinson is witnessing rather than creating." This invites first-time viewers into an inclusive story in a way that a standalone statue of a single player would not. That said, they also argue that "perversely, this 'tolerance branding' diminishes community acknowledgement of the impact Robinson's career and character had upon them. That is, by promoting themselves as historic beacons of equality, these cities or communities are effectively claiming that they were not in need of the transformation in hearts and minds that Robinson influenced."[50]

Some might agree. Yet again some might view this position as too ivory-towered, while others might counter that the argument lands better on Daytona Beach, a moderately progressive place in 1946 by the standards of Jim Crow Florida, than on Montreal. It is perfectly understandable that Daytona Beach wanted to mark a historic site of great significance to the American civil rights story and that replicating a popular existing statue was more economical than commissioning a new one. Those with less cynicism would simply conclude that the original Montreal statue, once relocated to Olympic Stadium, was a better than fine result that came out of a sustained, grassroots campaign to dutifully honor Robinson's legacy through public art.

The Expos made a much better effort in 1996 to mark the fiftieth-anniversary celebration of Robinson's Royals season than they did in 1986 with a hasty effort to fundraise for the Delorimier monument. Commissioner Peter Ueberroth had dedicated the 1987 season to Robinson's memory—it was forty years since his Dodger debut and fifteen since his death—but MLB was still many years away from an annual league-wide commemoration. The Expos decision to mark 1996 rather than 1997 as a golden Robinson anniversary was both assertive and appropriate even if it did not ultimately succeed in convincing baseball to adopt his Royals debut as a shared marker for baseball integration.

As always, though, the Expos held their first official Jackie Robinson Day commemoration on May 24, 1996, while the Dodgers were visiting rather than fully marching off on their own by setting a more locally meaningful date like his regular-season Royals debut or his first appearance at Delorimier Stadium. This time, they got a relatively well-attended game with just shy of twenty-eight thousand fans in the park. Rachel Robinson was on hand, as always, happy to tell familiar stories about her time in the city. Municipal authorities held their own commemoration the day before, and it was a busy weekend for baseball academics and fans who were treated to a Jackie Robinson symposium jointly organized by two local universities, one francophone, UQAM, and the other anglophone, Concordia University. The message there was that discrimination across the city had been reduced to the individual, rather than institutional, level, though much remained to be done to truly honor Robinson's legacy.[51]

The cabbie who transported Rachel Robinson from the Queen Elizabeth Hotel to the ballpark immediately recognized her and apologized for picking her up in old work clothes instead of a suit. She said he had nothing to apologize for and obliged his autograph request as he told her, "No child should ever grow up without knowing about Jackie Robinson, his courage, and the type of spirit he demonstrated."

Rachel had brought her grandson Jesse along for the trip, and she wanted to take him down to her old neighborhood on Avenue de Gaspé. They knocked on the door to her old apartment and had a friendly, impromptu chat with some of the people who had been living on the street since the 1940s. One very elderly neighbor told her that her child had played with the Robinsons back in 1946, but Rachel chalked this recollection up to a fading memory; her first was not born until after she left the city, after all. Another neighbor later clarified that the woman meant that it was Jackie, not Jackie Jr., whom her child remembered so fondly as a playmate, and it all suddenly made sense.[52]

The rest of baseball caught up the following year on April 15, which was highlighted by a Shea Stadium ceremony to mark the fiftieth anniversary of Robinson's Dodgers debut during the fifth inning of a Mets-Dodgers game. Acting Commissioner Bud Selig was on the field, along with Rachel Robinson and President Bill Clinton for the announcement that Jackie Robinson's No. 42 would be retired league-wide. (Legendary Yankees closer Mariano Rivera had taken 42 in Robinson's honor and was grandfathered in, keeping the number up to his retirement in 2013.)

Retiring a player or manager's number was an old baseball practice that went all the way back to 1939 when the Yankees were the first to bestow this honor on Lou Gehrig, who stumbled through a few games in April for the first time before accepting that amyotrophic lateral sclerosis (ALS) had effectively ended his athletic career. Nearly every franchise had retired numbers by then, the expansion teams of 1977 and those that came later excepted, but this had always been done on a team-by-team basis. Jackie Robinson, not Babe Ruth or Ted Williams or Sandy Koufax, was the first player to have his number retired across the entire sport.

Back in 2004, Jackie Robinson Day became the annual, league-wide celebration we know it as today. Superstar Ken Griffey Jr. first requested special permission to wear 42 on Jackie Robinson Day in 2007, and Commissioner Selig, with the blessing of Sharon Robinson, Jackie and Rachel's daughter, granted it. This act had the potential to show a connection between the past and the present in such a moving way that MLB ultimately encouraged players on every team to volunteer to wear 42 on April 15 as well. Six teams—the Dodgers,

Pirates, Cardinals, Phillies, Brewers, and Astros—chose to put their entire rosters in 42 uniforms.

Some notable Black players grumbled that letting the number circulate this broadly was watering down the profound meaning of Jackie Robinson as an athlete and cultural figure. Cleveland ace CC Sabathia suggested that it should have been restricted to just the Dodgers. Taking a different and very modest view was veteran Angels outfielder Garret Anderson, who felt the number was too heavy and that he did not deserve the honor of wearing it despite having received down-ballot MVP votes on three occasions. Griffey Jr. was surprised that so many other players wanted to follow his lead, but he thought that this was an extremely positive development.[53] Angels outfielder Torii Hunter later stirred up a minor controversy with comments that Latin players with some or mostly African ancestry should be categorized separately from Black Americans, the implication being they were not part of the Jackie Robinson legacy, but he later argued that his words had been taken out of context and misconstrued.[54]

Amid this diversity of opinion, Mets manager Willie Randolph put it like this: "Maybe the best thing about this year's tribute is that it came from the players," he said. "You hear these jokes that the modern player doesn't know anything about baseball history. But it's pretty clear that most of them do appreciate what Jackie Robinson did for them—for all of them."[55] Jackie Robinson Day has since become every bit as entrenched on the baseball calendar as Opening Day, the All-Star Game, or the playoffs, giving fans and players alike a regular opportunity to walk through these old stories about the integration era together.

Back in 2004, the Expos enjoyed just one of these league-wide Jackie Robinson Days in their thirty-sixth and final season. The cruel beginning to their demise actually began a decade earlier in August 1994, when the players' union (MLBPA) went on strike over a simmering dispute with owners over the potential imposition of a salary cap. The players saw this as a naked attempt to suppress salaries while owners took a bigger share of the profits for themselves. There was a widespread belief among players that owners had been colluding against certain high-profile players for years, the most egregious case coming in 1987 when superstar Andre Dawson had to take a 30 percent pay cut when he signed with the Cubs, then went on to win the NL MVP Award. No one really wanted to strike so close to the end of the regular season, but the players thought there was far too much at stake not to take action. Off they went to the metaphorical picket lines on August 12.

The MLBPA and owners spent the next month talking, bringing in federal mediators in a bid to salvage the playoffs, but they were unable to make any serious headway, and Bud Selig called off the rest of the season on September 14. For the first time since the modern World Series began in 1903, a period that saw a world war, the Depression, and another world war, there was no fall classic. Everyone lost, but none so much as Expos fans.

In the early 1990s the Toronto Blue Jays were a giant meteor that blocked out the sun in Canada's sporting landscape. The team had been good to great through the 1980s, winning division titles in 1985 and 1989, then it elevated itself to powerhouse status following a gutsy and franchise-altering December 1990 trade that brought in second baseman Roberto Alomar and outfielder Joe Carter for team icon Tony Fernández and first baseman Fred McGriff. Alomar and McGriff became Hall of Famers, while Carter and Fernández were both excellent players in their peak. The trade did not boost the overall talent level on the team so much as it better distributed it to areas of weakness and made room for John Olerud, the 1993 AL batting champion. The Blue Jays also used their substantial financial clout to add aging mercenaries like Dave Winfield, Jack Morris, Dave Stewart, and Paul Molitor. Annual attendance in the brand new Skydome, the first retractable-roof stadium in North America, hit four million per year in 1991 and stayed there until the strike. The Blue Jays had the biggest payroll in baseball during their World Series championship years in 1992 and 1993, and few Canadian baseball fans outside Québec bothered to make time for the Expos.

The Blue Jays of 1994, however, had a few too many aging or underperforming players to make a serious push for three in a row. Meanwhile in Montreal, the Expos had quietly brought in a first-class manager in Felipe Alou and handed him a roster loaded with talent.

He guided them to second-place finishes in the NL East in 1992 and 1993, then everything came together beautifully in 1994. It was as though the entire twenty-five-year-old Expos' model of low-budget scouting and development was finally about to pay off like never before.

When play stopped in August, the Expos held a 74-40 record—this translates to 106-56 over a full season, a single-season win total the Blue Jays had never come anywhere remotely close to—and they were six games clear of the second-place Braves. They had become, hands down, the best team in the National League, first in run prevention and third in scoring. Moises Alou and Canadian-born Larry Walker had blossomed into superstar outfielders. On defense, they were superb to a man. On the bases, every regular except catcher Darrin Fletcher could steal bases. Their top four starters were all in peak form, from stud newcomer Pedro Martínez to journeyman Jeff Fassero. The bullpen regulars were impenetrable. They had also been collectively unstoppable approaching the strike, going 20-3 over their final month's worth of games before play stopped.

Virtually everyone in Canada believes that these Expos would have punched their ticket to the World Series and given the Yankees a run for their money if the strike had been averted. All we do know is that we will never know for sure and that Expos fans were tormented by the what-could-have-been for the finest team in franchise history.

The magic had worn off by 1995 after Larry Walker departed as a free agent and many of the veteran 1994 stars were traded away because the team was operating at a loss and ownership said it could no longer afford them. The offense sputtered, the pitching fell to the middle of the pack, and the team finished sub-.500. They showed signs of life again in 1996 but were not much of a threat to the Braves in the end. Then they finished twenty-three games back in 1997, forty-one in 1998, and twenty-five in 1999, leaving all but the diehards with little reason to hope for a turnaround. Even with Pedro Martínez and Vladimir Guerrero, two of the brightest stars in the game, a general ennui had set in and the Expos became the worst-attended team in the National League. By 2001 the AAA Buffalo Bisons were even outdrawing them.

Sports radio chewed on plenty of scapegoats in the years ahead. Principal owner Claude Brochu was blamed for being either a cheapskate or an ineffective leader who had failed to convince other members of the consortium to spend on the team. Premier Lucien Bouchard got a little more sympathy for refusing to agree to public financing for a new boutique park downtown at a time when the provincial legislature was forced to make painful cuts to cherished social programs. The federal government had little incentive to help out so long as separatists made up most of the Québec delegation in Ottawa and their fellow travelers ran the provincial government. But worst of all in the eyes of Expos fans was Jeffrey Loria, who obtained a majority stake in the team in 2001, boosted payroll, and promised big changes, but then had no better luck on getting a new stadium built or convincing his partners to open their purse strings.

Some blamed the fans themselves for not coming out to support their team, but there were very legitimate fears that Olympic Stadium itself was simply unsafe. There were roof rips and collapses in 1989, 1991, 1998, and 1999, forcing a series of major-event and concert cancellations. There is a very good reason why the geriatric version of the Rolling Stones has always preferred Toronto to Montreal. Five people suffered minor injuries from falling debris and ice during the 1999 auto show roof failure. It was a miracle that no one was killed when a fifty-five-tonne beam collapsed in September 1991 onto the roof of a government office.[56] These incidents were so frequent and so potentially catastrophic that it is easy to understand why many families decided to steer clear of the park entirely.

Right after the 2001 World Series, MLB owners voted by a 28–2 margin to contract both the Expos and the Minnesota Twins, a proud small-market franchise with a loyal fanbase and a similarly awful Astroturf ballpark. The Twins got a last-minute legal reprieve, and as a result the Expos bought a little more time. They had done nothing to earn it, but scheduling for an odd number of teams would have been a nightmare. Loria then proceeded to sell his Expos stake to MLB and used the proceeds to buy the Florida Marlins, another troubled organization. The Expos effectively became a ward of the state, and a skeleton crew of front-office staff led by GM Omar Minaya tried to figure out a way to survive with a frozen payroll and what they assumed was just one more guaranteed season at the Big O.

Minaya made an understandable gamble in 2002, trading a dizzying package of prospects including Cliff Lee, Brandon Phillips, and Grady Sizemore to Cleveland for a half-season rental of ace starter Bartolo Colon. It was a desperate move motivated by misguided hope that a serious playoff push would bring a new owner candidate out of the woodwork, keeping the team in Montreal, and, hopefully, eventually righting the ship. The Expos finished above .500, but the move ultimately backfired, as they ended up a very distant twelve games back of the Giants for the NL Wild Card spot. That winter, Minaya had to trade Colon to the White Sox for a dramatically inferior prospect package.

The final gambit had been played, and the only thing that kept the Expos in Montreal for the 2003 to 2004 seasons was uncertainty over where they would be relocated. In the meantime, MLB tried to salvage some good from this bad situation by having the team play twenty of its home games at Hiram Bithorn Stadium in San Juan, a great novelty for Puerto Rican baseball fans that stoked some unrealistic expectations that the city might actually take the Expos permanently. The league announced during the final Expos home game in 2004 that the team would relocate to Washington DC for the following season.

The pattern of the past has been that Major League cities that lost their franchises to relocation usually got a new one to replace it sooner or later. Milwaukee lost two different Major League teams before it got a permanent one in 1970. Kansas City poached the Athletics in 1955, lost them after the 1967 season, then got the expansion Royals as a replacement in 1969. The original Washington Senators exited for Minnesota in 1961, then the expansion Senators left for Arlington, Texas, in 1972. Baseball fans in the national capital area at least had the nearby Orioles, a team that enjoyed several intermittent windows of greatness during the thirty-five years it took for Washington to regain a team of its own. The joy a new generation of Nationals fans took as play began in 2005 was coupled with Montreal's sorrow.

At present, twenty years out from the Expos' departure, the prospect of Major League baseball in Montreal looks about as likely as it did in 1945—maybe, someday; maybe someday soon, even. Until then, we all hope and wait.

The demise of the Expos meant that efforts to preserve and honor Jackie Robinson's memory in Montreal fell to artists and storytellers rather than government or club officials, a refreshing development that ushered in a wave of creativity that ultimately reached a broader audience.

In 1991 the national charitable organization Historica Canada launched the first in a series of short films called *Heritage Minutes* that have, over the past thirty years, become as quintessentially Canadian as No Name brand potato chips and complaining about the winter. By 2004 just over one hundred of these vignettes had been created to air during television commercial breaks or in movie theaters with the coming attractions.

Each has been seen by hundreds of thousands if not millions of Canadians. They are so well known that comedians have been lovingly parodying them for decades. Ask anyone—we all have our favorites—but most agree that the Jackie Robinson minute from 1997 is at the top or very near the top of the list, along with the Halifax Explosion of 1917, Winnie the Pooh, and Laura Secord. (For the last one, American readers should imagine a female Canadian version of Paul Revere during the War of 1812 whose name was borrowed in the twentieth century by a much-loved national chocolate-shop chain.)[57]

The production values are just good enough to convince most viewers to watch, from start to finish, what are essentially intellectual public service announcements to better inform Canadians about their own history. It is nearly impossible to imagine such a national undertaking in the United States, where history is more contentious and public educators in many states are circumscribed on if or how they can present certain social and cultural topics.

Each minute generally highlights individual or collective acts of bravery, inventiveness, sacrifice, or resilience across a broad cross section of Canadians. They come in English and French versions, but more recently an Inuktitut minute focused on Inuit artist Kenojuak Ashevak. The minutes also run head-on toward what would be considered controversial themes today in much of the United States, such as marginalization of Native peoples, extra-European immigration, civil rights, and LGBT-rights activism among them. A dozen look at sports, broadly defined, and Jackie Robinson is joined by old friend Rocket Richard, the Edmonton Grads (the most dominant women's basketball team of all time), the Vancouver Asahi (a powerhouse amateur baseball team made up of Japanese Canadians), Tom Longboat (winner of the 2007 Boston Marathon and one the greatest Native athletes from Canada), and Norman Kwong (the first Chinese Canadian to play in the Canadian Football League).

The wildly popular Robinson minute first aired in 1997 to coincide with the golden anniversary of his Dodgers debut. Journeyman actor Anthony Hylton played Robinson, while Vlasta Vrana, a regular on Canadian television since the 1970s, played the part of Branch Rickey.

The minute opens in a raucous Royals locker room as Branch Rickey walks in to present a suit-wearing Robinson to his teammates as their new second baseman. Rickey is enthusiastic, but Robinson says nothing and looks tentative, while viewers are left with the impression that the rest of the players are skeptical before the cutaway to the next scene that shows Robinson coming to the plate in a nighttime home game against Newark, as a bilingual PA announcement rattles through the stadium. The pitch comes in, and a fastball lands hard on Robinson's upper left buttock as the crowd erupts in boos. He is next seen coming up again, smashing a game-winning RBI single. Later, toward the end of the game, the crowd erupts into "Jack-ie, Jack-ie" chants until manager Clay Hopper points to Robinson to exit the dugout and take a curtain call for the fans. A middle-aged white fan in a business suit reaches over for a hearty handshake with a relieved, then smiling Rachel Robinson who puts her hand on her stomach. Here, in a split second, was a hint that while the Robinsons' firstborn was not delivered on Canadian soil, he did at least gestate there.

The narrator only joins for the minute's final ten seconds to note that "a record number of cheering Montrealers helped Jackie Robinson break baseball's color bar that year. He never forgot the city that launched his journey to baseball's Hall of Fame." It ends with a smiling, uniformed Robinson lifting his cap with his right hand, the bright stadium lights beaming down on him. In sum, this was a powerful, effective story that encapsulated Robinson's experience with Montreal fans even as the actor who played him uttered not a single word.

At a governmental level, American authorities in Canada rightly stood back for many years to let the municipal government, the Expos, and MLB take the lead on Robinson commemorative efforts. The historic election of Barack Obama as America's first Black president in 2008 did, however, inspire the American consulate in Montreal to mark Black History Month in 2011, the sixty-fifth anniversary of the Robinsons' arrival in the city, with a bilingual historic plaque at the Robinsons' one-time apartment at 8232 Avenue de Gaspé.

From the street at least, the assembled dignitaries and a few dozen onlookers saw the duplex much as it looked when it was built during the interwar years. Sharon Robinson braved the cold and wet snow as the family surrogate in place of Rachel, her mother, who was approaching ninety years old, but still sent a letter bearing gratitude. American Ambassador David Jacobson noted that there could be no Black president had Jackie Robinson not come first and paved the way for him. Consul Lee McClenny read a letter from Rachel Robinson that repeated something she had said on virtually every occasion she had returned in person: "In the end, Montreal was the perfect place for Jack to get his start. . . . We never had a threatening or unpleasant experience there, the people were so welcoming and saw Jack as a player and more importantly as a man." Sharon Robinson went into more detail with inherited recollections of her parents' fond memories of Montreal.[58] For the Robinsons, Rachel and Sharon, this all bore repeating because it was a genuine character witness of a broad group of people who may not have been fully aware of the role their city had played in a historic struggle. They wanted Montrealers to remember and share a story that was as much about them as it was about Jackie.

The 2013 release of the film *42* sparked much interest in Montreal partly because many ticket buyers rightly expected that their city would at least be an ancillary character in the story. Those who saw it in Cineplex theaters were treated with a minute-long prefilm clip that offered some important Montreal-specific content that did not make its way into *42* itself. This effort was a collaboration between producer and Expos superfan Eric Cohen and Jack Jedwab, the president of the Association for Canadian Studies and author of *Jackie Robinson's Unforgettable Season of Baseball in Montreal* (1996), a concise and accessible English-language account for general readers. Cohen explained their motivation: "As much as Jackie Robinson played a big part in the history of baseball, Montreal played a big part in the history of Jackie Robinson."[59]

The film 42 was not the end of the story, though, and there is every reason to believe a new generation of officials, artists, and storytellers in Montreal will continue to carry it forward whenever future anniversary years call for it.

Two new vibrant outdoor Jackie Robinson murals have appeared over the past decade, the first just a few minutes' walk from 8232 Avenue de Gaspé on the side of a dentist's office at 171 Jarry Street East. Vincent Dumoulin's piece from 2016 features a large Robinson from the letters up in a Dodgers uniform, swinging at a pitch with intense look of concentration on his face. Next to this figure is a second Robinson, staring straight ahead at the viewer in a home white uniform with *Montreal* written across it, again inverting the normal home-road club name–city practice as Jules Lasalle did in his statue from the 1980s. They both hint at a militance for civil rights that had spilled over into the world of sports. Occasional bits of the wall's original yellow brick peek through. Dumoulin painted in black, white, and gray, with just a few pops of Dodgers blue.

A second mural appeared in 2017 on the side of Coco Rico, a popular Portuguese chicken spot, two blocks off the northeast corner of Mount Royal Park. The Dumoulin mural was serious, but this one from Fluke, a busy street artist whose work has appeared all over the city and abroad, is vibrant and playful. Here, a nearly three-story uniformed Robinson is smiling, almost unnaturally so from joy with *Montreal* emblazoned on his chest, while a rainbow palette of stripes zig zag across the red brick wall on which the mural was painted. So many terrific murals are across the city—while en route to Coco Rico, this author was delighted to randomly walk past a brilliant, thirty-story black-and-white one of poet-songwriter Leonard Cohen on a high-rise apartment building—but this work may very well be the best of them all. Here's one Instagram take: "Everything about Montreal is pretty dope, but this mural of Jackie Robinson made the trip for me!"[60]

In the spring of 2016, a trio of local creatives—two Cirque du Soleil producers, Michel Lemieux and Victor Pilon, and a well-known Québec playwright, Michel Marc Bouchard—launched Cité Mémoire as a new vehicle to project outdoor video installations on some of the most striking buildings downtown and around the historic Old Port area. They were often set to music that can be as moving as the visual, with each an intricate collaboration from hundreds of actors, technicians, and support crews. The city, province, and Ottawa, along with various sponsors, helped fund this C$18 million (roughly $13.1 million at the time) endeavor, the largest of its kind anywhere in the world.

Over twenty of these installations went up between 2016 and 2019, and they were an absolute delight for anyone who happened to be walking by at night, particularly those who were not purposefully looking for them. Each required dozens of individual projectors. The videos were shown on such places as the side of a two-hundred-year-old basilica, straight at the leaves of a tree, or down onto a cobblestone alley. They all featured iconic or underappreciated denizens who represent various aspects of the city's identity. Many of these installations had an overt goal of promoting tolerance and understanding across cultural lines, reminiscent of the *Heritage Minutes* series. They appear to be semipermanent and are still running as of this writing in 2024.

The "From Marie-Josèphe to Jackie Robinson, 1734–1946" video is projected onto the side of a historic four-story building at 408 Saint-François-Xavier Street. The creators wanted to tell two powerful stories about Montreal's Black history; the first and better known one is of Jackie Robinson, and the second is the much lesser-known tale of an enslaved woman, Marie-Josèphe Angélique, from early-eighteenth-century colonial New France who was tortured and forced to confess to an arson and then hanged for it. Together, these two vignettes combine to present a vivid message of pride and shame as the viewers reflect on race relations within the city.[61]

The projection begins with Marie-Josèphe on hands and knees scrubbing the floor when a young white girl appears behind her and casts an accusatory index finger toward her. There is an age disparity of at least a decade, but the white figure looms at three times Marie-Josèphe's size to represent the racial power imbalance. She is left sobbing on the floor as three more disembodied white fingers appear to accuse her of something. She stands, exasperated, then begins to run toward the viewer and morphs into a uniformed Jackie Robinson running the bases, still toward the viewer, with a completely black backdrop. Flash bulbs go off over his shoulders as his figure grows bigger, as though he is getting closer to reaching home plate. He then reverts back into Marie-Josèphe standing in a long purple skirt and white blouse, hands cuffed together and eyes cast downward. There is no answer here as to whether she actually was an arsonist—historians debate whether she was an innocent scapegoat or had indeed started the fire as a justifiable act of vengeance against a cruel enslaver—but images of Marie-Josèphe engulfed in flames convey a sense of great injustice that we will never truly understand.[62] Jackie Robinson later appears standing at home plate before an adoring crowd in the thousands, as his triumphs take on added significance when juxtaposed with Marie-Josèphe's tragic pain.

Visitors to Montreal like you and me could make a delightful spring or summer day of visiting all the Robinson pilgrimage sites at Delorimier, Avenue de Gaspé, and Olympic Stadium, along with numerous pieces of public art scattered throughout the city, stopping when peckish for heaping poutine or a smoked meat sandwich, washed down with a glass of something cold from McAuslan Brewing or Unibroue. People like us will come looking for traces of him, but to many Montrealers Jackie Robinson has never really left.

Epilogue

> The teacher said to me—and this is in front of the class—he said I didn't have a history.
>
> —DOROTHY WILLIAMS, "Putting Black History in Canada on the Map," CBC News

The past never dies, and old battles are never truly won or lost, something Jackie Robinson knew all too well. He finished writing his autobiography the year he died, rounding out his preface on a downcast memory of his first World Series game:

> There I was, the black grandson of a slave, the son of a black sharecropper, part of a historic occasion, a symbolic hero to my people. The air was sparkling. The sunlight was warm. The band struck up the national anthem. The flag billowed in the wind. It should have been a glorious moment for me as the stirring words of the national anthem poured from the stands. Perhaps it was, but then again perhaps the anthem could be called the theme song for a drama called *The Noble Experiment*. Today as I look back on that opening game of my first world series, I must tell you that it was Mr. Rickey's drama and that I was only a principal actor. As I write this twenty years later, I cannot stand and sing the anthem. I cannot salute the flag; I know that I am a black man in a white world. In 1972, in 1947, at my birth in 1919, I know that I never had it made.[1]

Every April 15, baseball celebrates Jackie Robinson Day, and at random moments every year or two we are reminded that the events of 1946 and 1947 represented at best a partial victory. Vandals and censors will never give up challenging the popular narrative about his larger meaning to American society.

In 2021 someone shot up the Jackie Robinson birthplace marker in sleepy Cairo down in southwestern Georgia. He is the most famous son of that mostly Black town, and this is exactly what turned an innocuous historic plaque into a target during the Black Lives Matter protests that followed the police killing of George Floyd. The gunfire appears to have been centered on the words "Negro American" and "baseball's color barrier."[2] Point made.

In 2023 a county in Florida pulled Barbara Cohen's 1974 children's novel *Thank You, Jackie Robinson*, on the grounds that it dealt with provocative themes. The plot of this YA classic was semiautobiographical, built around the friendship the white author's brother developed with a Black chef who worked at their family's New Jersey hotel back in the 1950s. It was a shared love of the Dodgers and Robinson that had brought them together.[3] That was the dangerous idea within its pages.

Early in 2024 a Robinson statue at a youth league park in Wichita was cut off at the ankles, removed, then dumped in a trash can seven miles away after the thief made a failed attempt to melt it down.[4] MLB and generous donors immediately stepped forward with money for a replacement, but many were left skeptical of the police explanation that the crime had been motivated by a desire to sell the statue as scrap metal.

Isolated acts such as these will continue with demoralizing frequency. In those moments, it is best to remember the truth that *Washington Post* sports columnist Jerry Brewer shares: "Statues can be defiled. Books can be removed. But the Robinson spirit endures."[5]

When Dorothy Williams, the leading historian of Black Montreal, speaks of the Jackie Robinson myth, she can cite plenty of examples of local pioneers in education, politics, and the business world who found their success after 1946 in the face of barriers that should have been swept away generations earlier. They all had to fight like hell for everything they achieved. Nothing came easily.

One of them is Richard Lord, a bright student from a Caribbean immigrant family and a talented youth hockey player in the early post–World War II years. He won an athletic scholarship at McGill

University, a precious opportunity that would have allowed him to pursue an elite education in chemical engineering in his hometown, close to his tight-knit family. His transcripts and the sports-page game recaps did not reveal his race, however, and the admissions office at McGill had made an assumption. When the university found out he was Black, it rescinded his scholarship offer.

Undeterred, Lord applied to Michigan State College (now Michigan State University), which issued him a fresh athletic scholarship for the fall 1949 semester. The Spartans too had no idea they had just recruited one of the first Black players to lace up for college hockey until he actually got down to East Lansing in person, but to their credit they accepted him into their fraternity after they learned who he really was. On the ice, he turned into a hard-nosed defenseman who served as cocaptain in his junior and senior years. Off of it, he found time to be an active participant in Greek life while serving as president of a handful of social organizations. Imagine the surprise of some of his fellow expats from Ontario when they discovered the campus Canadian Club was led by a Black Montrealer.[6]

Lord made his career back home in chemical engineering, but he was also an active community leader who rose to become vice president of the Quebec Liberal Party, among many notable accomplishments. Throughout his adult life, he was an enthusiastic amateur hockey historian who championed awareness of Herb Carnegie, a talented, high-scoring center from Toronto who never got to live out his own Jackie Robinson story in the NHL. The owner of his hometown Toronto Maple Leafs reportedly stated in 1938 that Carnegie could play his way onto the team, but only if he could first turn into a white man. A decade later, the New York Rangers offered Carnegie an insultingly low offer to join their Minor League affiliate.[7] The accolades did catch up to him later in life, though, a victory that was as important to Lord as getting the Robinson statue moved from the trash-strewn park at Delorimier Stadium to Olympic Stadium.

When Lord looked at the differences between Canada and the United States in his early adulthood and middle years, he was envious of the Black-owned businesses and Black colleges in America that created opportunities that simply did not exist for people like him at home.

When Black friends visited him in Montreal, they thought it was remarkable that they could sit wherever they liked on public transportation or go into any bar or restaurant. "To them, Montreal was fabulous," he said. "But they had economic freedom. We had social freedom but not freedom to go into the institutions."[8] These were two flawed systems looking at each other in a funhouse mirror.

No one can make a convincing argument that six months of Jackie Robinson in 1946 magically fixed racism in Montreal. The record shows that it continued to rear its head in the ugliest of ways into his twilight years.

There is a broad standardization of Canadian universities these days. Most Americans would consider Canada's higher education system to have a very high floor in terms of funding, resources, physical infrastructure, and quality of instruction. There may be no Harvard or such, but there are no neglected state institutions or teetering liberal arts colleges, either, as the general standard ranges from very good to excellent. To an outside observer, Concordia University in Montreal looks much like all the others despite a unique history that does not always get the attention it deserves.

Concordia came together in 1974 as a merger of two small English-language institutions, the Jesuit-run Loyola College and Sir George Williams University. Sir George Williams began as an outgrowth of the YMCA and served the city's working poor, but it also opened its doors to Jews who were turned away from McGill, which had a strict quota system in place. It similarly became the university of choice for Black anglophones in and around Montreal, thanks to its reputation for tolerance in admissions. By the 1960s, Black students from the Caribbean came up in larger numbers to join them. Loyola followed a similar path, opening up to female students in the late 1950s, then to a growing pool of international students in the 1960s as Canada relaxed European preference immigration laws. There was, however, trouble brewing just beneath this progressive veneer.

The 1960s were the era of late-stage decolonization across most of Africa and the era of civil rights protests, then Black Power activism, closer to home just across the border in America. In Québec itself, a large and growing movement of francophone nationalists began rallying around the idea that they too could never seize control of their own destiny within the confines of the Canadian federation. The most hyperbolic public intellectual among their ranks, Pierre Vallières, a straight journalist turned revolutionary or terrorist leader—which fits better depends on one's politics—in the Front de libération du Québec, penned a 1967 essay "Nègres blancs d'Amérique" (White n——s of America) that claimed similarities between the plight of Black America and francophone Québec. Many Black students in Canada saw this turmoil at home and abroad and very much considered themselves part of a global movement fighting to overturn exploitation and inequality. This inevitably and rightly led to growing assertiveness by the end of the decade over issues that would previously have gone without an open challenge.

Canada's first and biggest Black-led student protest came as an outgrowth of Sir George Williams University's mishandling of very serious accusations of racist marking practices. By anyone's standard, students had caught a biology professor red-handed in the spring of 1968, just after Rev. Martin Luther King Jr. was assassinated in Memphis. A white student had copied a Black student's assignment, but when they were returned, the former's mark was several letter grades higher for no explicable reason other than the most obvious one. Six Caribbean students filed a complaint with the university administration, which discounted the claim, misplaced the paperwork related to it, and then ultimately chose to do nothing. Tensions simmered across campus into early 1969.[9]

A group of about four hundred students, Black and white, took over the university's computer lab on January 29 in a protest intended to draw attention to the administration's seeming indifference to racism on campus. The leaders included the future prime minister of Dominica, Rosie Douglas, and a future Canadian senator, Anne Cools. (In an interesting twist of fate, she lost considerable progressive credibility after quitting the Liberal Party in 2004 over its plans to codify same-sex marriage.) It appeared as though there was a workable solution roughly two weeks into the standoff that would have students leave the Hall Building in exchange for a promise that the university would reopen the investigation into the original racism complaint against

Professor Perry Anderson. The faculty stood with their colleague—what would happen if their books were opened to closer scrutiny?—and many of the students hedged out of concerns the deal would not be honored. The administration chose to force them out on February 11, and in came the riot police.

There were fist fights between students and police in the hallways, and thousands of computer punch cards with all of their precious data started flying out of ninth-floor windows. Then a fire started amid the melee around midday—started by whom, we will never know—and the protesters had no choice but to abandon their positions. About one hundred of them, over half white, were arrested as they exited the building, as jeering onlookers yelled, "Let the n——s burn!" It was all televised. Grandstanding politicians called for the deportation of any international students who had been involved. There was one death, C$2 million in property damage, and Canada's global reputation for relative tolerance was left in tatters.[10]

In the short term, Sir George Williams University cleaned up its procedures for dealing with student grievances, but it took forty-three years before Concordia formally apologized on its behalf. In the intervening years, the university has earned a well-deserved reputation, verging on notoriety, across Canada for fearless campus activism. Concordia students led the charge to divest from apartheid South Africa in the 1980s. In the 2000s they had become the most stridently pro-Palestinian in the country, rioting in 2002 to prevent Israeli Prime Minister Benjamin Netanyahu from speaking on campus.[11] For the past half century Concordia students have made it very clear that they will not stand by silently in the face of perceived injustice. The heavy hand in 1969 created a perpetual dissent machine in the end, and somewhere here is a lesson about human persistence.

So yes, Dorothy Williams is absolutely right to argue that there is a danger to buying into the Jackie Robinson myth that everything suddenly and cleanly changed for the better for Black Montrealers during the Royals' 1946 season. It is even possible that there really is little point in searching for Canadian or Québécois examples of mostly white communities that provided Black minorities with a small amount of latitude slightly earlier than their counterparts in the United States. Does this amount to nothing more than searching for a little less wrong in a troubled world?

Jackie Robinson could no more bring an end to racial inequity in Montreal or Canada than at home. He is, however, frequently invoked whenever Canadians try to inspire themselves to live up to the ideal of basic fairness for all. He passed through a society that was admittedly resistant to change longer than it should have been, but during that time he brought together a community within a community—a few tens of thousands of Royals fans in a sea of twelve million Canadians and three-and-a-half million Québeckers—that stood up proudly for a man who appealed to their better angels. Jackie or Rachel Robinson spent a half century reminding anyone who would listen at every opportunity that they had seen a collective, fundamental show of human decency at Delorimier Stadium and elsewhere in 1946 that still counts for something that matters today. That, in the end, is why this story is worth telling.

Acknowledgments

This book was an absolute pleasure to write from start to finish, even if every turn at the keyboard made this expat more homesick than usual. I would like to express my gratitude to my institution, Murray State University, for providing a significant grant through the Committee on Institutional Studies and Research that enabled me to visit several archives and repositories across the United States and Canada back in 2023. I also thank our University Libraries dean, Cris Ferguson, for generously backing my research trip with supplementary departmental funding.

Out on the road, I was very grateful for friendly service from supremely helpful librarians and archivists in Cooperstown at the National Baseball Hall of Fame and Museum; in Montreal at the McCord Stewart Museum, the Jewish Public Library, McGill University's Rare Books and Special Collections, Concordia University Library, Bibliothèque et Archives nationales du Québec (BANQ), and Archives de Montreal; and in Ottawa at Library and Archives Canada. They were all a credit to their trade.

My parents are and have always been wonderfully supportive people. I grew up listening to Stephen James McLaughlin's stories about Harmon Killebrew and Rocky Colavito socking dingers or getting booed at the old Tiger Stadium whenever we had a long car ride. My dad worked long hours when I was young, but he always made time on weekends to take me to card shows and stand in autograph lines, so much so that we both might have forgotten who convinced whom to pick up the hobby. We will get another ballgame in soon, either on your home turf in Vancouver or mine in St. Louis or Nashville. Judith Diane McLaughlin has never turned down a request to proofread anything I have ever written, and I suspect she never will. She got the first read of this manuscript, and I hope I have made her proud of me, not so much as a writer but for having the right sort of values.

I am still eternally grateful to Julie Paquette of Saint-Jérôme for all the time she invested two decades ago in Québec City helping this late starter get good enough at French to use it for research and writing. If a francophone Habs superfan from Québec and an Anglo Leafs guy from Ontario can become friends over beers and *La Soirée du hockey*, this world of ours is truly full of possibilities.

My first book was dedicated to my wife, Selina Gao, and our daughter, Olivia Sophie McLaughlin, but I cannot thank you two often enough. You have both humored my baseball obsession over the years even if you never quite understood it, so I thank you again for keeping me company during that long, meandering research trip through New York, Québec, and Ontario. What an amazing gift it has been sharing my life with the two of you.

Notes

PREFACE

1. Pierre Foglia, "Des remerciements . . . 25 ans après!," *La Patrie* (Montreal), September 7, 1969.

INTRODUCTION

1. In summer 2020 *The Washington Post*, then my go-to morning read, updated its writing style for racial and ethnic identifiers to capitalize both "B" in Black and "W" in White. The decision to capitalize Black was a perfectly justifiable response from media outlets to the horrific police killings of Breonna Taylor and George Floyd, which led to massive Black Lives Matter protests across the globe. I formatted the original version of this manuscript according to the *Post*'s style that fits with my personal values, but this has since been edited to conform with the University of Nebraska Press's house style and the *Chicago Manual of Style*.
2. Keegan Matheson, "Montreal Was Jackie's 'Paradise' in 1946," MLB.com, February 4, 2022, https://www.mlb.com/news/jackie-robinson-loved-playing-with-montreal-royals.
3. Dugas, "Montreal and Jackie Robinson," 356.

1. CANADA'S PLACE

1. Johnson and Aladejebi, *Unsettling Great White North*; and Mathieu, *North of Color Line*.
2. "Doc about Being Black in Chatham-Kent Gains Attention at Film Festivals across North America," CBC, January 28, 2021, https://www.cbc.ca/news/canada/windsor/chatham-kent-documentary-1.5890282.
3. Arenson, "Experience Rather Than Imagination."
4. A fanciful version of Mink's life story was turned into a 1996 TV biopic with Louis Gossett Jr. and Kate Nelligan called *Captive Heart: The James Mink Story*.
5. Greenham, "On Battlefront."
6. Joost, "Asian- and Black-Canadians."

7. "Curley Christian," The Military Museums (website), n.d., https://mural.themilitarymuseums.ca/panels/row12/240-curley-christian.
8. Dame, "Coloured Diamonds," 7.
9. Dame, "Coloured Diamonds."
10. "A Brief Team History," Breaking the Colour Barrier, University of Windsor Centre For Digital Scholarship, accessed March 11, 2025, https://collections.uwindsor.ca/BreakingColourBarrier/all-stars-history.
11. Wright, *Chatham Coloured All-Stars*, 99–118.
12. Ferguson Jenkins, "Interview With: Ferguson Jenkins," interview by Heidi Jacobs, Breaking the Colour Barrier, University of Windsor Centre For Digital Scholarship, October 1, 2016, http://cdigs.uwindsor.ca/BreakingColourBarrier/exhibits/show/oral-history/item/726.
13. Howell, "Black Baseball in the Maritimes," 103.
14. Trudeau, "Integration in Quebec."
15. Trudeau, "24 Years Before Jackie."
16. Trudeau, "Integration in Quebec."
17. Max Weder, "Indian Head and Canada's Greatest Baseball Tournament, 1947–55," Society for American Baseball Research, accessed August 12, 2025, https://sabr.org/journal/article/indian-head-and-canadas-greatest-baseball-tournament-1947-55/.
18. Spivey, "'To Canada with Love,'" 240.
19. Spivey, "'To Canada with Love,'" 245.
20. Williams, "Jackie Robinson Myth," 42–53.
21. Williams, "Jackie Robinson Myth," 82–83.
22. Kennedy, *True*, 7.
23. Mark Reynolds, "Toot Sweet: When Jazz Ruled Montreal," *The Beaver*, June-July 2001, 26–32, Concordia University Library Special Collections and Archives.
24. Halpern, "Malestrom."
25. Jonathan Montpetit, "Searching for Fred Christie, the Jamaican Immigrant Who Tried to End Legalized Racism in Canada," CBC, last updated December 17, 2019, https://www.cbc.ca/news/canada/montreal/fred-christie-montreal-supreme-court-1.5390316.

2. A MOMENTOUS SIGNING

1. Bruce Watson, "The Judge Who Ruled Baseball," *Smithsonian* magazine, October 2000, https://www.smithsonianmag.com/arts-culture/the-judge-who-ruled-baseball-68788790/.
2. The most vocal among them included Barry Larkin, Terry Pendleton, and Mike Schmidt.

3. Most notable are Heywood Broun (*New York World-Telegram*), Jimmy Powers (New York *Daily News*), Wendell Smith and Chester Washington (*Pittsburgh Courier*), Fay Young (*Chicago Defender*), Joe Bostic (*People's Voice*, New York), Sam Lacy and Art Carter (*Afro-American,* Baltimore), Mabray "Doc" Kountze (*Call and Post*, Cleveland), Dan Burley (*Amsterdam News*), and, last but not least, Lester Rodney, the sports editor of the communist *Daily Worker*, which surprised many nonleftist players and executives with its high-quality sports section.
4. Tygiel, *Baseball's Great Experiment*, 32; and Dreier, "Before Jackie Robinson."
5. Kahn, *Rickey & Robinson*, 59.
6. Dreier, "Before Jackie Robinson."
7. Wendell Smith, "'No Need For Color Ban in Big Leagues—Pie Traynor," *Pittsburgh Courier*, September 2, 1939.
8. Pietrusza, *Judge and Jury*, 417.
9. Cox, "Happy Helping?"
10. Dreier, "Before Jackie Robinson," 34.
11. John Thorn, "When Landis Met Robeson: What Was Said? What Was Done? How to Judge?," *Medium* (blog), July 6, 2020, https://ourgame.mlblogs.com/when-landis-met-robeson-dc10f951a8b.
12. Chris Lamb, "Catcher's Tears Were a Likely Inspiration for Rickey," *New York Times*, April 14, 2012, https://www.nytimes.com/2012/04/15/sports/baseball/branch-rickey-found-inspiration-in-catchers-tears.html.
13. Kahn, *Rickey & Robinson*, 155.
14. Kahn, *Rickey & Robinson*, 82.
15. Joseph Gerard, "Silvio Garcia," Society for American Baseball Research, 2016, https://sabr.org/bioproj/person/silvio-garcia/.
16. Kahn, *Rickey & Robinson*, 99; and Simon, *Jackie Robinson and Integration*, 60–63.
17. Cox, *Fine Team Man*, 6–7.
18. Bullock, "Playing for Their Nation."
19. John Rosengren, "GI World Series of 1945 Featured Diverse Heroes of the Diamond," National Baseball Hall of Fame, accessed July 22, 2024, https://baseballhall.org/discover/gi-world-series-of-1945-featured-diverse-heroes-of-the-diamond.
20. Simon, *Jackie Robinson and Integration*, 15.
21. Cox, *Fine Team Man*, 13.
22. UCLA *Baseball History: 1920–2007*, UCLA, accessed July 22, 2024, 98, https://ucla_ftp.sidearmsports.com/old_site/pdf/m-basebl/2007BaseballPages88-104.pdf.

23. Kahn, *Rickey & Robinson*, 98; and Trudeau, "Daily Operations," 24.
24. Pollard, *The League*.
25. Simon, *Jackie Robinson and Integration*, 18–22.
26. Brown and Terry, *Baseball's Fabulous Montreal Royals*, 77.
27. Kreuz, "Greenwade and His 007 Assignment," 100.
28. Brown and Terry, *Baseball's Fabulous Montreal Royals*, 93.
29. Honig, *Baseball When Grass Was Green*, 185.
30. Jackie Robinson to Clyde Sukeforth, July 21, 1972, BA MSS 44 Correspondence Collection, Giamatti Research Center.
31. Robinson, *I Never Had It Made*, 31.
32. Robinson, *I Never Had It Made*, 29; and LeMoine, "Jackie Robinson in 1945," 62.
33. Tygiel and Thorn, "Jackie Robinson's Signing," 164.
34. Rampersad, *Jackie Robinson*, 127.
35. Rampersad, *Jackie Robinson*, 128.
36. Stott, *Canadian Minor League Baseball*, 9–11.
37. Charlie Trudeau (1887–1935) came into the city from a south shore family farm and launched Canada's version of the Kennedy dynasty. His son Pierre Elliot Trudeau served as prime minister from 1968 to 1979 and again from 1980 to 1984, then his grandson Justin Trudeau served in the same role from 2015 to 2025.
38. Brown and Terry, *Baseball's Fabulous Montreal Royals*, 17–40.
39. Brown and Terry, *Baseball's Fabulous Montreal Royals*, 55.
40. Stott, *Canadian Minor League Baseball*, 10.
41. Kennedy, *True*, 17; and Brown and Terry, *Baseball's Fabulous Montreal Royals*, 89.
42. Gauvreau took an honorary commission as lieutenant colonel with the Fusiliers Mont-Royal in 1941.
43. "Jouer de couleur mis sous contrat par le club Montreal," *Le Canada* (Montreal), October 24, 1945.
44. Kahn, *Rickey & Robinson*, 191.
45. Dugas, "Montreal and Jackie Robinson," 357.
46. Dink Carroll, Playing the Field, *The Gazette* (Montreal), October 24, 1945.
47. Dink Carroll, Playing the Field, *The Gazette* (Montreal), October 25, 1945.
48. "Le Royal crée un précédent dans l'histoire du baseball organisé," *La Presse* (Montreal), October 24, 1945.
49. "Jack Robinson devient le premier joueur nègre à signer un contrat avec un club dans le baseball organisé," *Montreal-matin*, October 24, 1945.
50. Louis Gosselin, "Une bombe éclate dans le baseball," *La Patrie* (Montreal), October 24, 1945.

51. "Organized Baseball Opens Its Ranks to Negro Player," *New York Times*, October 24, 1945.
52. Dan Burley, "Bklyn Dodgers Hire Negro Star: Color Line in Baseball Crumbles as Shortstop Jackie Robinson Signs," *New York Amsterdam News*, October 27, 1945.
53. Marshall, *Baseball's Pivotal Era*, 130–31.
54. Brown and Terry, *Baseball's Fabulous Montreal Royals*, 95.
55. Anderson, "Great Leap Forward," 76.
56. Richard Goldstein, "Bob Feller, Whose Fastball Dazzled, Dies at 92," *New York Times*, December 15, 2010, https://www.nytimes.com/2010/12/16/sports/baseball/16feller.html?_r=1.
57. Jackie Robinson to Wendell Smith, October 31, 1945, BA MSS 44 Correspondence Collection, Giamatti Research Center.
58. Steve George, "250,000 See Feller-Paige Teams Play," *Sporting News*, October 30, 1946, 9.

3. COMING THROUGH ADVERSITY

1. Myrdal, Sterner, and Rose, *American Dilemma*, 100.
2. "Ray Elliot–1939–1945: 'Two Wars to Win,'" American Centuries (website), accessed July 23, 2024, https://americancenturies.org/activities/oralhistories/oralhistory-ray-elliott/1939-1945-two-wars-to-win/.
3. White, "Civil Rights," 38.
4. Michael E. Ruane, "'Greatest Generation' Runs Counter to Its Wholesome Image in Survey on Race, Sex and Combat during World War II," *Washington Post*, December 20, 2021, https://www.washingtonpost.com/history/2021/12/20/greatest-generation-survey-race-sex/; and "Attitudes of and toward Negroes," The American Soldier in World War II (website), accessed July 23, 2024, https://americansoldierww2.org/surveys/s/S32/q-0/tab-1.
5. Schwartz, *Trends in White Attitudes*, 55–79.
6. Sheinin and Bryce, "Baseball and Categorization," 121.
7. William C. Kashatus, "Philly's Gene Benson Was Winner on and off the Field," *Philadelphia Daily News*, April 16, 1999.
8. Burns, Burns, and McMahon, *Jackie Robinson*.
9. Burns, Burns, and McMahon, *Jackie Robinson*.
10. Burns, Burns, and McMahon, *Jackie Robinson*.
11. Chris Lamb, "Jackie Robinson—Crossing the Line," *Los Angeles Times*, February 27, 2012, https://www.latimes.com/opinion/la-xpm-2012-feb-27-la-oe-lamb-jackie-robinson-20120227-story.html.

12. Schnur, "Persevering on Home Front," 52.
13. Schnur, "Persevering on Home Front," 58.
14. Mormino, "GI Joe Meets Jim Crow," 24.
15. Lamb, *Blackout*, 64.
16. Oscar Major, Dans le monde sportif, *Le Samedi*, January 12, 1946, 10.
17. "Le lanceur Barney Lee s'est rapporté aux Royaux à Daytona Beach," *Montreal-matin*, March 9, 1946.
18. "Roland Gladu signe un contrat pour jouer à Mexico cet été," *Montreal-matin*, February 5, 1946.
19. Paul Parizeau, "De sol au lendemain," *Le Canada* (Montreal), February 8, 1946.
20. "Jackie Robinson aura sa chambre à part," *Le Front Ouvrier* (Montceau-les-Mines, France), January 5, 1946.
21. Charles Daoust, Et le spectacle continue, *Le Droit* (Ottawa), March 1, 1946.
22. Paul Parizeau, "De sol au lendemain," *Le Canada* (Montreal), March 7, 1946.
23. Jean Barrette, Autour des buts, *La Patrie* (Montreal), March 3, 1946.
24. Syd Thomas, Canadian Sport Snapshots, *Daily Record* (Sherbrooke, Québec), March 4, 1946.
25. Lamb, *Blackout*, 90.
26. "Jack Robinson est philosophe; de baseball Montreal ne s'en fait pas!," *La Presse* (Montreal), March 11, 1946.
27. Ian MacDonald, "Statue Honors Robinson," *The Gazette* (Montreal), May 18, 1987.
28. Lamb, *Blackout*, 95, 113.
29. Simon, *Jackie Robinson and Integration*, 92.
30. "Pourrait-il jouer à Québec?," *Le Nouvelliste* (Trois-Rivières), March 29, 1946.
31. Lamb, *Blackout*, 103–6.
32. "Le nègre Jackie Robinson reçoit une offre d'un agent recruteur mexicain," *Le Canada* (Montreal), March 20, 1946.
33. Zotique Lespérance, Commentaire sportifs, *La Patrie* (Montreal), March 17, 1946.
34. Lamb, *Blackout*, 136–44.
35. Lamb, *Blackout*, 154.
36. "Robinson Quits Game in Florida at the Request of Police Chief," *The Gazette* (Montreal), April 8, 1946.
37. Lamb, *Blackout*, 161–62.
38. "'Pas de négres, pas de parties,' dit Hec Racine," *Le Droit* (Ottawa), April 8, 1946.

39. "Une louable attitude," *Le Soleil* (Québec City), April 10, 1946.
40. Charles Daoust, Et le Spectacle continue, *Le Droit* (Ottawa), March 23, 1946.
41. Simon, *Jackie Robinson and Integration*, 93.
42. "Quelques potins sur le baseball," *Le Droit* (Ottawa), April 4, 1946.
43. "Un club rapide et combatif pour le gérant Clay Hopper," *La Presse* (Montreal), March 29, 1946.
44. "Le Montreal cède le 2e but Lou Rochelli au Saint-Paul," *La Presse* (Montreal), April 9, 1946.
45. Roper and Roper, "'We're Going to Give All We Have.'"
46. Lanctot, *Campy*, 129–32.
47. "L'alignement du Royal n'est pas encore connu: Les Dodgers de Brooklyn verront certes à nous céder quelques joueurs. Robinson et Wright," *Le Canada* (Montreal), April 12, 1946.
48. Charles Daoust, Et le Spectacle continue, *Le Droit* (Ottawa), April 15, 1946.
49. Stott, *Canadian Minor League Baseball*, 14–15.
50. Stott, *Canadian Minor League Baseball*, 208.
51. Scott Pitoniak, "Twenty-Five Years Ago, Big League Pioneer Larry Doby Received His Hall of Fame Plaque," National Baseball Hall of Fame, accessed July 23, 2024, https://baseballhall.org/discover/Twenty-five-years-ago-big-league-pioneer-Larry-Doby-received-his-Hall-of-Fame-Plaque.
52. Jerry Izenberg, "Izenberg: Larry Doby Should Be Honored by Newark," *The Star-Ledger* (Newark NJ), July 7, 2012, https://www.nj.com/sports/ledger/izenbergcol/2012/07/izenberg_larry_doby_should_be.html.
53. Jacobson, *Carrying Jackie's Torch*, 32.
54. Scott Pitoniak, "Twenty-Five Years Ago."
55. Jack Hand, "Negro Jackie Robinson Makes Dazzling Debut with Royals," *The Ottawa Journal*, April 19, 1946.
56. United Press, "Robinson's Debut a Roaring Success," *Brooklyn Daily Eagle*, April 19, 1946.
57. "Negro Ace Bats .800 For Royals," *Winnipeg Tribune*, April 19, 1946.
58. Stu Cowan, "Obituary: George Shuba Was First White Player to Shake Jackie Robinson's Hand with Montreal Royals," *The Gazette* (Montreal), October 1, 2014, https://www.montrealgazette.com/sports/obituary-george-shuba-was-first-white-player-to-shake-jackie-robinsons-hand-with-montreal-royals.
59. "Robinson-Shuba Monument," The City of Youngstown, Ohio (website), accessed June 4, 2024, https://youngstownohio.gov/robinson-shuba.

60. Wendell Smith, "Jackie Hits Homer, Scores 4 Runs as Royals Win First," *Pittsburgh Courier*, April 27, 1946.
61. "'Jackie's Excited, Has Tie Trouble, Almost Loses Shirt to JC Crowd," *The Gazette* (Montreal), April 19, 1946.
62. Benjamin Hill, "Forgotten Members of the 'Great Experiment,'" MiLB.com, February 14, 2007, https://www.milb.com/news/gcs-176859.
63. Wendell Smith, The Sports Beat, *Pittsburgh Courier*, April 20, 1946.

4. SETTLING IN

1. Mike Rosenbaum, "Examining the Percentage of MLB Draft Picks Who Reach the Major Leagues," *Bleacher Report* (blog), June 12, 2012, https://bleacherreport.com/articles/1219356-examining-the-percentage-of-mlb-draft-picks-that-reach-the-major-leagues.
2. Rachel Robinson, "A Working Pair Who Changed a World," *New York Times*, April 12, 1987.
3. "Montreal's Own Villeray Neighbourhood Has Ranked among the Coolest in the World for 2021," *Time Out Montreal*, October 6, 2021, https://www.timeout.com/montreal/news/montreals-own-villeray-neighbourhood-has-ranked-among-the-coolest-in-the-world-for-2021-100621.
4. Jean Dion, "Montreal se souvient de celui qui a écrit l'histoire," *Le Devoir* (Montreal), March 1, 2011, https://www.ledevoir.com/sports/317829/montreal-se-souvient-de-celui-qui-a-ecrit-l-histoire.
5. Kennedy, *True*, 12.
6. John Kalbfleisch, "From the Archives: Robinson and Montreal Were a Perfect Match," *The Gazette* (Montreal), October 7, 2017, https://montrealgazette.com/sponsored/mtl-375th/from-the-archives-robinson-and-montreal-were-a-perfect-match.
7. Kahn, *Rickey & Robinson*, 207–8.
8. Patrick Sauer, "The Year of Jackie Robinson's Mutual Love Affair with Montreal," *Smithsonian* magazine, April 6, 2015, https://www.smithsonianmag.com/history/year-jackie-robinsons-mutual-love-affair-montreal-180954878/.
9. Jackie Robinson, "Baseball Star Jackie Robinson Talks Race Relations in 1964," interview, *Youth Special*, CBC, April 7, 1964, video, 10:40, https://www.cbc.ca/player/play/video/1.3594894.
10. Robinson, *I Never Had It Made*, 65.
11. Marshall, *Baseball's Pivotal Era*, 132.
12. Anderson, "Great Leap Forward," 78.
13. Chris Lamb, "How Clay Hopper's Attitude Was Transformed by Jackie Robinson," *National Post* (Toronto), April 9, 2013, https://nationalpost

.com/42/how-clay-hoppers-attitude-was-transformed-by-jackie-robinsonhttps://nationalpost.com/42/how-clay-hoppers-attitude-was-transformed-by-jackie-robinson.

14. Branch Rickey, "'One Hundred Percent Wrong Club' Speech," January 20, 1956, Atlanta, LOC Branch Rickey Papers, https://www.loc.gov/collections/jackie-robinson-baseball/articles-and-essays/baseball-the-color-line-and-jackie-robinson/one-hundred-percent-wrong-club-speech/.
15. Kahn, *Rickey & Robinson*, 211.
16. Bill Johnson, "Spider Jorgensen," Society for American Baseball Research, accessed July 24, 2024, https://sabr.org/bioproj/person/spider-jorgensen/.
17. Brown and Terry, *Baseball's Fabulous Montreal Royals*, 104.
18. William Weinbaum, "The Legacy of Al Campanis," ESPN, March 29, 2012, https://www.espn.com/espn/otl/story/_/id/7751398/how-al-campanis-controversial-racial-remarks-cost-career-highlighted-mlb-hiring-practices.
19. Weinbaum, "Legacy of Al Campanis."
20. Gary Cieradkowski, "Johnny Wright: He Was Never Just the 'Other Guy,'" "Infinite Baseball Card Set" (blog), December 28, 2020, https://studiogaryc.com/2020/12/28/cyclone-joe-williams-2/.
21. W. M. Akers, "The Forgotten Men Who Broke Baseball's Color Line with Jackie Robinson," *VICE*, April 15, 2015, https://www.vice.com/en/article/qkqywx/the-forgotten-men-who-broke-baseballs-color-line-with-jackie-robinson.
22. Shawcross, *Queen Mother*, 458.
23. Kennedy, *True*, 13–14.
24. Simon, *Jackie Robinson and Integration*, 98; and Anderson, "Great Leap Forward," 79.
25. Jack Anderson, "Great Leap Forward," 79; Camille DesRoches, "La jeune Fontaine sera au monticule pour le Royal contre le Jersey City à l'ouverture de la saison cet apres-midi," *Le Canada* (Montreal), May 1, 1946; "Cy Buker lance une partie de deux coups sûr contre Rochester," *La Presse* (Montreal), May 24, 1946; and "Le Royal possède un club supérieur à celui de 1945," *La Presse* (Montreal), May 28, 1946, 17.
26. Kennedy, *True*, 40.
27. Brown and Terry, *Baseball's Fabulous Montreal Royals*, 108.
28. Phil Seguin, "Les Royaux victorieux dans leur joute d'ouverture locale, hier," *La Patrie* (Montreal), May 2, 1946; and Sam Lacy, "Montreal Fans Greet Jackie with Wild Acclaim," *Afro-American* (Baltimore), May 11, 1946.

29. Lacy, "Montreal Fans Greet Jackie."
30. André Rufiange, "Curieuse promenade dans le stadium," *Le Front Ouvrier* (Montceau-les-Mines, France), June 8, 1946.
31. Kennedy, *True*, 41.
32. Maria Anastasia Weekes, "Ivan Livingstone: Exemplary at All Levels," Montreal Community Contact (website), May 10, 2019, https://mtlcommunitycontact.com/ivan-livingstone-exemplary-at-all-levels/.
33. Ingrid Peritz, "Jackie Robinson's Wife Remembers a Welcoming Montreal," *The Globe and Mail* (Toronto), April 28, 2013, https://www.theglobeandmail.com/news/national/jackie-robinsons-wife-remembers-a-welcoming-montreal/article11602715/.
34. Gilbert Rogin, "One Beer for the Rocket," *Sports Illustrated*, March 21, 1960, https://vault.si.com/vault/1994/03/14/one-beer-for-the-rocket.
35. Pellerin, *L'idole d'un peuple*, 509.
36. Melançon, *Rocket*, 80.
37. Canadian Press, "J. Robinson est un bon deuxième but," *Le Nouvelliste* (Trois-Rivières, Québec), May 2, 1946.
38. Sam Maltin, "Jackie, Hockey Stars Visit War Veterans," *Pittsburgh Courier*, June 29, 1946.
39. "Vingt ans après, on ne l'a pas oublié," *Le Petit Journal* (Montreal), November 20, 1966.
40. Maurice Richard, "Le courage de Jackie Robinson," *La Presse* (Montreal), May 26, 1996.
41. Oscar Major, "Dans Le Monde Sportif," *Le Samedi*, February 2, 1957, 13, 29.
42. Trudeau, "Punching above Its Weight," 291.
43. "Drummondville bat Sherbrooke à deux reprises," *La Tribune* (Sherbrooke, Québec), June 30, 1947; and "Lou Shapiro et Dean remportent les deux victoires au dépend du Drummondville samedi dernier," *Le Courrier de Saint-Hyacinthe*, August 1, 1947.
44. "Expos Honour Maurice Richard," CBC, June 2, 2000, https://www.cbc.ca/news/canada/expos-honour-maurice-richard-1.229251.
45. "Les sports à Drummondville," *Le Soleil* (Québec), August 13, 1947.
46. "The Origins of the Song Alouette," Gateway Arch National Park, July 1, 2020, video, 3:01, https://www.nps.gov/media/video/view.htm?id=E46A4746-F603-1CE5-53D29A10438EBB3B.
47. "Robinson May Play Football for Montreal," *Sherbrooke* (Québec) *Daily Record*, May 13, 1946; and Charlie Daoust, "Jack Robinson jouera pour Montreal contre les Riders de 'Baldy' Baldwin," *Le Droit* (Ottawa), May 11, 1946.
48. Oscar Major, "Dans Le Monde Sportif," *Le Samedi*, June 15, 1946, 9.

49. “Moody, Trawick Join Montreal’s Top Pro Grid Team,” *Pittsburgh Courier*, September 7, 1946.
50. Valentine and Darnell, “Football and ‘Tolerance,’” 62, 64.
51. Dave Zirin, “Montreal: Adopted Home of Jackie Robinson, John Carlos, and Now Michael Sam,” *The Nation*, May 26, 2015, https://www.thenation.com/article/archive/montreal-adopted-home-jackie-robinson-john-carlos-and-now-michael-sam/.
52. Jim Popp, “Michael Sam Backed by Alouettes GM,” interview by Les Carpenter, *Guardian*, June 25, 2015, https://www.theguardian.com/sport/2015/jun/25/montreal-alouettes-michael-sam-jim-popp-interview.

5. GLORY

1. Allan Woods, “Mordecai Richler Would Have Enjoyed Montreal Memorial Controversy,” *Toronto Star*, March 13, 2015, https://www.thestar.com/entertainment/books/mordecai-richler-would-have-enjoyed-montreal-memorial-controversy/article_7d7829ea-7539-5d2d-b845-1cb4376709af.html.
2. Richler, *Dispatches from Sporting Life*, 221.
3. Richler, *Dispatches from Sporting Life*, 225.
4. Jean Barrette, Autour des buts, *La Patrie* (Montreal), August 11, 1946.
5. Sam Maltin, “Montreal Shifts Robinson to Third Base; Hold Batting Lead,” *Pittsburgh Courier*, September 27, 1946.
6. Kennedy, *True*, 48.
7. Sam Maltin, “Jackie Denies He Will Quit Baseball and Return to School,” *Pittsburgh Courier*, August 24, 1946.
8. For more on the topic, see Alpert, *Out of Left Field*.
9. Greenberg, *Story of My Life*, 191.
10. Sam Maltin, “Tells Bob How Jackie Led League,” *Pittsburgh Courier*, September 21, 1946.
11. Dink Carroll, “Royals Halt Bears’ Late Rally to Win 7–5; Take Series Edge Despite 5-Run 9th,” *The Gazette* (Montreal), September 12, 1946.
12. Dink Carroll, “Les Burge Belts Royals to 2–1 Win over Bears—Orioles Deadlock Series,” *The Gazette* (Montreal), September 13, 1946.
13. Zotique Lesperance, “Commentaires sportifs,” *La Patrie* (Montreal), September 15, 2024.
14. Dink Carroll, “Royals Take Series Edge by Winning 2–1—Chiefs Eliminate Baltimore,” *The Gazette* (Montreal), September 17, 1946.
15. Dink Carroll, Playing the Field, *The Gazette* (Montreal), September 17, 1946.
16. Dink Carroll, “Rioting Marks Victory Which Sends Royals into Governor’s Cup Final,” *The Gazette* (Montreal), September 19, 1946.

17. Carroll, "Rioting Marks Victory."
18. Berra and Kaplan, *Ten Rings*, 14.
19. Lloyd McGowan, "Four Newark Bears Fined $200 for Playoff Ruckus," *Sporting News*, October 2, 1946, 25.
20. Dink Carroll, "Royals Drop First Game of International League Finals to Syracuse, 5–0," *The Gazette* (Montreal), September 20, 1946.
21. Dink Carroll, "Royals Tie Cup Finals, Overcome 10–2 Syracuse Lead to Win by 14–12," *The Gazette* (Montreal), September 19, 1946.
22. Dink Carroll, Playing the Field, *The Gazette* (Montreal), September 28, 1946.
23. Lakshmi Gandhi, "What Does 'Sold Down the River' Really Mean? The Answer Isn't Pretty," NPR, January 27, 2014, https://www.npr.org/sections/codeswitch/2014/01/27/265421504/what-does-sold-down-the-river-really-mean-the-answer-isnt-pretty.
24. Julia Mattingly, "How Racism Is Built into Louisville's Infrastructure," Louisville Political Review, October 1, 2021, https://loupolitical.org/2021/10/01/how-racism-is-built-into-louisvilles-infrastructure/.
25. Wendell Smith, "Brooklyn Dodgers to Evade Race Issue, Train in Cuba," *Pittsburgh Courier*, September 28, 1946.
26. Gary Belleville, "October 3, 1946: Jackie Robinson's Heroics Put Montreal on Verge of First Junior World Series Title," Society for American Baseball Research, accessed June 26, 2024, https://sabr.org/gamesproj/game/october-3-1946-robinsons-heroics-put-montreal-on-verge-of-first-junior-world-series-title/.
27. "Jackie, Mates Near Little World Series," *Afro-American* (Baltimore), September 28, 1946; Gary Belleville, "October 2, 1946: Jackie Robinson Leads Montreal to Thrilling 10-Inning Victory over Louisville," Society for American Baseball Research, accessed June 26, 2024, n2, https://sabr.org/gamesproj/game/october-2-1946-jackie-robinson-leads-montreal-to-thrilling-10-inning-victory-over-louisville/; and Jedwab, *Jackie Robinson's Unforgettable Season*, 47.
28. Robinson, *I Never Had It Made*, 50.
29. Belleville, "October 2, 1946."
30. Sam Lacy, "Robinson Victim of Rebel Boos in Series: Evades 2 Vicious Spiking Attempts Goes Hitless, But Proves Power on Defense as Team Wins, Loses," *Afro-American* (Baltimore), October 5, 1946.
31. Kahn, *Rickey & Robinson*, 219–20.
32. Dink Carroll, "Royals and Colonels Split at Weekend—Brooklyn Cards End in Deadlock; Montrealers Capture Opener 7–5 but Louisville Comes Back 3–0," *The Gazette* (Montreal), September 30, 1946.

33. Dink Carroll, Playing the Field, *The Gazette* (Montreal), October 2, 1946.
34. Kennedy, *True*, 57.
35. Robinson, *I Never Had It Made*, 51.
36. "Robinson's Brilliance Highlight of Series; Batting, Fielding Factors as Montreal Takes Title," *Afro-American* (Baltimore), October 12, 1946.
37. Dink Carroll, "Jackie Robinson Is Hero as Royals Edge Colonels 6–5 to Tie Up Series," *The Gazette* (Montreal), October 3, 1946.
38. Dink Carroll, "Royals Squeeze 5–3 Victory from Colonels to Lead Series 3 Games to 2," *The Gazette* (Montreal), October 3, 1946.
39. Dink Carroll, "Royals Win Little World Series for First Time in Their History," *The Gazette* (Montreal), October 3, 1946.
40. Sam Maltin, "Fans 'Mob' Jackie in Great Tribute," *Pittsburgh Courier*, October 12, 1946.
41. Brown and Terry, *Baseball's Fabulous Montreal Royals*, 112.
42. Maltin, "Fans 'Mob' Jackie."
43. Robinson and Smith, *Jackie Robinson*, 110.
44. *Jackie Robinson during Preseason Game in Louisville, 1956*, caption, *Herald-Leader* (Lexington) Archive, April 10, 2016, https://kyphotoarchive.com/2016/04/10/jackie-robinson-during-preseason-game-in-louisville-1956/.
45. Focus on Race Relations, "60th Anniversary of the Freedom March on Frankfort," press release, Kentucky State University, accessed June 26, 2024, https://www.kysu.edu/news/2024/02/mlk-march-on-frankfort.php.

6. HOMECOMINGS

1. Polner, *Branch Rickey*, 174.
2. Cox, "Happy Helping?," 68.
3. Rhiannon Walker, "Forgotten Fridays: How Disappointing Contract Terms Threatened Jackie Robinson's Debut," *The Athletic*, last modified January 30, 2024, https://www.nytimes.com/athletic/3145949/2022/02/25/forgotten-fridays-how-disappointing-contract-terms-threatened-jackie-robinsons-debut/.
4. Kahn, *Rickey & Robinson*, 126, 131.
5. Irv Goldfarb, "1947 Dodgers: Spring Training in Havana," Society for American Baseball Research, accessed July 15, 2024, https://sabr.org/journal/article/1947-dodgers-spring-training-in-havana/.
6. Allen and Walker, *Dixie Walker of Dodgers*, 158.
7. Richard Sandomir, "A Dissident Can Now Embrace the Legacy," *New York Times*, April 5, 1997, https://www.nytimes.com/1997/04/05/sports/a-dissident-can-now-embrace-the-legacy.html.

8. Harvey Araton, "The Dixie Walker She Knew," *New York Times*, April 10, 2010, https://www.nytimes.com/2010/04/11/sports/baseball/11walker.html.
9. "Dodgers, Bosox Win Opening Games," *The Gazette* (Montreal), April 17, 1947; "Marchildon permet aux Athletics de vaincre les Yankees—les Dodgers ont raison du Boston—Newhouser triomphe," *Le Canada* (Montreal), April 17, 1947; "Les Dodgers débutent par une victoire," *Le Devoir* (Montreal), April 17, 1947; "Beau début de Jack Robinson; Eddie Lopat a battu Bob Feller," *Montreal-Matin*, April 17, 1947, 14; "Brooklyn Debuts with a Win—the Royal Is the Victor," *La Presse* (Montreal), April 16, 1947; and Arthur Daley, "Opening Day at Ebbets Field," *New York Times*, April 16, 1947.
10. Corbett, "The 'Strike' against Jackie Robinson," 91.
11. Mike Lackey, "May 13, 1947: Jackie Robinson Makes First Appearance in Cincinnati with Dodgers," Society for American Baseball Research, accessed July 15, 2024, https://sabr.org/gamesproj/game/may-13-1947-jackie-robinson-makes-first-appearance-in-cincinnati-with-dodgers/.
12. "Rookie of the Year," *Time*, September 22, 1947, https://time.com/6258524/jackie-robinson-time-cover-1947/.
13. J. G. Taylor Spink, "Rookie of the Year . . . Jackie Robinson; Gains Award on Basis of All-Around Ability," *Sporting News*, September 17, 1947, 3.
14. Baseball had just one Rookie of the Year in 1947, not separate ones for the National League and American League as we know today.
15. Bert Souliere, Horizons sportifs, *Le Devoir* (Montreal), January 7, 1957.
16. Charlie Daoust, Et le spectacle continue, *Le Droit* (Ottawa), January 7, 1957; and Jean Chartier, "Randonnée sportive," *La Tribune* (Sherbrooke, Québec), January 7, 1957.
17. "The Two Number 9s, Maurice Richard and Jackie Robinson," EX1999-02.1–5.090, c692, McCord Stewart Museum.
18. Mike Petriello, "The L.A. Browns? How One Day in '41 Changed MLB," MLB.com, December 25, 2020, https://www.mlb.com/news/featured/the-story-of-the-los-angeles-browns-changed-baseball-forever.
19. Kurt Blumenau, "September 22, 1953: Satchel Paige, Don Larsen Lead St. Louis Browns to Their Final, Win," Society for American Baseball Research, accessed June 27, 2024, https://sabr.org/gamesproj/game/september-22-1953-satchel-paige-don-larsen-lead-st-louis-browns-to-their-final-win/.
20. Taylor Spink, "'Third Major Must Come Soon'—Rickey; Believes New Loop May Be International," *Sporting News*, May 21, 1958, 1–2.
21. Brown and Terry, *Baseball's Fabulous Montreal Royals*, 173.

22. Warren Corbett, "Rickey's Folly: How the Continental League Forced Baseball Expansion," Society for American Baseball Research, accessed June 27, 2024, https://sabr.org/journal/article/rickeys-folly-how-the-continental-league-forced-baseball-expansion/.
23. "Jackie Robinson Offered Job as Montreal Manager," *Afro-American* (Baltimore), March 31, 1951.
24. Bert Souliere, Horizons sportifs, *Le Devoir* (Montreal), October 10, 1956.
25. "Dodgers Offer Robinson Montreal Post: Jackie May Be First Tan Mgr," *Michigan Chronicle* (Detroit), October 13, 1956.
26. Fitts, "Sayonara Jackie Robinson."
27. "Montreal fait une demande officielle d'admission dans la Ligue continentale," *Le Droit* (Montreal), September 2, 1959.
28. Claude Harrison Jr., "People in Sports: Jackie Robinson to Manage Montreal's Baseball Squad?," *Philadelphia Tribune*, September 19, 1959.
29. Puerzer, "Jackie's Last Stand," 282.
30. Brodie Snyder, "Sportbeat: TV-Radio; Expos on English TV: The Picture Clears Up," *The Gazette* (Montreal), June 3, 1972.
31. "Il joua ici pour $600 par mois," *Le Devoir* (Montreal), October 25, 1972.
32. Rhiannon Walker, "Jackie Robinson's Final Public Appearance: 50 Years Ago at 1972 World Series," *The Athletic*, October 21, 2022, https://www.nytimes.com/athletic/3702849/2022/10/21/jackie-robinson-world-series-1972/.
33. Jackie Robinson, "Jackie Robinson's Speech—October 15, 1972," posted August 28, 2020, by Oakland Athletics, YouTube, 9:17, https://www.youtube.com/watch?v=0hNF65zWB6km.
34. *Jackie Robinson*, October 25, 1972, photograph, *Le Devoir* (Montreal), cover; *Dead at 53 Years*, October 25, 1972, photograph, *Montreal-Matin*, cover; "Une rue ou un parc Jackie-Robinson," *Montreal-Matin*, October 26, 1972; "Jackie Robinson: Conduit à son Dernier Repos," *Montreal-Matin*, October 28, 1972; "Il s'est souvenu!," *La Presse* (Montreal), October 27, 1972; and "Le maire Drapeau n'a pas oublié Robinson," *La Presse* (Montreal), October 28, 1972.
35. Roland Sabourin, "Robinson est parti sans avoir vu un gérant noir," *Le Soleil* (Québec), October 25, 1972.
36. Jack Todd, "The 40-Year Hangover: How the 1976 Olympics Nearly Broke Montreal," *The Guardian*, July 6, 2016, https://www.theguardian.com/cities/2016/jul/06/40-year-hangover-1976-olympic-games-broke-montreal-canada.
37. Keri, *Up, Up, and Away*, 351.

38. Kevin Glew, "Gary Carter Beloved in Montreal: Former Expos Bat Boy," CBC Sports, February 6, 2012, https://www.cbc.ca/sports-content/baseball/opinion/2012/02/gary-carter-beloved-in-montreal-former-expos-bat-boy.html.
39. Mordecai Richler, "The All-Star City Has No Champion to Call Its Own," *New York Times*, July 11, 1982.
40. Rachel Robinson,"1982 MLB All Star Game," interview by Howard Cosell, July 13, 1982, posted September 27, 2016, by ClassicPhilliesTV, YouTube, 4:00:23, at 4:00–5:20, https://www.youtube.com/watch?v=loTK8sD_Vyo.
41. Roger LaBonté, "Des sportifs ont créé hier à Montreal une bourse scolaire 'Jackie Robinson,'" *Le Devoir* (Montreal), September 8, 1966; and Ted Blackman, "Quick as You Can Say: 'Jackie Robinson Day,'" *The Gazette* (Montreal), September 8, 1966.
42. Geoff Moore, "Memories Are Mementoes of the Ultimate Boy of Summer," *The Montreal Downtowner*, July 11, 1984, Archives de Montreal.
43. "Le RCM propose un projet pour rendre hommage à Jackie Robinson," *La Presse* (Montreal), April 13, 1984.
44. Harvey Shepherd, "Jackie Robinson Memorial Sought," *The Gazette* (Montreal), April 16, 1984.
45. Angèle Dagenais, "Quatre motions du RCM sont défaites au conseil," *Le Devoir* (Montreal), April 25, 1984.
46. Mark Sullivan, "Drapeau Ego Blasted," *The Express* (Montreal), April 29, 1984.
47. "Tribute to Jackie Robinson," Montreal Expos, press release, August 11, 1986, Hommage à Jackie Robinson, 11 août 1986, Archives de Montreal.
48. Michael Farber, "Swing and a Miss at Lunch to Honor Jackie Robinson," *The Gazette* (Montreal), September 4, 1986.
49. "Des 'n—— lovers' ont lancé la carrière de Jackie Robinson," *Le Journal de Montreal*, August 12, 1986.
50. Stride, Thomas, and Smith, "Ballplayer or Barrier Breaker?," 2183, 2185.
51. Mario Cloutier, "Le fier Jackie Robinson; Il y a 50 ans, il devenait le premier joueur de race noire de l'histoire du baseball majeur," *Le Devoir* (Montreal), May 25–26, 1996.
52. Myra Virgil, "Meeting Rachel Robinson, a Moving Experience," paper presented at Jackie Robinson, a Part of Montreal's History, Conference Papers, 50th Anniversary Celebrations of Jackie Robinson's Presence in Montreal, May 25, 1996, 57–59, Jackie Robinson Papers, GV865.R6 J33 2000, Giamatti Research Center.

53. "'We're Killing the Meaning' of Jackie Day," NBC Sports, last modified April 13, 2007, https://web.archive.org/web/20120307172358/http://nbcsports.msnbc.com/id/17964581/.
54. Torii Hunter, "A Hurtful, Unfortunate Episode," *Torii's Storiis* (blog), March 10, 2010, http://toriihunter.mlblogs.com/2010/03/10/a-hurtful-unfortunate-episode/.
55. Bill Pennington, "A Measure of Respect for Jackie Robinson Turns into a Movement," *New York Times*, April 13, 2007, https://www.nytimes.com/2007/04/13/sports/baseball/13jackie.html.
56. Canadian Press, "From Falling Concrete to Shredded Roof, a Timeline of the Olympic Stadium's Struggles," CBC, November 10, 2017, https://www.cbc.ca/news/canada/montreal/montreal-olympic-stadium-problems-1.4397761.
57. "The Top 10 Heritage Minutes," *Maclean's*, June 29, 2013, https://macleans.ca/society/life/the-top-10-heritage-minutes/.
58. "Jackie Robinson's Plaque Unveiled Where They Lived in Montreal," *Montreal Gazette*, posted February 28, 2011, YouTube, 1:37, https://www.youtube.com/watch?v=HYGaHAAVYBo.
59. "Cineplex Pre-Show Honours Jackie Robinson's Montreal Baseball Roots to Preview New Biopic," *The Gazette* (Montreal), March 18, 2013, https://montrealgazette.com/entertainment/cineplex-pre-show-honours-jackie-robinsons-montreal-baseball-roots-to-preview-new-biopic.
60. @laurencewholmes, "Everything about Montreal is pretty dope," Instagram, August 31, 2021, https://www.instagram.com/laurencewholmes/p/CTP_TfHLCwU/.
61. Susan Schwartz, "Cité Mémoire Makes History in Old Montreal," *The Gazette* (Montreal), last updated July 15, 2020, https://montrealgazette.com/entertainment/arts/cite-memoire-makes-history-in-old-montreal; and "Cité Mémoire Walking Tour in Old Montreal," posted February 16, 2024, by Ambi Travel,YouTube, 1:10:59, https://www.youtube.com/watch?v=mVgqVL68oLk.
62. Cigdem Talue, "The Placing of Angélique," McGill University, April 16, 2021, https://www.mcgill.ca/race-space/article/reading-group-contributions/placing-angelique.

EPILOGUE

1. Robinson, *I Never Had it Made*, iii.
2. James Wagner, "A Marker Honoring Jackie Robinson Was Defaced. M.L.B. Helped Replace It," *New York Times*, last updated January 30,

2022, https://www.nytimes.com/2022/01/27/sports/baseball/jackie-robinson-mlb-georgia.html.

3. Jerry Brewer, "The Fight over Jackie Robinson," *Washington Post*, June 4, 2024, https://www.washingtonpost.com/sports/interactive/2024/jackie-robinson-myth/.
4. Heather Hollingsworth and Thomas Peipert, "Jackie Robinson Is Rebuilt in Bronze to Replace Kansas Park's Stolen Statue," Associated Press, NPR, May 28, 2024, https://www.kcur.org/sports/2024-05-28/jackie-robinson-statue-wichita-kansas-stolen-art-castings.
5. Brewer, "Fight over Jackie Robinson."
6. Tim McRoberts, "Remembering a Spartan: Dick Lord," *Michigan State University Archives and Historical Collections*, February 27, 2020, https://msuarchives.wordpress.com/2020/02/27/remembering-a-spartan-dick-lord/.
7. Ian Halperin and Max Wallace, "Black Hockey Players Fight Racism in NHL," *The Varsity* (University of Toronto), December 1, 1986.
8. René Bruemmer, "Montreal's Black Pioneers: They Paved the Way for Others," *The Gazette* (Montreal), last updated March 13, 2019, https://montrealgazette.com/news/local-news/montreals-black-pioneers-they-paved-the-way-for-others.
9. Douglas Quan, "50 Years Later: How Racism Allegations against a Montreal Professor Turned into the Greatest Student Riot in Canadian History," *National Post*, January 28, 2019, https://nationalpost.com/news/canada/50-years-later-how-racism-allegations-against-a-montreal-professor-turned-into-the-greatest-student-riot-in-canadian-history.
10. David Austin, "How the 1969 Sir George Williams Affair—Canada's First Major Black-Led Student Protest—Changed the Country," CBC, November 1, 2023, https://www.cbc.ca/documentaries/black-life/how-the-1969-sir-george-williams-affair-canada-s-first-major-black-led-student-protest-changed-the-country-1.7009058.
11. Iness Rifay, "50 Years of Concordia Student Activism: A Timeline," *The Link*, September 5, 2023, https://thelinknewspaper.ca/article/50-years-of-concordia-student-activism-a-timeline.

Bibliography

ARCHIVES AND MANUSCRIPT MATERIALS

Archives de Montreal, Histoire Monument Jackie Robinson, D3020–86, Montreal.

Concordia University Library Special Collections and Archives, Tina Brereton fonds, P074, Montreal.

Giamatti Research Center, National Baseball Hall of Fame, Cooperstown NY.

Jewish Public Library, Sam Maltin Fonds, Montreal.

Library of Congress, Branch Rickey Papers, Washington DC, https://www.loc.gov/collections/branch-rickey-papers/about-this-collection/.

Library and Archives Canada, Charles Mayer Fonds (1911–1971), R5797–0-9-F, MG30-C76, Ottawa.

McCord Stewart Museum, Collection Alain Choquette (1896–1980), Montreal.

McGill University Archives, Austin "Dink" Carroll Fonds, CA MUA MG4151/08, Montreal.

PUBLISHED WORKS

Allen, Maury, and Susan Walker. *Dixie Walker of the Dodgers: The People's Choice*. Tuscaloosa: University of Alabama Press, 2010.

Alpert, Rebecca. *Out of Left Field: Jews and Black Baseball*. New York: Oxford University Press, 2016.

Anderson, Jack. "A Great Leap Forward: Jackie Robinson and the View from Montreal." In Nowlin and Sparks, *Jackie Robinson: Perspectives on 42*, 75–85.

Arenson, Adam. "Experience Rather Than Imagination: Researching the Return Migration of African North Americans during the American Civil War and Reconstruction." *Journal of American Ethnic History* 32, no. 2 (Winter 2013): 73–77.

Berra, Yogi, and Dave Kaplan. *Ten Rings: My Championship Seasons*. New York: William Morrow, 2003.

Brown, William, and Scott Terry. *Baseball's Fabulous Montreal Royals: The Minor League Team That Made Major League History*. Montreal: Robert Davies Publishing, 1996.

Bullock, Steve. "Playing for Their Nation: The American Military and Baseball during World War II." *Journal of Sport History* 27, no. 1 (2000): 67–89.

Burns, Ken, Sarah Burns, and David McMahon, dirs. *Jackie Robinson.* Episode "Jackie Robinson: Part 1." Aired April 11, 2016, on PBS. PBS streaming.

Corbett, Warren. "The 'Strike' against Jackie Robinson: Truth or Myth." *Baseball Research Journal* 46, no. 1 (Spring 2017): 88–94.

Cox, Joe. *A Fine Team Man: Jackie Robinson and the Lives He Touched.* Lanham MD: Lyons Press, 2019.

———. "Happy Helping? Inside Commissioner Chandler's Role in Jackie Robinson's Great Quest." In Nowlin and Sparks, *Jackie Robinson: Perspectives on* 42, 68–72.

Dame, Stephen. "Coloured Diamonds: Integrated Baseball in the Canadian Expeditionary Force 1914–1918." *Journal of Canadian Baseball* 1 (2022): 3–19.

Dreier, Peter. "Before Jackie Robinson: Baseball's Civil Rights Movement." In Nowlin and Sparks, *Jackie Robinson: Perspectives on* 42, 27–37.

Dugas, Marcel. *Jackie Robinson, un* été à *Montreal.* Montreal: Éditions Hurtubise, 2019.

———. "Montreal and Jackie Robinson." In North, *Our Game, Too*, 356–63.

Fitts, Robert K. "Sayonara Jackie Robinson: How an American Hero Finished His Career in Japan." In Nowlin and Sparks, *Jackie: Perspectives on* 42, 213–18.

Greenberg, Hank. *Hank Greenberg: The Story of My Life.* Edited by Ira Berkow. New York: Times Books, 1989.

Greenham, Craig. "On the Battlefront: Canadian Soldiers, an Imperial War, and America's National Pastime." *American Review of Canadian Studies* 42, no. 1 (March 2012): 34–50.

Halpern, Monda. "The 'Malestrom' at Christie Pits: Jewish Masculinity and the Toronto Riot of 1933." *Canadian Jewish Studies (Études juives canadiennes)* 28, no. 1 (2019): 12–33.

Honig, Donald. *Baseball When the Grass Was Green: Baseball from the Twenties to the Forties Told by the Men Who Played It.* Lincoln: University of Nebraska Press, 1993.

Howell, Colin. "Black Baseball in the Maritimes: 1880–1980." In North, *Our Game, Too*, 101–7.

Jacobs, Heidi L. M. *1934: The Chatham All-Stars Coloured All-Stars' Barrier-Breaking Year.* Windsor ON: Biblioasis, 2023.

Jacobson, Steve. *Carrying Jackie's Torch: The Players Who Integrated Baseball—and America*. Chicago: Lawrence Hill Books, 2007.

Jedwab, Jack. *Jackie Robinson's Unforgettable Season of Baseball in Montreal*. Montreal: Les Éditions du CIDIHCA, 2021.

Johnson, Michele A., and Funké Aladejebi, eds. *Unsettling the Great White North: Black Canadian History*. Toronto: University of Toronto Press, 2022.

Joost, Mathias. "Asian- and Black-Canadians at Vimy Ridge." *Canadian Military Journal* 18, no. 1 (Winter 2017): 45–55.

Kahn, Roger. *Rickey & Robinson: The True, Untold Story of the Integration of Baseball*. New York: Rodale, 2014.

Kennedy, Kostya. *True: The Four Seasons of Jackie Robinson*. New York: St. Martin's Press, 2022.

Keri, Jonah. *Up, Up, and Away: The Kid, the Hawk, Rock, Vladi, Pedro, Le Grand Orange, Youppi!, the Crazy Business of Baseball, and the Ill-Fated but Unforgettable Montreal Expos*. Toronto: Random House Canada, 2014.

Kreuz, Jim. "Tom Greenwade and His 007 Assignment." *The National Pastime* 27 (2007), 96–100.

Lamb, Chris. *Blackout: The Untold Story of Jackie Robinson's First Spring Training*. Lincoln: University of Nebraska Press, 2004.

Lanctot, Neil. *Campy: The Two Lives of Roy Campanella*. New York: Simon and Schuster, 2011.

LeMoine, Bob. "Jackie Robinson in 1945: From Boston 'Tryout' to a Negro Leagues Star." In Nowlin and Sparks, *Jackie Robinson: Perspectives on 42*, 61–67.

Marshall, William. *Baseball's Pivotal Era, 1945–51*. Lexington: University Press of Kentucky, 1999.

Mathieu, Sarah-Jane. *North of the Color Line: Migration and Black Resistance in Canada, 1870–1955*. Chapel Hill: University of North Carolina Press, 2010.

Melançon, Benoît. *The Rocket: A Cultural History of Maurice Richard*. Vancouver: Greystone Books, 2009.

Mormino, Gary R. "GI Joe Meets Jim Crow: Racial Violence and Reform in World War II Florida." *Florida Historical Quarterly* 73, no. 1 (1994): 23–42.

Myrdal, Gunnar, Richard Sterner, and Arnold Rose. *An American Dilemma: The Negro Problem and Modern Democracy*. Vol. 1. New York: Harper & Brothers Publishers, 1944.

North, Andrew, ed. *Our Game, Too: Influential Figures and Milestones in Canadian Baseball*. Phoenix AZ: Society for American Baseball Research, 2022.

Nowlin, Bill, and Glen Sparks, eds. *Jackie: Perspectives on 42*. Phoenix AZ: Society for American Baseball Research, 2021.

Pellerin, Jean Marie. *L'idole d'un peuple, Maurice Richard*. Montreal: Les Editions de l'Homme, 1976.

Pietrusza, David. *Judge and Jury: The Life and Times of Judge Kenesaw Mountain Landis*. South Bend IN: Diamond Communications, 1998.

Pollard, Sam, dir. *The League*. 2023; Dallas TX: 2929 Productions. Hulu streaming.

Polner, Murray. *Branch Rickey: A Biography*. Jefferson NC: McFarland, 2007.

Puerzer, Richard. "Jackie's Last Stand: Jackie Robinson's Last Public Appearance and His Appeal for the Integration of Major-League Baseball Management," In Nowlin and Sparks, *Jackie: Perspectives on 42*, 281–84.

Rampersad, Arnold. *Jackie Robinson: A Biography*. New York: Random House, 2011.

Richler, Mordecai. *Dispatches from the Sporting Life*. Guilford CT: Lyons Press, 2002.

Robinson, Jackie. *I Never Had It Made*. As told to Alfred Duckett. New York: Harper Collins, 1995.

Robinson, Jackie, and Wendel Smith. *Jackie Robinson: My Own Story*. New York: Greenberg, 1948.

Roper, Scott C., and Stephanie Abbot Roper. "'We're Going to Give All We Have for This Grand Little Town': Baseball Integration and the 1946 Nashua Dodgers." *Historical New Hampshire* 53, no. 1–2 (Spring-Summer 1998), 2–19.

Schnur, James Anthony. "Persevering on the Home Front: Blacks in Florida during World War II." In *Florida at War*, edited by Lewis N. Wynne, 49–69. Saint Leo FL: Saint Leo College Press, 1993.

Schwartz, Mildred A. *Trends in White Attitudes toward Negroes: Report No. 119*. Chicago: University of Chicago, 1967. https://www.norc.org/content/dam/norc-org/pdfs/NORCRpt_119.pdf.

Shawcross, William. *The Queen Mother*. New York: Knopf, 2009.

Sheinin, David, and Benjamin Bryce. "Baseball and the Categorization of Race in Venezuela." In *Race and Transnationalism in the Americas*, edited by David Sheinin and Benjamin Bryce, 121–39. Pittsburgh PA: University of Pittsburgh Press, 2021.

Simon, Scott. *Jackie Robinson and the Integration of Baseball*. Hoboken NJ: Wiley, 2002.

Spivey, Donald. "'To Canada with Love': Satchel Paige and Baseball Diplomacy." *The International Journal of the History of Sport* 32, no. 2 (2015): 238–49.

Stott, Jon C. *Canadian Minor League Baseball: A History Since World War II*. Jefferson NC: McFarland, 2022.

Stride, Christopher, Ffion Thomas, and Maureen M. Smith. "Ballplayer or Barrier Breaker? Branding through the Seven Statues of Jackie Robinson." *The International Journal of the History of Sport* 31, no. 17 (2014): 2164–96. https://doi.org/10.1080/09523367.2014.923840.

Swanton, Barry, and Jay-Dell Mah. *Black Baseball Players in Canada: A Biographical Dictionary, 1881–1960*. Jefferson NC: McFarland, 2009.

Trudeau, Christian. "Daily Operations in the United States Negro Baseball League, 1945–46." *Baseball Research Journal* 54, no. 1 (Spring 2025): 24–30.

———. "Integration in Quebec: More than Jackie Robinson." In *Dominionball: Baseball above the 49th*, edited by Jane Finnan Dorward, 23–24. Cleveland: Society for American Baseball Research, 2005.

———. "Punching above Its Weight: The Quebec Provincial League." In North, *Our Game, Too*, 290–99.

———. "24 Years before Jackie, There Was Charlie Culver." *Baseball Research Journal* 49, no. 1 (Spring 2020): 15–19.

Tygiel, Jules. *Baseball's Great Experiment: Jackie Robinson and His Legacy*. New York: Oxford University Press, 1983.

Tygiel, Jules, and John Thorn. "Jackie Robinson's Signing: The Real Story." In *SABR 50 at 50: The Society for American Baseball Research's Fifty Most Essential Contributions to the Game*, edited by Bill Nowlin, 162–75. Lincoln: University of Nebraska Press, 2020.

Valentine, John, and Simon C. Darnell. "Football and 'Tolerance': Black Football Players in 20th-Century Canada." In *Race and Sport in Canada: Intersecting Inequalities*, edited by Janelle Joseph, Simon Darnell, and Yuka Nakamura, 57–80. Toronto: Canadian Scholar Press, 2012.

White, Steven. "Civil Rights, World War II, and U.S. Public Opinion." *Studies in American Political Development* 30, no. 1 (2016): 38–61.

Williams, Dorothy. "The Jackie Robinson Myth: Social Mobility and Race in Montreal, 1920–1960." Master's thesis, Concordia University, 1999.

Wright, Miriam. *The Chatham Coloured All-Stars and Black Baseball in Southwestern Ontario, 1915–1958*. Waterloo ON: Wilfrid Laurier University Press, 2023.

Index